# TEXT & PRESENTATION, 2019

*Edited by* Amy Muse

The Comparative Drama Conference Series, 16

McFarland & Company, Inc., Publishers
*Jefferson, North Carolina*

Excerpts from "Summer and Smoke" and "The Eccentricities of a Nightingale" by Tennessee Williams, from *The Theatre of Tennessee Williams*, Vol. 2, copyright © 1971 by The University of the South. Reprinted by permission of New Directions Publishing Corp.

ISBN 1054-724X
ISBN (print) 978-1-4766-7038-6
ISBN (ebook) 978-1-4766-4058-7

© 2020 The Executive Board of the Comparative Drama Conference.
"A Conversation with Branden Jacobs-Jenkins" © 2020 Branden Jacobs-Jenkins.
All rights reserved

*No part of this book may be reproduced or transmitted in any form or by any means, electronic or mechanical, including photocopying or recording, or by any information storage and retrieval system, without permission in writing from the publisher.*

Front cover image: Playwright Branden Jacobs-Jenkins, right, in conversation with Baron Kelly during the keynote interview at the Comparative Drama Conference at Rollins College (courtesy Jamie Renee Hoffman / Rollins College).

Printed in the United States of America

McFarland & Company, Inc., Publishers
   Box 611, Jefferson, North Carolina 28640
      www.mcfarlandpub.com

# Contents

*Acknowledgments* .................................................. vii

*Preface* ............................................................ 1

A Conversation with Branden Jacobs-Jenkins
BARON KELLY ........................................................ 5

*A Raisin in the Sun* at 60: A Conversation
TERESA GILLIAMS, NATHANIEL G. NESMITH, JANNA SEGAL,
BARON KELLY *and* BRANDEN JACOBS-JENKINS ....................... 27

Radical Resurrections: A Performance History of John Brown's
Body
VICTORIA LYNN SCRIMER ............................................. 49

Deep When: A Basic Design Philosophy for Addressing Holidays
in Historical Dramas
MICHAEL SCHWEIKARDT ............................................. 63

Uncanniness and Alienation in Lisa D'Amour's *Detroit* and
*Airline Highway*
M. SCOTT PHILLIPS .................................................. 78

Precious Resources: Cultural Archiving in the Post-Apocalyptic
Worlds of *Mr. Burns* and *Station Eleven*
PAUL D. REICH ...................................................... 96

Past the Lyrical: Mythographic Metatheatre in Marina Carr's
*Phaedra Backwards*
PHILLIP ZAPKIN ..................................................... 113

Infidelity, Adaptation, and Textuality: Directing Late Medieval
and Early Modern French Farce
SCOTT D. TAYLOR ................................................... 130

Rectories Meet "One-Hour" Rooms: Williams on Summery and
   Eccentric Loves
   JEFFREY B. LOOMIS .................................................. 148

A Portrait of the Krapp as a Young[er] Man: Michael Laurence's
   *Krapp, 39*
   WILLIAM HUTCHINGS ............................................... 161

Waiting for Rothko
   DOUG PHILLIPS ...................................................... 174

***Review of Literature: Selected Books***

Simon Critchley, *Tragedy, the Greeks, and Us*
   DOUG PHILLIPS ...................................................... 189

Trevor Boffone, Teresa Marrero and Chantal Rodriguez, eds.
   *Encuentro: Latinx Performance for the New American Theater*
   OSVALDO SANDOVAL-LEON ......................................... 193

Lopamudra Basu. *Ayad Akhtar, the American Nation, and Its Others
   After 9/11: Homeland Insecurity*
   MAHWASH SHOAIB .................................................. 197

Max Shulman and J. Chris Westgate, eds. *Performing the Progressive
   Era: Immigration, Urban Life, and Nationalism on Stage*
   PATRICK MIDGLEY ................................................... 200

Selby Wynn Schwartz. *The Bodies of Others: Drag Dances and Their
   Afterlives*
   ALICIA M. GOODMAN ............................................... 204

David Palmer, ed. *Visions of Tragedy in Modern American Drama*
   MELISSA RYNN PORTERFIELD ....................................... 207

Index ...................................................................... 211

# Acknowledgments

That creating *Text & Presentation, 2019*, my first issue as editor, has been such a pleasure is due entirely to the frequent and generous support I've received from so many. Christine Stevens deserves the first and greatest thanks. Graduate student in the MA program in English at the University of St. Thomas, Christine was editorial assistant extraordinaire, copyediting with a sensitive ear for sentence rhythms and a keen eye for grammar and mechanics, gamely taking on one task after another while juggling her own load of coursework. I wish her every success as she moves into a career in editing and publishing. Graley Herren and Jay Malarcher, most recent past editors of *Text & Presentation*, answered my many questions, however mundane or panicked, promptly and with good cheer. I am grateful for their encouragement and role-modeling, and for the assists of my editorial team, Kevin J. Wetmore, Jr., Associate Editor, and Michael Schwartz, Book Review Editor. Bill Boles, director of the Comparative Drama Conference, has been my tech support, timesaver, and booster throughout, providing transcripts of the keynote interview and roundtable discussion on *A Raisin in the Sun*, and prepping the lovely photograph of Branden Jacobs-Jenkins that graces our cover. That photo and the one accompanying the keynote interview were taken by Jamie Renee Hoffman, and Andrew McIntosh videotaped and transcribed both the keynote event and roundtable discussion. I am very grateful to Branden Jacobs-Jenkins for his energizing and thought-provoking interview that had us buzzing all weekend and for his brilliant contributions to the discussion of *A Raisin in the Sun*, and to Noah Rubenstein, Jacobs-Jenkins's assistant, for all his swift and able help with transcript editing. Our editor at McFarland & Company, David Alff, has been gracious, patient, kind, and helpful at each stage of the process.

The Comparative Drama Conference and I want to express gratitude for the support we receive from our home institutions. At the University of St. Thomas, English Department chair Olga Herrera granted me course release time and funds to hire an editorial assistant. She and our administrative assistant Andy Leet arranged for me to teach a professional editing course and involve our English majors and graduate students in the *T&P* process. My colleague Andrew Scheiber performed valiant service at a crucial moment. I appreciate their enthusiasm for bringing *Text & Presentation* into our department. Rollins College has been an excellent home for the CDC, and we are thankful for the financial support from the Department of English, the Writing Minor, the Theatre Department, the Office of the Dean of the College of Liberal Arts, the Thomas P. Johnson Distinguished Artist Fund, and the Office of the President. Our deepest thanks to President Grant H. Cornwell for his support and his inspiring welcome address at the 2019 conference; Dean Jennifer Cavanaugh; Provost Susan Singer; Dr. Gail Sinclair, director of the Winter Park Institute; Dr. Paul D. Reich, chair of the Department of English; David Charles, chair of the Department of Theatre; Jessica McKown, English Department administrative assistant; Aubrey Correiro, conference coordinator; and Jamie Renee Hoffman, senior conference coordinator.

No issue of *Text & Presentation* could ever be created without the collaborative spirit, academic expertise, and intellectual support of the editorial board, many of whom served as thoughtful, encouraging reviewers of manuscripts. I thank them all: José I. Badeness, S.J. (Loyola Marymount University), William C. Boles (Rollins College), Miriam Chirico (Eastern Connecticut State University), Stratos E. Constantinidis (The Ohio State University), Ellen Dolgin (Dominican College), Verna A. Foster (Loyola University Chicago), Yoshiko Fukushima (University of Hawaii, Hilo), Kiki Gounaridou (Smith College), Jan L. Hagens (Yale University), Karelisa Hartigan (University of Florida), Graley Herren (Xavier University), William Hutchings (University of Alabama–Birmingham), Baron Kelly (University of Louisville), Jeffrey B. Loomis (Northwestern Missouri State University), Ian Andrew MacDonald (Bowdoin College), Jay Malarcher (West Virginia University), Elizabeth Scharffenberger (Columbia University), Michael Schwartz (Indiana University of Pennsylvania), Janna Segal (University of Louisville), Laura Snyder (Stevenson University), Tony Stafford (University of Texas–El Paso), Kevin J. Wetmore, Jr. (Loyola Marymount University), and Kelly Younger (Loyola Marymount University). We are all sorry to say goodbye to Tony Stafford, longtime board member and welcoming face at the conference. Tony, we wish you all the best for a happy retirement.

I would also like to thank the authors whose work appears in these pages. Your insightful readings of dramatic literature and performance, your archival research and manuscript analysis, and your pedagogical innovations are a real contribution to the field, and I am honored to publish them in *Text & Presentation*. Many thanks, too, to the specialists in a range of subfields who generously served as peer reviewers; you must of course remain anonymous but have my deep appreciation. Thank you to all the participants who made the 2019 Comparative Drama Conference such a lively and stimulating experience, and to all the scholars, emerging and veteran, who submitted work to *T&P* this year. I enjoyed reading everything that arrived on my e-doorstep and wish I had enough room to include every excellent essay I received. May they all find good homes.

*Text & Presentation* would not exist without the Comparative Drama Conference. Deepest gratitude to our current director Bill Boles for his dedication to the ongoing success of the conference, his hard work behind the scenes throughout the year, his organizational savvy and creative problem-solving, and his enviable unflappability. He makes us look forward to reconvening in Orlando each spring.

I'll close with gratitude for my home base: for my warmly supportive colleagues and friends Kanishka Chowdhury, Alexis Easley, Liz Wilkinson, and Martha Johnson, and for Doug Phillips, who lets me know I am where I should be.

# Preface

Each annual volume of *Text & Presentation* features attractions and hot spots of the previous year's Comparative Drama Conference. The joined names in this publication—"text" and "presentation"—indicate the scope of the work presented and productive tensions in play at the conference and published here. The Comparative Drama Conference brings together scholars, critics, playwrights, translators, dramaturgs, directors, designers, and performers from across the country and around the world, who share their discoveries about dramatic literature from every era and many national and cultural traditions; theatre theory, history, and production; performance in theory and practice; and theatricality in non-dramatic genres. It is truly global and comparative.

We have Karelisa Hartigan to thank for this. Now Professor Emerita of Classics at the University of Florida, she founded the Comparative Drama Conference in 1977. Over the forty-two years that have ensued since then, the conference has grown substantially. We are lucky to have had stable and resourceful leadership. From 2000 to 2005, the conference was held in Columbus and led by Stratos E. Constantinidis (The Ohio State University); from 2005 to 2011, it moved to Los Angeles, where it was ably directed by Kevin J. Wetmore, Jr. (Loyola Marymount University); and from 2012 to 2016, Laura Snyder (Stevenson University) steered the conference in Baltimore. Since 2017 we have gathered in Orlando under the direction of William C. Boles (Rollins College). This year's meeting, held April 4–6, 2019, at the DoubleTree Hotel in downtown Orlando and on the attractive grounds of the Rollins College campus, attracted nearly 200 attendees from around the globe, presenting scholarly papers or sharing their views in roundtable discussions. Staged readings of two full-length plays, arranged by our resident dramaturg, Janna Segal (University of Louisville), are a regular feature of the CDC; this year's offerings were Meghan Brown's *The Tasters* (directed by Rachel Carter) and Brian T. Silberman's *The Yip* (directed by Eric Zivot). Attending live theatre together is also a CDC tradition, and on Thursday evening conference participants were treated to a production of Caryl Churchill's *Top Girls* by Mad Cow Theater of Orlando; Mad Cow artistic director Mitzi Maxwell, *Top*

*Girls* director Tony Simotes, and set designer Eric Craft joined scholars Kerri Ann Considine (University of Tennessee–Knoxville), Rebecca Cameron (DePaul University), and Deborah Kochman (Florida State University) the following day to discuss the production with conference attendees. Another signature event at the CDC is Author Meets Critics, in which the author of a recent book in drama and theatre studies is invited to converse on stage with two critics, one of whom has reviewed the book for that year's *Text & Presentation*. We welcomed author Frances Babbage, who discussed her book *Adaptation in Contemporary Theatre: Performing Literature* with its reviewer, Verna A. Foster (Loyola University Chicago)—who responded in part with an adaptation of her own of Borges's short story "Borges and I"—and with Ann M. Shanahan (Purdue University).

That afternoon we also presented the annual Philadelphia Constantinidis Essay in Critical Theory Award, a prize for the best article on Greek drama or theatre published during the previous year, endowed by former conference director Stratos Constantinidis in memory of his late mother. It was given to Marilynn Richtarik (Georgia State University) for her essay "Reality and Justice: Seamus Heaney's *The Cure at Troy*," published in the *Journal of Irish Studies*, no. 13 (March 2018), 98–112. Essays for this award may address any aspect or period of Greek theatre, so long as the essay is comparative in nature and published in English in a journal or anthology (in any country). The deadline for nominations is December 31. Nominating letters and electronic copies of the essays (converted to Adobe PDF) should be emailed to the Constantinidis Award Committee Chair Elizabeth Scharffenberger at *es136@columbia.edu*.

On Friday evening we were transported to the lovely city of Winter Park, where Rollins College makes its home, for the keynote conversation between playwright Branden Jacobs-Jenkins (who is now co-directing the playwriting program at the University of Texas–Austin) and Baron Kelly (University of Louisville). Saturday morning's highlight was a roundtable discussion of the sixtieth anniversary of Lorraine Hansberry's *A Raisin in the Sun*, featuring Branden Jacobs-Jenkins, Baron Kelly, Janna Segal, and scholars Teresa Gilliams (Albright College) and Nathaniel G. Nesmith (Scholar-at-large).

All of the essays you'll encounter in *Text & Presentation, 2019*—a variety of research papers, performance and production studies, interviews with practitioners, and exploratory essays—began their lives as papers at the Comparative Drama Conference. Expanded versions were submitted for consideration, then double-blind reviewed by experts in the field, and the accepted essays were revised in response to reviewer suggestions. This volume, *Text & Presentation, 2019*, contains nine scholarly essays, transcripts of our keynote events, and six reviews of new books in drama and theatre studies. The range of subjects addressed includes performance theory, scenic design pedagogy, theories of adaptation and direction, analyses of classic and contemporary drama, and connections between visual art and theatre. In other words, a fairly typical year at the Comparative Drama Conference.

Playwright Branden Jacobs-Jenkins was a warm, witty, and incisive keynote speaker and amiably agreed to join the roundtable discussion on the legacy of *A Raisin in the Sun*. The transcripts of these two events form the first two essays of this volume and should give any readers unfamiliar with the CDC an excellent sense of the intellectual vibrancy and collegiality of the conference. The Comparative Drama Conference has long been known for its generosity to graduate students, and in recent years has added two prizes for the best graduate student papers submitted to *Text & Presentation*. The winners not only see their work in print in *T&P* but also receive financial assistance to attend the conference the following year. The Anthony Ellis Prize for the Best Paper by a Graduate Student was established to honor the memory of Tony Ellis, late scholar of early modern Venetian and Shakespearean drama and longtime friend of the CDC. Victoria Lynn Scrimer (University of Maryland) has won the prize for the second year in a row; her essay, "Radical Resurrections: A Performance History of John Brown's Body," is an artful exploration of how the idea of abolitionist John Brown's body has fired the moral imagination of many a writer (playwright, songwriter, poet) for over a century now. The Joel Tansey Memorial Award for Graduate Student Travel to the CDC was dedicated in honor of Joel Tansey, award-winning scholar of French literature and former Assistant Editor of *Text & Presentation*. Michael Schweikardt (Pennsylvania State University) has won the prize for his paper, "Deep When: A Basic Design Philosophy for Addressing Holidays in Historical Dramas," an argument and instructional guide for teaching scenic designers to go beyond merely decorating the stage to using scene design to build the visual world of the play.

The two essays that follow those prize-winners focus on plays that are taking our pulse, staging the economic, political, and cultural anxieties of our era. M. Scott Phillips (Auburn University) examines Heidegger's theory of the uncanny and how the stresses of the 2008 financial crisis hit residents of Detroit and New Orleans in "Uncanniness and Alienation in Lisa D'Amour's *Detroit* and *Airline Highway*." Paul D. Reich (Rollins College) ruminates on the question of what cultural texts we would preserve after the fall of our civilization in his essay "Precious Resources: Cultural Archiving in the Post-Apocalyptic Worlds of *Mr. Burns* and *Station Eleven*," a comparative study of Anne Washburn's innovative drama, *Mr. Burns, a Post-Electric Play*, and Emily St. John Mandel's best-selling novel.

"Past the Lyrical," by Phillip Zapkin (Pennsylvania State University), continues a long CDC tradition of fine papers on dramatic adaptations of Greek myth; his essay digs into Marina Carr's "meta-mythical" retellings of the Phaedra story in her 2011 play *Phaedra Backwards*. Also exploring theories of adaptation, but of late fifteenth- and seventeenth-century French farces, Scott D. Taylor (University of Southern California), in "Infidelity, Adaptation and Textuality: Directing Late Medieval and Early Modern French Farce," turns our attention to the director-as-writer creating adaptations of *La farce de Maître Pathelin* and Moliere's *Les précieuses ridicules* that are accessible to contemporary audiences.

Our final three essays are by figures familiar to participants at the Comparative Drama Conference and readers of *Text & Presentation*. Tennessee Williams scholar Jeffrey B. Loomis (Northwestern Missouri State University), in his essay "Rectories Meet 'One-Hour' Rooms: Williams on Summery and Eccentric Loves," returns to his deep knowledge of the Williams archives to ponder distinctions between sexual intimacy as illicit or spiritual love in the drafts of the Alma Winemiller stories that became *Summer and Smoke* and *The Eccentricities of a Nightingale*. William Hutchings (University of Alabama–Birmingham) continues his series of interviews with contemporary playwrights, this time investigating Michael Laurence's theatrical response to Beckett, "A Portrait of the Krapp as a Young[er] Man: Michael Laurence's *Krapp, 39*"; his essay includes an artist's statement by Laurence as well as a conversation between the two. And Doug Phillips (University of St. Thomas), known to *T&P* readers for his aesthetic and philosophical explorations, offers "Waiting for Rothko," a wry and moving meditation on waiting and thinking in John Logan's 2009 play *Red*, about Mark Rothko's late-1950s commissioned paintings for the Four Seasons restaurant in New York City. The volume concludes with six book reviews, on subjects from classical Greek tragedy to contemporary Latinx performance, the playwright Ayad Akhtar, plays of the Progressive Era (1890–1920) in the United States, drag dances, and tragedy in modern American drama, an impressive range selected and coordinated by our Book Review Editor, Michael Schwartz.

The Comparative Drama Conference seeks original research on any aspect of dramatic literature, theory, criticism, performance, production, translation, or history. We are eager to see work that crosses national and cultural boundaries, that is multidisciplinary, and that breaks new ground and attracts new audiences. Only papers presented at the annual conference are eligible for consideration in that year's volume of *Text & Presentation*. Proposals are due each year in early November; information and updates can be found on our website: http://blogs.rollins.edu/drama/. On behalf of the executive board, I invite all readers of this volume of *Text & Presentation* to share your research with us at a future conference.

*Amy Muse* • *University of St. Thomas*

# A Conversation with Branden Jacobs-Jenkins

*Transcript of Keynote Panel: April 5, 2019*
*Presiding:* BARON KELLY

## Abstract

*The keynote address at this year's Comparative Drama Conference was a conversation with playwright Branden Jacobs-Jenkins. His plays include* Everybody *and* Gloria, *both Pulitzer Prize finalists;* An Octoroon *and* Appropriate, *both Obie Award winners; and* Neighbors. *He is the recipient of a MacArthur "Genius Grant" Fellowship, the Charles Wintour Award for Most Promising Playwright, the Windham-Campbell Prize for drama, the Benjamin H. Danks Award from the American Academy of Arts and Letters, the PEN/Laura Pels Theater Award, the Steinberg Distinguished Playwright Award, and the inaugural Tennessee Williams Award. In this wide-ranging conversation with director and scholar Baron Kelly (University of Louisville), Jacobs-Jenkins addresses anxieties of whiteness and representations of blackness in American drama, experiences of identification in the theater, the legacy of African-American playwrights in the contemporary theater, and challenges of casting.*

**Baron Kelly [BK]:** Let me just start out by saying that this is an intense and truly wonderful honor for me to be on the stage with you.

**Branden Jacobs-Jenkins [BJJ]:** Likewise.

**BK:** Thank you, brother. Thank you. Let's start off by having you talk a little bit about your grandmother and the strong presence for you that she's been in your life—the sense memory of the safety and majesty of childhood.

**BJJ:** You want me to talk about her? Yeah, okay, this is a very interesting way to start. I mean, I don't mind it. Ironically enough, I am formulating a play about my grandmother—I can feel it coming and I'm, like, resisting it so you're kind of tapping into my thoughts right now. Well, my grandmother, her name was Helen Marie Tate, she was a schoolteacher in Camden, Arkansas. It's unclear when she was born because she lied about her age, but she passed when I was a young pup. I would spend the summer with her because my mother was a single mother in D.C. and she would ship the kids off to Arkansas in the summer because she just wanted a break. And so I spent every summer of my childhood until my grandmother passed in Camden, Arkansas. And when I talk about the sense memory of that, it's oddly—I've always admired writers who have a very ingrained sense of place, a geography, like Dominique Morisseau or Sam Hunter, Annie Baker (it's funny to use those people's last names because they're my friends)—and I feel like the place that for a long time my imagination went to whenever I began writing about anything was Arkansas. And it was just because I grew up in D.C. when it was like the murder capital of the world, so you didn't spend a lot of time hanging out in D.C. So my idea of the outside is still in some ways based on my memories in Arkansas.

And my grandmother is important because she was a playwright. It's funny the stories you tell yourself; for a while I was like, oh, I found this by myself, but it was my mom who said, do you not recall that your grandmother wrote these adaptations of Bible stories for her church that were very popular? And, from what I understand, somewhat avant-garde. And the minute she told me that, I had this flood of remembering the sound of her typewriter late into the night, because she'd be working on these plays really late. She also directed them herself. She did the props herself. And the deep irony here is that I would be put in her plays, in these pageants. And the first thing I remember playing was a bunny and that was sort of why, yeah, it all came full circle twenty-odd years later and I'm literally in a bunny costume in my own play. And I think that's where I got the taste of what theater was. I still remember her rehearsals, her running these rehearsals. I have this really intense memory of when she made these swords out of wood, like scimitars. And I remember in a rehearsal, I accidentally hit another guy in the head with it and I remember being like oh, theater is dangerous! This is why you rehearse things: you make sure this doesn't happen. And my very first memory of the theater (I guess she was doing this for like market research) was that she took me to this play that was essentially like a Passion Play, like a crude form of a Passion Play. And it was a play about Jesus. We were in this wild sort of stadium seating outdoors. And my memory is of Jesus ascending to the heavens on this sort of elevator—like what we call it a trap elevator that goes up, but it's wrapped in black plastic, like garbage bags, I guess to mask that it's not—like Jesus isn't just floating up there. And I remember the car ride home and it being very late and I was very confused and wondering, was that *Jesus*? I didn't understand that it wasn't real; my

A Conversation with Branden Jacobs-Jenkins (Kelly) 7

**Baron Kelly, left, interviews playwright Branden Jacobs-Jenkins (courtesy Jamie Renee Hoffman/Rollins College).**

first memory of the theater was asking, did we just see Jesus? Was that Jesus? So she really is the beginning—if you have to give anyone the credit, she's sort of the beginning of the bug in a lot of ways.

**BK:** When you were 13 years old, you saw a production of *Waiting for Godot* at Studio Theatre. And I read something that you said: all of your work is trying to recreate that experience.

**BJJ:** Yeah. Yeah.

**BK:** You had those really intense sense memories of not knowing what was going on but being completely riveted. You know what I mean? That's similar to a person that I've written about and we talked about today, Earle Hyman, who also was similarly riveted by Ibsen when he was 13 years old. Let me ask you a question about—

**BJJ:** Are you going to ask about that? Because the point that I think gets lost is that production is a very famous and controversial production in Washington, D.C., at the Studio Theatre. It was color-blind. So Didi and Gogo were played by black actors, locally well-known black actors. And the [Beckett] estate tried to shut it down. The accusation was that they were changing Beckett's language and their argument was, no, we're actually just speaking English. But I think because of that controversy, a lot of middle-class blacks at the time were taking their kids to see this, whereas normally you'd see other work. And it was a very significant—and retrospectively to psychoanalyze myself, I think it was important that I was seeing these bodies occupy this modernist space. In a way that I never saw again, to be honest. And that was a very important kind of thing I've held onto for a long time.

**BK:** You flip things around in your work where you analyze whiteness—the whiteness of Miller, O'Neill—and you've said everyone is always writing about race, that artists of color get labeled as writing about race when actually if you look at every classic American play, they're all about race. Maybe you could unpack that a little bit.

**BJJ:** Yeah, that idea began to formulate for me around the time of *August: Osage County*. I had this profound experience with a play by Lydia Diamond called *Stick Fly* that had gone to Broadway and I was crying—it's just one of three times I've cried while watching a show on Broadway—and I realized I was identifying in a way that I'd never been invited to identify ever in the theater. And it was really strange, and I was like, oh my God, this is what everyone else has been experiencing. And I remember that the reviews of it at the time by Charles Isherwood, who no longer is reviewing, accused it of being too melodramatic and not being enough about social issues. And I recalled that when *August: Osage County* happened, the reviews were like, it's good old-fashioned melodrama and there's nothing wrong with that! So very early on I was perceiving a double standard that I felt no one was talking about. And sort of following that breadcrumb trail, I began to realize that there was a different expectation put on artists of color, and specifically black playwrights, when it came to telling stories about family. And this sort of became the impulse behind my play *Appropriate*. I went back and thought, okay, I'm going to read all of these plays, influenced very much by Arthur Miller's incredibly influential essay "Tragedy and the Common Man" and this moment of believing that the American drama's value was in recasting social tragedy, a social drama, into the domestic space. I'm going to try to trace this archaeology of why we think this is anything. And it took me back to O'Neill, which is where we all think American theater starts, which is so silly.

When I began to assemble this kind of canon of American family dramas, I realized that they were all about anxieties of whiteness. That the O'Neill play *Long Day's Journey*, which we all think of as the peak of the mountain, is totally about his family's spiritual turmoil of releasing their Irish roots to become white. And then I remember reading *Streetcar* (people rarely read *Streetcar*; people cheat and watch the movie and think it's *Streetcar*, which is a great movie), and you know, the first moments of *A Streetcar* are a black and a white woman talking, and the black one makes a dick jo—oh, sorry: the black one makes a joke about, oh, about Stanley's meat. [*laughter*] And then when (spoiler alert!) when Stanley is assaulting Blanche, when Williams is depicting this assault, he cuts away to the image of a white woman being mugged by a black woman. And I was like, God, this is so interesting. They're all using… they all have a feeling or point of view on how blackness is used on stage. But no one marks that in the discussions about them as classics.

**BK:** What do you think about when in the second act of *Streetcar* the vendor comes on and says, "hot tamales"—

**BJJ:** "Red hot, red hot, red hot." It's funny you say that. I remember—I read *Streetcar* like twice a year, but I remember reading it in high school and I didn't understand, I had no idea what was going on. But I remember thinking I would really love to play this vendor, who has the one line and comes on and goes "red hot." I was like, I'd be really good at that. But it never panned out. The point being that I realized there was a story in all of these major works about American life. They were all about the panic around racial tension, but it wasn't—you know, even *Death of a Salesman* is all about this unmarked, maybe Jewish family next door. It was just odd that it was a thing we didn't talk about.

But then when you look at something like *The Piano Lesson*, it's considered to be about the legacies of history, whereas I really feel a family story in that before I feel anything. All ghost stories are family stories in some way. I remember when Bruce Norris, at the moment of *Clybourne Park* or a little bit after—by the way, the thing I remember thinking about *August: Osage County* is like, we're going to talk about this woman in the attic, this quote "Indian in the Cupboard," and then *Clybourne Park* happened and I remember reading all these weird interviews with Bruce where he was saying he would watch *A Raisin in the Sun* and not know who he was supposed to identify with except for Karl, the white guy who came in, and I was like, wow, that's really interesting. Here I am going to all these [plays about white families] and I know how to identify with the family, but oddly you're having a hard time identifying with a family that doesn't look like you. This was an odd moment for me. And it really spun me out. I guess I've been making work about that moment of, well, the tension between how experience is narrated after the fact, but also the moment of identification in the theater and what's so important about that: being able to identify across identity or rethink the way that you think you have access to certain stories.

**BK:** I can piggyback on that because in your play *Neighbors*, let's say, there's a representation of blackness in that play—

**BJJ:** There's several—

**BK:** Several, and the audience is to interrogate perhaps what is authentically black and what, if anything, we are really talking about in that play. Can you talk a little bit about that for people who probably don't know that play?

**BJJ:** Yeah. You sort of just summed it up really neatly. It's a play that I— I was also twenty-two or twenty-three when I started writing that play and I wanted to write sort of the Last Play. This is also pre–Obama. I wanted to write like.... I was sort of getting annoyed by this: I was just out of college, I was just out of school, and I was suddenly feeling like I was being asked in the industry to step aside from the students that I had been going to school with for the last four years, and to bring something into a creative space that no one else was being asked to bring in. Like I felt this sort of expectation was preceding me that I hadn't been trained for, if that makes sense.

And I was expected to know more about something than anyone else I knew, knew about it. I remember feeling like, okay, I'm going to do this play that it seems everyone wants me to make, but I'm going to just do it so crazy that no one would ever ask me to do it again. [*laughter*] I remember feeling that. I was going to write like the Last Black Play or something. I was going to write the play that literally summed up the origins to the, what I thought— you know, August [Wilson] had just passed, and so I was like, what's that next step after August? And I still think it's the next step, which is a story about an interracial family that isn't, you know, that feels.... So I wanted to mash those two poles up. I somehow thought if I could take the two ends of history and smash them together then we would be done. And so in that play, you have a family that's drawn from real minstrelsy archetypes. I've fudged a couple of people, but only advanced scholars will notice. And I wanted to put a black man on stage who, quote, "talked white." I wanted to put a young mixed-race girl on stage who didn't know where she was in terms of her allegiance. And I thought somehow by really saturating the theater space, or the theater container, with the different versions of blackness that itself had generated over the years, we might somehow get closer to the reality, the realization, that the theater is not going to—you know the joke about, the thing about race, is it's the greatest theater game ever. It's like when we all kind of went after Rachel Dolezal; it's like, why are we going after her because she's playing the game against us? So I felt somehow in the theater, if I could make a play that pointed out the absurdity of trying to represent a thing that wasn't real, it might bring people to another plane of thought or something.

**BK:** Was it a breakthrough moment for you as an artist?

**BJJ:** Oh, totally. Yeah. I mean, I thought, I really thought it would be the last play about the issue, but it just opened a door that I've been living in for the last ten, twelve, thirteen years. And it's funny, I just was—there are whispers about reviving that play, which is so odd that we'd be talking about a revival and I am just a baby. But we went back and read through it and it was interesting to hear me working out my—I could feel the ideas that I was working through and how they would become other plays. It was really interesting.

**BK:** Because that launched you. Was it sort of traumatizing in a way for you?

**BJJ:** Yes, it was very traumatizing for different reasons. It was traumatizing because I wrote it, and we were sort of unprotected by the institution that produced it in a way that was, that I think they feel actually quite a lot of shame about now, to be honest. And the press at the time was crazy. It felt crazy. We were supposed to be doing this like it was a workshop production in their 72-seat theater with a quarter of a normal budget, but we got more press coverage than any show that season got, despite being promised that we wouldn't have that coverage. Someone had leaked the play to the press, and they basically were like, we're going to write about it whether or not you say anything. So then—and I was just a baby, I mean I was just a kid, I had no idea what any of this was. I expect it to be protected in ways that it wasn't. And I felt very confident in my intellectual thought, I mean, I felt, I actually feel like I got through it very well, obviously, but it was, it was a lot to take in. And I think about if it had premiered now, with Instagram and Twitter and, you know, people putting petitions up to take shows down, I have no idea how it would fare now. But at the time it was truly traumatic. I mean, I ran away; I moved to Berlin the day after it closed and lived there for two years because I couldn't handle it. But it was funny because I remember when I got this review by Charles Isherwood, one of his more famously eviscerating crazy reviews, which was awesome to me because at the time I was working for Hilton Als and John Lahr, so I actually knew how to read criticism with a grain of salt. And I realized he was asking me questions in the review and I was like, that's a good sign, actually; I got the critic to ask questions out loud.

And I remember seeing Mark Ravenhill, who was randomly in town and someone had set us up for a meal or a lunch, and I was being down on myself about my mean *Times* review, and he said some things I'll never forget. And one of them was, if anything this has just made you *more* interesting. I was like, oh. And then he said, it would have been a problem if they *did* like it because what you're doing ultimately is critiquing a system that they are active participants in creating. So if they had liked it, I would ask you to be frightened that you hadn't completed—you hadn't done your thing. And that was important to me. That advice carried me through the next few years, and the next few plays, when I really sat and thought about what he was saying. Because it did feel like I was embarking on some sort of—I needed to shift something even if it was just an inch, in a better or different direction, when it came to questions of representation in the theater.

**BK:** [*To the audience*] How many of you know Branden's adaptation of *An Octoroon*? Okay. Many.

**BJJ:** Thank you. So nice.

**BK:** What a lot of people don't realize—before we get into *An Octoroon*—is that African American theater artists in the early part of the twentieth century also would put on, like, stage Irish, stage Italian. There would be whiteface with particular black actors in performances, particularly in New York City. And so here we have Verna Foster, where's Verna? [*Indicating her in the audience*] We were talking about Dion Boucicault today in the elevator. The first time I became aware of Dion Boucicault was when I was doing research on the nineteenth-century great British actor, Henry Irving—and how Irving made his early career doing the melodramas of Boucicault. And Boucicault was part of a group of French writers who were reinventing this particular form of theater. They were codifying it in a particular way. And what I think is interesting about what Branden has done to the play is that he is speaking to today through working through the original script, because there's only about maybe, what, 70–80 percent of the—

**BJJ:** I would say less than that.

**BK:** Less than that. And what do you think the issues are in working with that particular form of melodrama today? Do you think that audiences understand that the emotions have to be particularly large in melodrama, that you're writing of particular histories with characters that—you've condensed characters in that play? If you can speak to representation again: what does that mean?

**BJJ:** Well, the funny thing about melodrama, that whole thing got me on this kick of trying to ask the question of, well, what is American theater? What are we talking about? Like, why do we pretend that it just happened twenty years ago? It started honestly with me thinking through O'Neill and being like, O'Neill had influences, and there's a play of his I'm obsessed with and have been trying to adapt forever and haven't figured out, called *The Emperor Jones*. And I forgot where I was reading this, but *Emperor Jones* kind of climaxes, in terms of the height of its believability, in the slave auction fantasy. And I remember reading something that drew a connection between that and *The Octoroon*, the idea of this sensation scene being a slave auction. And I was like, oh right, he himself is sort of metabolizing this history in some ways to remake it or rethink it. And the funny thing about *An Octoroon* and melodrama is that it still very much lives with us. I mean, it just became film—it moved into film, and so audiences are actually far more acclimated to that style of storytelling than they admit to themselves. And it was interesting to watch, I think part of the success of the play early on was people walking in with a certain like, this isn't going to get me, it's an old fart museum piece. But when it works on you, you're like, oh my God, I love this feeling of people doing too much! The human body exerting that much energy and emotion, it's just a thing we love to see—it's circus, it's sensation ultimately that became really important in that regard. I also felt like that play landed because we're still obsessed with what people are. We still are obsessed with who is what, and we're still playing the big theater game of race being like, you know, what do you think she is? What is she, what is she, what is she not, and literally all the play is about—

**BK:** The tension between what you see and what you've been told.

**BJJ:** Yeah. What you get and what you think someone is; what you first thought, what you feel someone is. You know, we're in a really interesting moment of confusing feelings with facts, and that is melodrama. Melodrama is playing on your feeling to give you a sense of illusion. And it became an important playground for me and taught me a lot.

**BK:** And in the nineteenth century there was a multiple consciousness that black people lived in certainly, and in New York City in the pleasure gardens, all of a sudden white people were seeing, you know, the working folk dressing up on one day of the week and enacting this sort of whiteness, particularly down in the Village in these pleasure gardens. And that totally disrupted a lot of people. They didn't know what to think about that kind of stuff.

**BJJ:** Yeah. Eric Lott's book *Love and Theft* was a huge deal for me and for a lot of my plays. But my big aha! moment with *The Octoroon* when I was adapting it, was when I realized that no black people were in the company. I had this green book called something like *Plays about Slavery* that I got from my Barnes and Noble. (*To the audience:* If you edited it and you're here, thank you!) I remember reading the dramatis personae and there's all this attention paid to the color of the various slaves. I was like, why would he care if someone was yellow or light brown? And I realized it was all about makeup—that he was telling a story through makeup and vision. And that's really when that play popped open for me: this question of, right, this was probably a troupe of more or less white actors who were capitalizing on a curiosity about race. There was a desire to represent realistically this race question. And I was like, oh my God, that's it, it's about that desire. It's about that need for something—which was more important to me than the play itself.

**BK:** Which character did he play?

**BJJ:** Boucicault? Well, famously he played Wahnotee, but then he took over, I believe Scudder, which I cut out, well, combined him in my play, but for me that was an important moment too because I realized what it meant for—well, I don't know; I have a whole read on Boucicault that I can't honestly confirm, but I think he was actually incredibly sly about representation, whether or not it was conscious. I think he very intentionally cast himself as "the drunk," and he was this Irish guy. He was Anglo-Irish, and his entire career as an actor was based on him touring the region, and there were these reviews that were like, he's so good in this Shakespeare, you couldn't even tell he was Irish. But then he gets to London and they're like, this guy's Irish, get him *outta* here! And I think that for me, that's the story of a person wrestling with the weird double standards of a form that makes a pretense towards democracy and openness and transgression. And he comes to America and he takes on the part of the American stereotype of the drunk illiterate. But if you look closely enough at that character (and I get read all the time for my treatment of that character), if you really read closely what he's doing, he's made a character who actually speaks four languages and who actually is like, this is the only real site of nobility in the piece. But because we don't understand his language, we dismiss him as a clown. And I was like, God, that is such a sophisticated piece of construction conceptually as a playwright to work your way into. And the fact that he played it was like him pointing the arrow at something, which I thought was really cool.

**BK:** When you got a chance to work with his work, though, did you as a playwright have to get intimate with another person's work to figure out this other person's process and their choices?

**BJJ:** Yep, totally. As much as you can. It was very eerie because I feel like I don't believe in spirits and stuff, but I got really—I would be reading that play and I'd be like, oh…. And this is a testament to his writing, honestly, because he never really wrote to publish; from what I understand, everything we have of his are weird cue scripts that were found in an attic somewhere that people put together, and I would read a thing and I'd be like, oh my God, I can see his staging. I see exactly why he wrote it this way because this person's behind a rock and this person's coming from stage right. When you get that deep with someone, it's like archaeology; you're piecing together a practice. You do start to feel like you're in some kind of uncharted territory ultimately. Because I—look, I'm one of a handful of playwrights who actually does go into JSTOR and read academic writing; I'm always ordering the most obscure book on like morality theater from Amazon marketplace. It's a mess; my house is a mess. But yeah, I did feel like I learned so much from him. And I found this unpublished half of an essay that he wrote—one copy of it happens to live in the New York Public Library—where he's outlining his, it's called "Art of Dramatic Composition," and he's outlining his ideas of the theater and I completely absorbed those ideas. I felt the scholar in him, I felt the guy kind of trying to wrestle with Aristotle in some odd way. And the truth is, I find *The Octoroon*— I mean he's written a lot of really amazing stuff—but *The Octoroon* is his last because it's actually not, it's not a melodrama because Zoe is not resolved and in some funny ways, it's like a melodrama that becomes a tragedy and that's what makes it really singular in his oeuvre.

**BK:** So, in a way, language is a conceit of peeling away, of feeling, sort of like Ibsen, like with *Peer Gynt* and the onion: the layers are peeled away to get to what's going to happen there.

**BJJ:** Well, yeah, and I mean there's still—when I read *The Octoroon* there are things I still catch, like this motif of snakes and toxin and poison that follows Zoe. I mean, it took me 20,000 reads to be like, oh my God, even on a *line* level, he's weaving in almost musical phrases, these images that haunt certain performers. This level of composition; I don't know anyone who's sustaining that now. You know, it's really amazing to be that in touch with a master in that way.

**BK:** How does spectacle animate your creative process?

**BJJ:** How does it animate my creative process? I mean, I believe in it. I believe it's the secret to a good play. There's a lot of cynicism around it in the theater. I think people don't believe that spectacle is possible in the theater. So you get a lot of talky, very serious plays about issues without thinking like maybe we want a little *mo'* than that, you know? I have never seen someone leave a play and be like, oh my God, that scene where they talk about that issue? [*laughter*]

The things that ultimately define the theater are those illusions of reality that Aristotle and Boucicault and all those guys talk about, and the heart of that is spectacle. And that's what those old guys are incredible at; they really find a way to turn that spectacle in a new and fresh way. Whereas I feel like we have a lot of writers today who—and these are my friends—who don't quite know how to generate that energy or why to generate that energy. And I think that's really interesting. But when spectacle really works, you're almost in a spiritual place. You're in a place of speechlessness, you're in a place of, of overwhelmed—you're in your body the most somehow, in my opinion, when you're facing spectacle.

**BK:** At dinner tonight with my friends we were talking about how the size of a house can matter—whether, you know, a 99-seat house as compared to a 2000-seat house, and then how the play has to be able to transfer for the audience. I know that you care about how the audience feels, or if the audience can feel something, and if they can feel something together perhaps.

**BJJ:** Yeah. That's the question of scale, which is the big challenge facing my cohort of writers. There's been a kind of boom in the arts in which every major theater in New York opened up a black box in a basement that would be, you know, where the young writer would start out. And so everyone began to pitch their work to that kind of scale and space. And I think this is why you have—like, Annie Baker's voice was very influential in a huge generation of people because it was this study of a sort of naturalism where it's about small gestures and scrutinizing interior states through very small things. And the reason why that took off as an aesthetic was because it really works like gangbusters in a small space. But then this thing happened where suddenly everyone had to go upstairs and be in their like 300- or 400-seat house. That's the proscenium space. And no one knew how to build in that room, how to build to scale. I mean, when you watch something like *Angels in America,* you want to jump off a bridge because you're like, this is a play that fills an entire theater! I mean from the back of the house to the balcony, and to get that sort of technical awareness, you do have to kind of teach yourself and it's becoming harder and harder for people to do that, to figure that out.

**BK:** And you, you're so adaptable—

**BJJ:** Oh, please—

**BK:** You go and write a play like—

**BJJ:** You're so sweet. I'm struggling to write it—

**BK:** What about *Gloria*? It's the flip end, the other side of that, where you have a bunch of people working in an office and it's about artistic ambition and how certain things can drive people to a particular state. Did that come from another place where you said in yourself, in your artistic process, let me explore this, as opposed to what you were doing in *An Octoroon,* because there were other issues?

**BJJ:** Oddly, I think it came out of *An Octoroon; Gloria* initially, I think, was an investigation of sensation. It was me learning from Boucicault about what it is to bring people close to a realistic depiction of the horrible—or suffering, rather—because I remember there's a line from the Boucicault essay where he's like the pure intention (I'm kind of botching it, so if there are Boucicault people here, please forgive me), the intention of theater is to bring an audience as close to possible to the truest illusion of suffering. That is all it's for. And that really stuck with me; for me, *Gloria* is all about suffering. The religious resonance of the title is not an accident. It is trying to think about purification and being in work and in life and death and all these things—and talking about and thinking about it. For me, that play's very much connected to *An Octoroon*. And it's because of *Octoroon* and the work I found—the kind of patch I stumbled in thinking through what doubling was—that led to the doubling of *Gloria*. So they're all kind of a continuum to me. They're all me investigating something else—the last thing asked of me to do.

**BK:** Have there been casting decisions that you've ever questioned?

**BJJ:** Yes. You mean in general? Well, yeah. But yes, there have been, especially with *Gloria* because I feel like, I think I go out of my way to, if you look at the casting breakdown, everything is sort of either in quotes or like—you know, I get a lot of.... These are the only two plays where I really leaned into how absurd I think cast lists are. *An Octoroon* has like fourteen different variables in order of my preference, which drives people nuts, but it's on purpose, because I think it's ultimately an insane errand to ask me.... Let me stop. So: *Gloria, Gloria* sort of devolves into list-questions. And the last one on that list is this guy named Lorin, who's "unclear," it's unclear what he is, and that's intentional because I want you to hire the actor who you just don't know what he is. And this is how that actor who doesn't get any work—honestly, because he's working in a field that's got very codified ways of looking at people. And I get a little disappointed when I see a production of it where it's a random, lovely, very good actor, but like a random Caucasian guy, you know? Because I feel like it's an opportunity to be slightly more adventurous in any direction. And it's sad when it sort of lands there. But otherwise, no, I think I'm open to the challenge of how hard—I mean, listen, I wrote a play called *Everybody* that literally requires you to cast five random people; it could be anything, any night. This question of casting is very important to me, and I think it's rooted in my own experience of being cast or not cast as a kid. And it's always, I always go into every piece with a bit of cynicism where it's like, in truth, people are going to cast whoever they want to cast, so how do I let people know that I'm watching. [*laughter*] Ultimately, I want people to own their own choices, so if you're going to go against me as a writer, I want that to be clear to people that that's what you're doing. Because that says more about you than anything else.

**BK:** What about in the rehearsal process? How present are you, so that perhaps if an actor has a question about something, can they come to you?

**BJJ:** Well, for a premiere, I'm very present. I mean I'm there every day with the director. We're working through the piece. The way I more or less build plays now is I write something and start folding actors in right before it's finished to just get a sense of who might be right for the part. And that's when they really ask the questions. Because I tell my students all the time, the thing people don't realize is that as a writer, this is like my entire involvement in a piece [*gesturing a level with one hand*]. And then this is the actors' involvement in the thing [*gesturing a level with the other hand*], and this is how much we overlap [*bringing hands together to show "very little"*]. And that is called rehearsal, you know? The task of rehearsal is downloading everything I know into other people's bodies so they can do something with it. And I take that very seriously, because otherwise the only people who can mess up your show are actors; they can do whatever they want at the end of the day. [*laughter*] So yeah, I try to be as available as possible, especially in those early productions because it feels important.

**BK:** What about the legacy of Wilson, Hansberry, Adrienne Kennedy, Alice Childress in your work?

**BJJ:** Their influence is as important if not more important than Williams and Miller and O'Neill. I've been on this real kick recently about coherence and how I think that there's always this phenomenon—there's one right now happening with all of these trend pieces about hey, look at all these black playwrights, where did they come from? And it's like, well, this happens every ten years, so we all show up and then everyone forgets and then there are new ones and there are new trend pieces. While the truth is there is a very strong tradition that we have that is uniquely American of black writers, black American writers—

**BK:** And Kennedy has not been done as often—

**BJJ:** Well, Kennedy herself will tell you she was saved by the academy. I mean she says she wouldn't have anything if it wasn't for the people sitting there writing about her and getting her down there. But Adrienne's work, her work on interiority, black interiority, is completely influencing everyone who's working right now in some significant way. And she's really kind of our—she's the hook into Albee and that branch of the American theater tradition. I had a very Oedipal relationship with Wilson for so long. But it's, funnily enough, I've just been talking to a guy named Michael R. Jackson, who's a musical theater writer, and I was saying I have really been missing Wilson; in these six months or so I have really been appreciating what his project was more than I ever have. Really seeing the space he carved out conceptually is powerful.

And Hansberry—I am obsessed with Lorraine, who is *not* obsessed with Lorraine Hansberry who knows one thing about her?—she really, I think doesn't quite.... I wrote a review of a biography of hers that just came out, and I was just sort of shocked by how little is known about her, but if you work in the theater, you feel her influence very vividly. Everyone's doing *A Raisin in the Sun* all the time and forever. It's one of those plays that's always being done in the world somewhere, which is really profound.

The person that I think is super under-sung is Lloyd Richards, because Lloyd Richards—why is there not a biography of Lloyd Richards?—is the architect of everything we're living inside of, not just in terms of people of color working, but he reinvented new play development. With the O'Neill Theater he completely rewrote the way that new plays were written and developed and that work, that program, has been copied by places like Sundance. Anything now that is devoted to identifying emerging artists or developing new work is all because of Lloyd. It's unbelievable. His stewardship of the Yale Rep gave us Angela Bassett, Courtney Vance. This man—I'm obsessed with figures like this who really do redirect the current. So in terms of this legacy, I feel very humbled by the legacy, and I proselytize about this legacy because it's truly like.... I mean, the only play I've ever seen—that I've ever gone back and seen three times was Ruben Santiago-Hudson's revival of *The Piano Lesson* because it blew. my. mind.

**BK:** At Signature.

**BJJL** Yeah, at Signature. I just think it's almost impossible to make work like that anymore. If you look at the brilliance of how that was developed and the way that he was able to tap into regional communities and it was, it's just like you can't—I was joking with someone who saw *The Ferryman* that all American playwrights I know, we're all kind of annoyed, I mean we all respected it, but we're like, yeah, but no one lets *us* do that. No one lets us put seventeen people on stage and a goose and a cat and a rabbit and a baby, you know? We're all sitting here making our three-character dramas in a kitchen. Of course it feels good! We all want to make that! But we don't have the infrastructure here to sustain that kind of bigness of imagination. But August and Lloyd built that for themselves and the difference it made is legion; it's completely amazing.

And Alice Childress, first of all I think she's having a moment—I have a feeling she's going to have a moment. If you really look at what she did, even *Trouble in Mind*, all this work about representation now goes back to her; she was the first person to open up this conceptual space of the black theater artist commenting on theater-making. And that's what half of us are doing right now, while the other half are doing something else. It's amazing.

**BK:** *Wine in the Wilderness.*

**BJJ:** *Wine in the Wilderness, The Wedding Band....* Yeah, it's so.... And her novels, her novels are amazing, too, but no one talks about those. She's fallen between the cracks, but she opened the first door for a lot of people. You know *Trouble in Mind* was supposed to be the first play by a black woman on Broadway, and then she said no, because the producers wanted to change it. And so then Lorraine became the first—you know, it's these near misses.... It's not enough to just celebrate one person. It's celebrating the network of people that make that person possible. You know what I mean?

**BK:** I do. Tennessee Williams had Audrey Wood as his agent and confidante. Is there someone that you've had in your artistic life that has served like an Audrey Wood?

**BJJ:** Not really. Um, didn't he fire Audrey Wood at some point? [*laughter*] Yeah. I don't. I have a good little tribe of buddies who I will share things with when I feel like they're ready. I'm in a bit of a writers' group with some writers, but I don't have anyone I, like, hit Print and immediately hand it to them. Not even—my agent's always like, you never give me anything until the last minute! And I'm like, I know! I don't know why that is. I guess I'd rather.... There are actors who I will always call on to be there for the first read. But that's less about wanting their notes and more about hearing what they do with it. Because I think I learn more from watching other people work with the work than I do from them telling me what they think.

**BK:** So do you trust someone in the process? You have a couple of stepparents that you trust with your plays, I think. Do you listen to them if they talk about a particular line or particular section?

**BJJ:** Yeah, I think—what the stepparents are that I'm referring to are my directors. I have four or five directors who I cycle between depending on what the play is calling for. Sometimes the play will be like, I think that's my stepparent and I'll go, Lileana, I think this is your play. Lileana Blain-Cruz is one of them. I've known her for a long time. And the process is about the illusion I'm trying to create, whether it's coming through on the page, and it's about sort of being in the—like Sarah Benson and I are developing a thing now that I've been sort of mulling over.

**BK:** From Soho Rep.

**BJJ:** Yeah, at Soho Rep; she directed the original *Octoroon* and we have a really crazy—we lock into each other creatively in a really amazing way. And I feel like the experience with her is like holding hands with someone in the dark, trying to find out what's in the room, and she's really game for that stuff, but not every director is like that.

**BK:** What about your work internationally? Like in London? The reception there—

**BJJ:** Yeah, I've been very fortunate; London was very lovely to me. I'm still very promising to them, which is great. It's been interesting because for so long my work was dismissed as being too American and I've noticed a substantial shift in the last three to four years where suddenly there was curiosity about what I was doing and there was actually a bigger interest in what I was doing formally. There's a lot of energy around American playwriting right now as it's perceived internationally. And it's weirding me out because we all complain all the time; we're texting all the time, lots of sad emojis, about how this is the worst, this is the pits. But then when you go to London or you go to Berlin, people are like, what's going on over there? And we're suddenly like, oh, are we doing something great? We were just hanging out. [*laughter*]

I think it has to do with the tradition that we were very lucky to have over here of the '60s; I think Albee made something happen where he broke off the mainstream and invested in the fringes. And so you had people like Fornes, you had Shepard, you had this Guare moment, you had this moment that actually is the defining locus of what's important about American drama in the last half of the twentieth century. And those people all became the teachers that taught the people who taught all of us now. And so every—it's funny, in London Caryl Churchill is not, well, now she's coming back in fashion, but for so long no one cared about Caryl Churchill. But every playwright on this side of the pond, from me going back to Tony Kushner, the first person out of their mouth in terms of influence might be Caryl Churchill. So there's something about form that we have over here that's really important, and apparently this formal knowledge is the thing that we're kind of disseminating again across the pond.

For example, Anne Washburn is having a huge moment in London right now. She could not get arrested in New York; I mean, she couldn't get a theater over 99 seats over here, except for *Mr. Burns*. And in Germany, where, you know, they think of themselves as the "formal-ist of the formal," even they are like, you guys are doing something with language that we can't quite figure out and what is that? It's like a breadth of thought…. So it's a really exciting time to be an American playwright because people are up, we've done something we didn't realize we'd done and that's kind of cool to see disseminated. In terms of my own work, the only play that's traveled very far is *Gloria*; it's been done in Korea, it's been done in Uruguay, it's been done everywhere. And I'm shocked. I'm shocked that people do this play everywhere they do a play, and it seems to go over well; I can't tell you why, but it feels very humbling and nice to be seen by people who otherwise would have called you too American or something. It feels like I'm tapping into something in a way. Which feels great.

**BK:** Let's give it up for this man. [*applause*]

**Audience member:** I would like to thank you very, very much for this. We truly do appreciate it. And I'm going to ask two very quick questions. Number one is you said that you left an experience and moved to Germany and stayed in Germany for two years. Can you expand upon that, also explaining what you gained in the process? And the second question is, would you also expand upon when you mentioned that you worked with two people I found very interesting, Hilton Als and John Lahr. Can you also talk about what you gained from them? Thank you very much.

**BJJ:** I went to Germany because, um, well, I just had to get out of New York, basically. But I had gone there under the guise of what is still a project in process; I was interested in this phenomenon of the mischlingskinder, the mixed-race war children in Germany, and it was born out of my getting there and realizing that I was being read as American first and black second. And that's because they have a very specific relationship to that image that has to do with occupation. And it really inverted my own personal narratives of status in a way that was profound to me. Also, the more research I did into the black presence in Germany during the wars, I found the connections between that and the Civil Rights Movement, and I was like, there's something to be said about blacks and race and the Cold War. And I was sort of sniffing it out. And I'd also had an experience with a play of mine there that's called *The Change* (which I've since disowned and no one will ever see; I burned all copies [*laughter*]) which has one black actor, and in the German translation they cast a Middle Eastern actor, but they put them in a grass skirt. And I was like, what is going on? I wanted to understand American blackness outside of the context of America and see how it traveled. And it did—I mean, it was actually in Germany that I wrote *An Octoroon* and *Gloria*, kind of back-to-back while being exposed to that different way of thinking, and that different dramaturgy really transformed the way I thought about what adaptation was and what a theater event could be in scale because everything that happens there happens at a massive scale. But really it was about me kind of thinking through all the things that James Baldwin already thought through: like being black abroad, and "Stranger in the Village," and I finally read *Notes of a Native Son* while I was there and I was like, oh God, I've been scooped, there's nothing to say. So that was sort of the Germany experience—also just being in a different language and understanding how language training changes your thought; that was really important for me.

In terms of working with Hilton and John, that was a total accident because I was…. I sort of flung myself out of graduate school—I was pursuing a PhD in performance studies at NYU and I just had this, like, panic attack and I was just: I've got to get out of here. And I got the first job I could, which happened very luckily to be an editorial assistant in the fiction department of the *New Yorker* magazine. And it was just my luck that the fiction department housed the editors who edited John Lahr, who at the time was lead critic, and Hilton was the secondary critic. And at the time I was also secretly pursuing the theater on my own, and I had this day when I just randomly brought a show up to one of them; I was just sort of like, well, I saw this show, I think you should see this show. And they would see the show. And I realized, and they also realized, that when they saw something that they liked, they wrote better about it. And so over time I became this like Man in Havana for John and Hilton and sort of tried to steer them into the direction of work that I thought they would connect to—just knowing them and knowing what their tastes were. And I watched it make a very significant difference in the life of some of these artists who I'd come across. I think Hilton is honestly one of the finest critics we've ever had in this country. It was interesting to watch him be born as a theater critic in some ways; it was really moving. And then my job became to go to the Drama Book Shop; he'd be writing about, let's say, Lynn Nottage, and I'd have to go to the Drama Book Shop and buy all the Lynn Nottage plays and we'd talk about the plays. It was like a sentimental education in some real ways.

But I kind of hid my own identity for a very long time, which I think kind of frustrated them at the end, because they didn't really know I was a playwright until I was about to leave the job.

**Audience member:** My questions are about race and casting. So here at Rollins [College], to see what plays can be selected for the students to direct in the student theater, we have a committee to read plays and then we vote on what plays could make it to the next year. And one thing that came up in one of our meetings was is the play that you're voting for castable? Now I, in my experience, what I have encountered is that we tend to default to—when we read the character list, if it doesn't specify that a character is white, Puerto Rican, Asian, black, we just default to white. What are your thoughts on that? Do we all default on that? Or when it comes to a play like *Gloria*, where you specified this character needs to be white, this character needs to be black and so on, if I understood correctly, you said that you wouldn't mind if a director goes against you and color blinds, uh, Gloria, and mixes it around a little bit, but then again you have lines [in the play] like Dean against Kendra where they cannot attack each other's ethnicities. So what are your thoughts on, on those two things?

**BJJ:** I think that the big thing we're all coming to terms with, or some of us at least are coming to terms with, in this moment is about how we do think of whiteness as a default, we think of whiteness as a neutral category and we are now learning that is not what it is. Again, race is a theater game, guys: like, you identify as white; white is not genetic. My family just did a 23andMe and we were shocked to find out we were 26 percent white. We don't know what we're doing about that yet; we've got a family meeting coming. [*laughter*] So it's like waking up to the reality that it's a fiction, guys, it's a construction. And how do we break out of that and get more specific in our work? Because if we really think about it, how do we think about these plays themselves as being propaganda for a certain racialized system when we look back at these works? That's important. In terms of castability, that's really deep that y'all do that. I think the thing to remember, too, and to fight for, is that you're in an educational institution, so the end result has to be the maximum education for all parties involved. And that sometimes means casting against type. Because you're not— no one here is taking a show on the road, it doesn't have to make any money, so we're not even going to start talking about the market and who wants to see what. I am always advocating for students to fight for the thing that they think they're going to get the most out of educationally. That's why your parents pay for you to be here. That's what theater programs are for. [*applause*] Aw, that's so sweet.

And this final question is what *Gloria* is. So, *Gloria*: in some ways it's a play about how people are commodifying their identity. And how they're weaponizing it in situations. So of course, if a director casts Kendra as not an Asian American, they're going to look like a bad director. And so in some ways I'm reminding people to read the play carefully. It's funny how much I talk about my cast list—it's my fault, I shouldn't mess with something, don't fix what's not broken—but I put "white" and "black" in quotes because I'm asking you to really tell me what you mean. What do we think we're doing when we're casting white and black people? What does that mean? Are they black-identified? What is someone who looks "black"? Black *how*? That's really the fine grain I'm challenging theater-makers to think about in terms of inhabiting or realizing a script in some way. Because ultimately it's about how we live in a system where we place value systems on bodies that are on stage differently. And we're trying as a society to move that. We're trying to figure out how to transform that, but you have to kind of *out* the problem before you can solve the problem, right? And so my fantasy is that in fifty years you can't do *Gloria* because those categories don't exist. Or you do it as a history piece and then what does that mean? But you have to really think about what is the meaning of a body? Not all bodies on a stage, sadly, at this moment, mean the same thing. And that reflects how we treat people in the world because we're just reflecting what's happening out in the audience. So how we, as artists, push or develop or challenge those ideas is really the point.

**Audience member:** Hi, Branden, thank you so much for being here. A lot of your groundbreaking works are adaptations of pieces that existed before. I got to see *Everybody* at Signature and will trek up to Yale to see *Girls* in October. Can you tell us a bit more about your process in adapting these pieces? Also: what makes for a good adaptation, in your opinion?

**BJJ:** Well, I have first of all to give myself permission to adapt because I—you know, I had this aha! moment with *Everybody* that the very essence of drama is adaptation. And I wish someone would just point out to me the exact moment when we felt like "original stories" was the premium, because the Greeks were adapting, Shakespeare was stealing and combining and doing all kinds of amazing stuff. So I was like, okay, I can just do this. I can just be in it. The pieces I'm drawn to all have a kind of Benjaminian aura of meaning that I'm after in some way. It becomes about me having to feel super-knowledgeable about that text object and what it was and why it's important *now*, why we think of it as important now. And then also: what is the sensory experience of it that the original author intended? And then I think about my job as a form of adaptation, or an adaptation-translation, that I really want to recreate. I hate when we treat theater like a museum. I just hate that because it's a live form and I always want the piece to ring out *for us*—the way, again, it's like the Benjaminian idea of translation where I want to refresh the language of theater *now*. That's always what my intent is. And I always think about it in such weird linguistic terms—is it Saussure or Sapir, that linguistic idea of drift in language? I think that the theater language drifts, and that's okay, but you want to bring back the ideas to our language now in some way. So that's where I start. I'll have this experience—with *Everyman*, weirdly, my experience of it, even though that play's been very good to me and means a lot to me, I kind of began to turn on the original piece. I was like, oh, this is actually not as good of a play as I thought it would be, and that wound up making the adaptation a little difficult because I wasn't as much in awe of it as I returned to it again and again, as I was by Boucicault. And *The Bacchae* is proving horri—it is so hard! I mean, that play is such a mic drop, it's like the mic drop of all playwriting. It's like, how do you—I mean, I feel embarrassed, and I'm also like, why did I say yes? It's humbling. It's like a communion with the dead when you're adapting; you're trying to understand someone who's not here to make themselves clear and it's a humbling act in some way.

**Audience member:** I've been writing about how audiences respond to shock in theater, and so I was reading a bunch of reviews of *Gloria* and looking through the Chicago reviews of the Goodman production and I found a very interesting review. A lot of them seemed very vague for a review, and then there was one that published the letter that the Goodman had sent to them that said, you can't talk about the details of the plot. And I'd be really interested to hear the sort of process of that. What were the discussions like about trying to protect the Act One ending moment and then how it went?

**BJJ:** My big lament is that it's very difficult to surprise people in the theater. It's like how you can't get lost anymore when you write a play because of cell phones. It's truly difficult to create a genuine experience of surprise in the theater. Early on with *Gloria* we knew we had to get ahead of it. So there were all these letters sent out to people saying "please don't spoil it." Of course they do spoil it—very aggressively, I'll say, as if to punish me. But for whatever reason, with this story, I think what happens is that people realize the joy and value of the surprise, and they protect it for each other. That's what I've noticed. When people talk about it, they'll say I told my friend I don't want to talk about it, just go see it and then I'll talk about it—and that's great for me because that's another ticket sale. But I'm watching one audience member take care of the other and valuing the aesthetic experience of a piece. And I think that's what's really amazing about it. The real trick of *Gloria*, though, is signage because everyone wants to trigger-warning the crap out of everything, and it's wild because I actually don't think that many people need trigger warnings like signage about it. But a theater will make you believe that you need to spell out the whole plot of something before they walk in and it's like, no, I think people want that [experience of surprise]. That being said, I have sat in many audiences of *Gloria*, and there is only one time when it was actually a group of, like, high school kids who were in the city on some theater journey, who, when they got to that point—I mean, the screams, I still think about the screams and get chills. And I'm like, did I harm children? I don't know. That's the only time when I began to question the shock of it in some way. But otherwise I feel like people go to the theater to feel things. That's actually all people want, and we kind of lie to ourselves and pretend that's not the case.

**BK:** Let's give it up for Branden Jacobs-Jenkins. [*applause*]

# *A Raisin in the Sun* at 60: A Conversation

---

*Transcript of roundtable discussion, April 6, 2019*
*Panelists: Teresa Gilliams (Albright College),*
*Nathaniel G. Nesmith (Scholar-at-large),*
*Janna Segal (University of Louisville),*
*Baron Kelly (University of Louisville),*
*Branden Jacobs-Jenkins (University of Texas–Austin)*
*Moderator:* William C. Boles *(Rollins College)*

## Abstract

*The year 2019 marks the sixtieth anniversary of Lorraine Hansberry's* A Raisin in the Sun, *which premiered on Broadway March 11, 1959. It was the first Broadway play written by an African American woman, and the first with an African American director (Lloyd Richards). To commemorate this occasion, the Comparative Drama Conference held a roundtable discussion among two scholars (Gilliams and Nesmith), a dramaturg (Segal), and a director (Kelly), along with playwright Branden Jacobs-Jenkins, whose 2010 play* Neighbors *is a response to* A Raisin in the Sun. *The panelists discussed approaches to teaching* A Raisin in the Sun, *especially to students unfamiliar with redlining real estate practices and the real dangers of violence faced by the Younger family; the play's multiple protagonists and constructions of black identity; Hansberry's innovative "proto-intersectional dramaturgy"; and* Raisin's *impact on the American canon, European drama, and today's generation of playwrights.*

**Teresa Gilliams (TG):** I'd like to talk a bit about the way that *A Raisin in the Sun* features in a specific class I teach at Albright College. It's a synthesis course, which is the capstone General Studies course, and I framed the course with the question, "What is grit?" I use *A Raisin in the Sun* the way that I use many of the other texts—I also teach Toni Morrison's *Song of Solomon*, Ta-Nehisi Coates's *Between the World and Me*—to help students begin to grapple with values: what it is to have values, how some of the values that they maintain have been inherited by their families and maybe haven't been questioned. But I also use it to challenge them to interrogate the merits of examining race. Many of them are really uncomfortable with the discussions of race. Many of them—it's a predominantly majority white student body, and for many of them, their encounter with a black professor is something that never even enters their mind until they, oh, you know, enter my classroom. And so *A Raisin in the Sun* I use as a foundation for our examination of racial identity, of stereotypes, of class issues. But also to talk about who we are, how we become who we are, and what matters most to us. And I typically ask them to write some kind of paper that helps me understand who they are in relation to their family because it gets them to begin thinking about the presentation, the way that Hansberry centralizes family, and the conflicts that occur within it.

What I found most challenging in terms of teaching the course is that students tend to bring their own, you know, they bring their own experiences and have a difficult time really unpacking what it means to grow up without the privileges they have or to kind of imagine or envision growing up perhaps in a single-parent household. So we start with examining the extent to which black families have always been extended. I talk about my own engagement, having been informed by my great-grandparents, my grandparents, my uncles and aunts who all lived within a three-block radius, and what that meant for me. Like the fact that I could not disentangle my own notions of who I am from all these people in this web from which I grew.

I do that so that even when they begin to talk about their own family systems, we have diverse perspectives. We're all kind of sharing and they can begin to open their minds. But I also talk about the importance of ancestry, of love, the ancestor figure that is significant in the texts. And that's Walter Lee, Sr. Even though he's not present, he still bears a great deal of influence on the way that the family interacts and what he does in terms of leaving this money to the family, what it produces in them, kind of the internal conflicts. We also talk about gender identity, why there's this clash between Beneatha and Walter and what it means for Walter to suddenly be without his father figure, what it means for him to become a man and become responsive to his wife and to his son as he's trying to model for his son what success looks like.

Most recently when I taught the class, we had also just finished reading a text by Thomas Chatterton Williams called *Losing My Cool*. And in each of these texts we were looking at black masculinity, particularly hypermasculinity and how this hypermasculinity is almost always functioning as a response—well, as a coping mechanism. It's fronting, you know, like you have it together when in fact you're just fretful about not having it together. And one of the things that was so significant about our looking at these, um, in the intertextuality at work in the relationships between Walter and Ruth and Thomas and [his girlfriend] Stacey—I don't know if you all are familiar with the text [*Losing My Cool*], it's a memoir—is that neither one of them was able to truly honor the romantic partnerships in which they were. And as we disentangled them, many of my students were able to come to terms with the fact that both these men were on a journey. And so at the heart of our examination of *Raisin* is this quest. What is it that the family wants? What kind of journey is Walter on? What does he want to get out of it? In the panel I was just on, one of the panelists said that at the core, the key question is What is freedom to me? What is freedom to you? Walter is trying to find himself. And so I framed the core, the fundamental question as "What is grit?" But in order to get to the answer, you have to start very personally. You have to start with, okay, who am I in relation to my family? Who am I in relation to the values that I stand by, that I say shaped my life, but also how do those things help shape the way that I respond to others in a way that keeps me accountable to myself?

**Nathaniel G. Nesmith (NN):** Well, I'm going to be very, very brief. First of all, this is a great turnout—I didn't anticipate so many people. I circulated a handout, an email conversation with Margaret Wilkerson, who is the leading Lorraine Hansberry scholar; you will see that I talked about two questions with her, which we will open up once we move forward. One is there is supposed to be an alternative ending to *A Raisin in the Sun*, and the second one is about the gender identity of Lorraine Hansberry. Once you have read Wilkerson's comments, we can start to engage and have a conversation about those two questions, which I think are very important and they will certainly come up at some point. Also, I wanted to mention that I have done extensive research on the original production of the play and its reception and hope to share some of this with you today. This work includes interviews with Lloyd Richards, the original director of *A Raisin in the Sun*. I had many conversations with Lloyd talking specifically about the play and also about Lorraine Hansberry. In addition to Lloyd, I've also talked to Douglas Turner Ward, who was in the original production, about the production and about Lorraine Hansberry. Playwright and scholar William Branch is another person I interviewed who knew Hansberry. These are all people who were very influential in reference to her career and her life. I also interviewed Philip Rose, the producer of the Broadway play. Once Rose read half of the play, he decided that he wanted to produce it. There's so much misinformation about Lorraine Hansberry. I would like to say certain

The *Raisin in the Sun* poster for the University of Louisville production directed by Baron Kelly.

things are not actually correct, and I've had people who've told me stuff that is just not true. So I'm going to give you my historical perspective in reference to speaking with all these people who knew Lorraine Hansberry, had dealings with Lorraine Hansberry, and particularly in reference to her sexuality and so forth.

**Janna Segal (JS):** This semester, I have had the good fortune of teaching Introduction to Dramaturgy, a practicum course in production dramaturgy new to the University of Louisville Theatre Arts Department's curriculum. The course was designed to train emerging theatre artists in the fundamentals of production dramaturgy so that they could learn how to best function as a dramaturg on a production, and how to best collaborate with a dramaturg on a production team. These skills have been instilled through the hands-on experience of dramaturging Dr. Baron Kelly's upcoming U of L production of *A Raisin in the Sun*, which opens on April 11, four days after we return from this conference (but who's counting?). Among the dramaturgy students' many contributions to this forthcoming production is the collection of images running in the background of our presentation today. These images were included in the dramaturgical research packet the students created in support of this revival of *Raisin* at a university that is situated in downtown Louisville, at the center of a city grappling with a long, complicated, and ongoing legacy of segregation.

On the first day of the class, I asked the students if they had previously read or seen *A Raisin in the Sun*. All of them had previously encountered it either in high school, in college, or both. Because of their familiarity with the play, on the second day of class, I came up with an exercise inspired by Chapter 1 of Lenora Inez Brown's *The Art of Active Dramaturgy*. Titled "Beginning the Dramaturgical Process: Letting Go of Bias," Brown's first chapter stresses that when we "approach a play for the first or fifth time," dramaturgs need to release whatever "personal baggage or bias" we bring to the play in order to "fully engage" with it on its own terms, unencumbered by preconceptions. In order to let go of whatever bias they carried about Hansberry's play from their previous academic exposure to it, I asked these budding dramaturgs, who had not yet been required to re-read *Raisin* for my class, to write down their preconceptions about the play. At first, most of their responses were symptomatic of that student-specific form of PTSD that is triggered by the mere mention of the title of a canonized text students have been required to read more than once. They collectively described the play as "long," "overly dramatic," "overly realistic," and of "weighty importance." They also collectively offered a reaction distinct from this perhaps more expected classroom response to a frequently taught play. One student's quip in particular best expressed this shared bias: "Everything is Walter Lee's fault."

To these students in 2019, "Everything [was] Walter Lee's fault." When he first appeared on a Broadway stage in 1959, Walter Lee garnered a more empathetic response, even on New York City's Great White Way. Indeed, in his review of the original production, *New York Times* theatre critic Brooks Atkinson wrote, "The play is honest. [Hansberry] has told the inner as well as the outer truth about a Negro family in the south-side of Chicago at the present time. Since the performance is also honest and since Sidney Poitier is a candid actor, *A Raisin in the Sun* has vigor as well as veracity and is likely to destroy the complacency of anyone who sees it." In Atkinson's estimation, Poitier's Walter Lee was above reproach. Rather than the cause of the family's problems, Walter was the "vigor"ous vector of the play's truth, and the means by which the "complacency" of Broadway spectators would be "destroy[ed]."

But that was then and, to be honest, I wasn't completely surprised by the students' scapegoating of Walter Lee. As I told them that day, finding fault with Walter Lee recalled something Hansberry herself said about what she considered the play's dramatic "flaw." Hansberry said, "Fine plays tend to utilize one big fat character who runs right through the middle of the structure, by action or implication, with whom we rise or fall. A central character as such is certainly lacking from *Raisin*. I should be delighted to pretend that it was inventiveness, as some suggest for me, but it is, also, craft inadequacy and creative indecision. The result is that neither Walter nor Mama Younger loom large enough to monumentally command the play. I consider it an enormous fault if no one else does" (qtd. in Wilkerson, "Lorraine Hansberry" 43). We could spend some time unpacking Hansberry's conception of Aristotelian structure as quintessentially "fine," or her self-disparaging dismissal of a play with competing protagonists or no clear protagonist as indicative of "craft inadequacy." As a dramaturg, though, I'm more interested in the self-diagnosed "creative indecision" over the play's protagonist. "Indecision" can be a source of creativity, and this particular version of "creative indecision" accounts, at least in some way, for the play's endurance. It's here, in this indecisive space between conflicting forces or sources of a central character, that I think every production and adaptation of Hansberry's script can make creative choices that resonate with a specific target audience.

Since that class session, I have routinely asked the students to tell me how the play would be different if the protagonist were neither Walter nor Mama. They have conceived of the drama as Beneatha's play, as Ruth's, as Asagai's, as George's, as Bobo's, as the Moving Men's, and even as Mama's plant's play. They have also studied Robert O'Hara's *Etiquette of Vigilance*, which reinterprets *Raisin* through the lens of an adult Travis Younger, and Bruce Norris's *Clybourne Park*, which envisions the play through the past and present lives of Karl Lindner. We have also explored the possibility of a non-living heroic figure driving the action of *Raisin*. We have talked about the looming "photo of Big Walter" as a protagonist or antagonist since, as Hansberry's stage directions state, it is his paternal "spirit" which "suffuses the play." And we have explored the leading role played by the 1950s, south-side of Chicago setting, which, according to Atkinson's review of the original production, was among the reasons *A Raisin in the Sun* could be called a "truth"ful representation of "a Negro family" living in "the present time" in which the play was first produced.

Our 2019 revival of *Raisin* might also have as its protagonist another Midwestern city altogether, the one where most of the audiences attending will be returning after they, like Mama at the play's conclusion, leave the Chicago south-side apartment meticulously constructed inside the theatre. In the second week of the semester, after my students had re-read the play for the second (for some) or fifth (for others) time, I asked them to answer what Michael Mark Chemers identifies as the fundamental dramaturgical question: "Why this play [ ... ] at this moment [ ... ] in front of this audience?" (108). In response, the students drew parallels between the housing segregation the Youngers face and the housing segregation plaguing Louisville. They talked about the income disparity the Youngers experience and that which exists in our city. They spoke about the play's emphasis on dreams as an antidote to the despair many feel in Louisville in the wake of the 2016 presidential election, especially as our city is a blueberry sandwiched between two mega-MAGA red states: Kentucky and Indiana. It was this conversation about the script's relationship to a city that plays such a central role in their lives that led them to see the drama afresh. For them, the city immediately outside their theatre was perhaps what Hansberry described as what she felt was lacking in her play, that "one big fat character who runs right through the middle of the structure, by action or implication, with whom we rise or fall." The connections they drew between the play's urban landscape and their own helped them move past the burden of what they had been taught was the "legacy" of Hansberry's drama. Unburdening the script of their prior educational encounters with it and reinterpreting it through the fault lines in their city has helped them to re-imagine it for an integrated, public university audience in Louisville, Kentucky, that it is doubtful Hansberry could have envisioned when *A Raisin in the Sun* opened sixty years ago.

**Baron Kelly (BK):** In certain circles of people in California and New York, they call me the griot about black theater because a lot of actors don't know their history anymore. A lot of actors of color don't know their history anymore. They're not being taught in the schools the right way. I truly believe in history and I truly believe in legacy. I've been in many professional productions where I've been in dressing rooms where people tell me I hold court because I'm talking to actors about particular things that they were not taught in their programs. And I even mean Yale, Juilliard, various other schools. And this has just been a part of who I am. So I'm in the generation that's behind Morgan Freeman. And the people that I was influenced by in New York City, people that have passed on, like Hal Scott—I don't know if anybody in this room even knows who Hal Scott was—and various other directors and actors who were not big names, but they had a tremendous influence on particular actors in classes at that particular time in New York City. I'm now at the University of Louisville, which has the only program in the nation with a graduate certificate in African American theater; we have the African American Theatre Program. None of the HBCUs have a graduate certificate in African American theater. Which basically means we have X amount of dollars that are given to us, to our department, to be able to present plays that deal with the African and African American diasporic experience on the stage. And it doesn't necessarily—it's not a segregated program by any means. And so when we have these season discussions about plays, the director of the African American Theatre Program, our colleague Johnny Jones, and also Janna Segal had this great idea about doing *Raisin* because we were in a board meeting and Johnny brought up the idea of *A Raisin in the Sun*, being that it's the sixtieth anniversary of this play. And I said, now, that's very interesting because if I was going to work with the actors at the University of Louisville, undoubtedly we were going to have to have community people come in because we wouldn't be able to fill all of the roles. Particularly I knew I was going to have to find an actress to play Lena Younger. And we have been very fortunate to have found a great community actress who is absolutely wonderful playing the role of Mama.

 I grew up in New York City at a time when a third of the people that I grew up with are dead: a third of the people that I grew up with are dead, a third have been in and out of jail most of their lives, and the other third have done well for themselves, you know, civil service jobs, post office or whatever, and raising their families. And when I've thought about this play—and I've seen a number of productions of this play in my lifetime over the years and I've seen productions that have been sanitized to a particular way and just don't look lived-in to me—what I've been interested in trying to do, at least at the University of Louisville and particularly now that I have a chance with this play, is to try to get the actors to have some kind of a lived-in experience of this play. And so far I think I've been pretty successful—as Janna has said, we have another few days before it opens and here we are, and we have a graduate student who is, you know, running the play for pace and it's up on its feet. And when I've thought about this play, there are two questions—and I just said it in the plenary that Teresa was on and Alan Nadel [*points to him in the audience*] was in the room—of where does Beneatha sleep or where did Beneatha sleep. People don't think about that. And so that's one way that I start to go into the play to start to ask questions to the actors so that they can start to get their synapses firing, so that they can get their imagination firing. Because I tell them, this play to me is the effect of anti-black terrorism on a particular people and a society and the small and individual choices that people make that push or that can push history forward. The explosive natures that can be within, uh, a confined space. I've lived that myself and I try to get the actors to understand this. I know what it's like to stand in the kitchen and see mice and rats running around. I know what it's like for my mother to stand between brothers and to stop them from fighting when weapons are going to be coming out. I remember I went back to my mother's house and I saw a bullet hole through the dining room window, and I said, what the hell is that? And she said, oh, somebody was looking for your brother. Just so casually.

And so when I talked to actors about this, even though this kind of stuff is not within the play, I try to get them to understand about the given circumstances of the play and what is happening outside of this play. And how in the play, a large part of the action is structured in the kitchen. What does the kitchen signify in that play? The kitchen signifies nurturing; the kitchen signifies where the family tries to come together, even though there are squabbles. And I try to get the actors to really understand this and live in this. And one thing that I find with a lot of young actors, and it's not just [August] Wilson that actors have trouble with, and I'm talking about young African American actors, it's that writers—and this brilliant writer here [*indicating Branden Jacobs-Jenkins*] can talk about it more so than I can about punctuation, syntax, and language. A lot of actors go like this [*gestures rushing through the play*]. They don't pay attention to that. Hansberry writes very specifically; I can hear it and when I'm in the audience in the theater when the actors are running it on the stage or they're running through sections of the play, I say stop, there's a comma there, isn't there? That means something. There's a semi-colon there isn't there? Can't you hear the build in the line? They can't hear it anymore. Because they're, you know, they've dumbed everything down. I'm speaking very generally. They've dumbed everything down to television and film. They can't, they don't understand about marrying truth to size. We talked a little bit about this last night [in the keynote conversation with Branden Jacobs-Jenkins] with melodrama and how particular emotions need to come out. And I think a lot of young actors shy away from it. And so I'm trying to get them to understand in this lived-in experience the explosiveness that can happen, but also the intergenerational love that can happen. There's so much love in this play. And I think I said it last night. Yuko [Karahashi] and I were talking that there's love, you hurt the people that you love the most. We can be awfully cool, you know, in relationships and with people that we love. We say things to hurt people. So anyway, I'm trying to get the actors to have a lived-in experience in this play, to pay attention to the given circumstances, to create the life of the play and also pay attention to the poetry of the language in this play.

**Branden Jacobs-Jenkins (BJJ):** I feel like I come to Hansberry as a devotee, a pupil of history. And I find that the kind of obsession I'm having over her and her work right now is from a very selfish place, but it's about thinking through the kind of conceptual work she might've felt she was doing in the writing of *A Raisin in the Sun*, and thinking through it as a kind of conceptual object that is taking on ideas of canon. She's actively putting herself in conversation (at a time where this seemed like crazy) with Arthur Miller, and thinking—it's useful to think through the large shadow that he cast and continues to cast over American drama, especially as we think about realism or naturalism as a privileged stylistic space to tell certain stories. I always have to remind my students how radical of an act it was. I'm very moved to hear this quote that she felt there was a fault, a craft fault or something. What is going on, Lorraine? But you know, part of that is about, I guess in some ways it had been taught to me that what she winds up doing to this notion of a monolithic kind of tragedy centered around one person is a bit of a prism job on the way that the women are actually treated. She creates a more equalized playing field in terms of an affective accessibility with all these different characters. And even the idea—you know, I always think that there's something really beautiful about Beneatha, Lena, and Ruth all coexisting and holding equal weight in the same kind of dramatic world. And that she's asking us to complicate our ideas of black femalehood somehow or is finding like a proto-intersectional dramaturgy that actually is part of its lasting power in some ways to me. I do want to think about how this engagement with Miller that she begins get sort of furthered in August's project, especially around *Fences*, and also think through the way that it feels like the world is trying to save Miller from himself right now professionally—there's a lot of cross-cast, under-cast, double-cast versions of *All My*—you know, "All My Deaths."

**BK:** *The Crucible.*

**BJJ:** *Crucibles*. Yeah. There is value in Lorraine's—she felt that it was necessary to create a black presence in that space in terms of theater history, but also theater as a social space. Um, I really love this detail of Douglas Turner Ward in the original production, and I didn't know that. It is like the 15,000th mark on the wall of how she created a nexus, a historical nexus, a literary nexus, a professional nexus that is sort of still paying dividends. It's also reminded me of a similar panel I was on about August's legacy a few years ago, where the big point I kept trying to make was that part of his—yes, he was this extraordinary artist, but what can be forgotten is that he was an economic force, he actually enabled careers to happen beyond his pen. And I think that *Raisin* is one of those plays that's apparently been nonstop: every day in history, since it's opened, there's been a production of *A Raisin in the Sun*. Think about how the providing of those opportunities actually does a significant amount of work to build up the presence of black artists in any given industry.

**William C. Boles (WCB):** Now, with the introductory comments out of the way, you can talk amongst yourselves, if you want to respond to what someone said, and then we'll turn to the audience.

**BJJ:** I'm kind of curious about how the tragedy of this play and of Lorraine is that we don't know what she could've written after. I mean, we know what she wrote—she wrote *The Sign in Sidney Brustein's Window*. But I always am fascinated by the idea that there seems to be no indication that she was going to return to these characters, even to this milieu; that somehow her future work was going to try to be ballistic and all over the place. And I wonder if that's something that anyone ever tries to unpack—that because of her just-like-that dying, should we now associate *Raisin* with her and somehow use it to hold all of her aesthetic impulses? Because it seems like there could have been something more to her aesthetic project in the long run. I mean, it's all speculation, I'm just curious, but I don't have any thoughts about that.

**NN:** Well, one of the things is Lorraine Hansberry just died so young. She actually had a very short career. Her career was something like five years, and that was pretty much it. Of course, she did *Young, Gifted and Black*, which was actually extended by Robert Nemiroff, her former husband. So that was pretty much it. And I think if you consider it a factor, if you're saying, "well, you know she died in five years and she was diagnosed with cancer two years before she died," you're looking at someone with a very, very short career. You're talking about perhaps three years. And now that's just in reference to what else she could have been thinking about. I mean, I know she thought that she was going to do—from talking with Margaret Wilkerson and various people—she clearly thought that she was going to do a great deal. The real fact was when she was diagnosed with cancer, she didn't even know she had cancer for a very long time because it was told to Robert Nemiroff that she had cancer, but it wasn't told to Lorraine Hansberry.

It was particularly interesting talking to Douglas Turner Ward because I have probably twenty hours of conversation with Douglas Turner Ward, and for two of those hours we're talking about Lorraine Hansberry. This is material I'm going to use at some point. I'm open to all types of questions in reference of people that I've talked with. You mentioned Earle Hyman, I've talked to Earle Hyman also.

**BK:** He did it [*Raisin*] in London.

**NN:** Yeah, June '59, of course. And that didn't get a good review or anything, but he certainly did it there.

**JS:** I'd like to go back to this idea of proto-intersectional dramaturgy, that phrase, which I now want to steal if that's okay. Is it copyrighted? So the notion of proto-intersectional dramaturgy today in terms of where her work may have gone: we think about, you know, *Sidney Brustein's Window* and certainly I think that is an intersectional drama. And I think that probably its intersectionality is why it failed at the time when it was initially done. Um, and, and what a visionary, I think, thinking about the way in which that quote that I gave is so sort of, in some ways really tragic to me is that she's judging her work according to, as you described it, this standard that's this really privileged stylistic space. And she's imagining that what she brings to that space is somehow a fault, but actually that creative indecision, that's, that's the juice, right? That's the exciting stuff. I think she was really bold. And it's exciting to imagine what she would've done. I think that those, uh, who are doing—or were, during the production, but also like you [*indicating Branden Jacobs-Jenkins*] engaging with it in their own dramas are doing, we're, we're getting a taste of what she may have brought about through your re-envisioning of it. And that is my gateway plug for *Neighbors*, which is brilliant.

**BJJ:** Okay!

**BK:** This play's been done all over the world, *A Raisin in the Sun*'s been done all over the world, and somebody sent me an article about a Polish production that was done in the 1960s. And of course at that time, Poland was still under communism and all of this sort of stuff. And so there are resonances in this play that various people pick up, even though the actors have to put on blackface and all of that. And just recently, within the past six years, I believe, there was a production that was done in Sweden. So have you guys thought about what the pull of this play is for, you know, like Eastern European countries or any of that stuff?

**TG:** I don't have an answer to that question, but I am fascinated by the idea that Lorraine Hansberry used Walter Lee to kind of create these, well, using self-directed stereotypes to bring people into their awareness of their own racism or their own expectations of, of black identity. And I think in terms of what she would have done down the road, to your point, Janna, she was very courageous. She was unafraid to speak about the elephant in the room. And I think had she lived, she would've continued to kind of push the envelope. It's troubling when you read that scene where Walter says he's going to go in and, you know, just become this buffoon when he knows in fact how damaging that would be, how incredibly deathly it would be, for his own mother or for his son, anybody to, to watch. But in terms of his confrontation with that stereotype, it brings him to greater awareness about just how debilitating that is. Not just for him, but for the entire community. And so I think it, I mentioned earlier, it provides deep self-directed stereotypes. Hansberry saw that it was a springboard for clarification of values in the black community, but also to kind of call to attention those who believe that this in fact was still black life in the 1950s.

**BJJ:** I'd like to speak to the question of its appeal in European, Eastern European countries. I think it's rooted in the fact that it's working in a very recognizable drama of social realism that all of those countries have a relationship to, and I think that there's—I mean, I'm sure there were a lot of people telling the same tale at that time, but she did kind of break ground in that space for black subjecthood. And I think there's a novelty, for many people, in encountering what is essentially an Ibsen- or Odets-kind of feeling drama that's populated very unselfconsciously with black life. I think ultimately that's why it winds up translating. And what's funny is that we've just so metabolized this approach to black storytelling, that we forget the radical nature of what she was attempting and how it sits. So strangely, especially when you look at her other dramatic works, it sits formally quite strangely. It didn't seem like she was going to return to these kinds of stories again, if you just look at where she was going next. And I think we always overlooked that in some ways. I think about that moment with Walter Lee and how in some ways, August spends a lot of his career responding to that moment. That we're kind of constantly portraying black men sort of signifying, and for economic reasons. And again, it's that thing where I feel like you really are watching the ground laid for a whole space for blackness to occupy in American theater between those two artists. And Lloyd [Richards] is oddly—I mean I'm obsessed with Lloyd, he's like the, it's almost the master builder in some ways behind these two moments, these two poles of argument.

**WCB:** If I could just throw in a real quick question for Branden, about *Neighbors*, since Janna mentioned *Neighbors*. There's an anthology of plays that respond to *A Raisin in the Sun* [*Reimagining A Raisin in the Sun*] and obviously *Clybourne Park* is there, and two other plays, and Branden, *Neighbors* is there, but it doesn't seem to, on reading it, it doesn't seem to exactly be a response to Hansberry. So what was your response to its inclusion in the volume?

**BJJ:** Rebecca Rugg edited that, and I had asked the same question where I was like, I don't know what you're talking about, but…. I mean, this is also… how many years ago was this? This was maybe ten years ago. But we had a lot of conversations about George C. Wolfe and how *Raisin* cast a mold for how we began; a new kind of forging of black archetypes began in that space, which was only reinforced by the popularity of its production. But also, the aha! moment I had about a lot of these plays was that they ensure the lifespan of a certain kind of actor. It creates a—like, for example, you [*indicating Baron Kelly*] found a Lena in the community. I bet she has some familiarity with Mama's part. And you know, Ruth always wins the Tony. It's like: what is it about these plays that creates these rivets? But then you have to think about who's excluded from those tracks in some way. And so George came along in the Eighties and was saying okay, I want to talk about this Mama and our comfort around "the Mama" and his "Last Mama on the Couch Play" is for me really the centerpiece, the kind of thesis of *The Colored Museum*. I think that was really what I was in conversation with as I was writing *Neighbors*. Just trying to think through what are the different kinds of iterations or constructions of blackness we now have swimming in the theater, authored both by lovely white people in blackface and lovely black women writing in the Sixties, and how are these things in conversation each other? And how do we know what's problematic and what's not? Is the theater even a space in which we can get to something real about blackness? Because I think that's partly why—this is the proto-intersectional dramaturgy of the play, and this is why I feel she's smartly co-opted that Miller idea that family has to be the kind of scale in which we think through American identity. Because it becomes a space in which we enact the tensions of belonging and difference. And I think that she kind of creates this prism of a concept of black family that she's building out here where it's like a constant negotiation between different parties who are coming into history at different moments.

If you look at the continuum of Lena-Ruth-Beneatha, we're talking about a very broad stretch of female consciousness building. I think that that's what was the genius, the allegory she found in that, which ultimately refused a clear definition. That's the genius of Mama at the end saying we're going anyway; whether or not we like it, the choice has to be made. And then we're going to start this renegotiation on the next page. And that, to me, didn't land on a place or a space of meaning; it didn't try to codify what blackness was. You can't point to that play and say, oh, this is the black part.

**WCB:** Thank you. Now we're going to open the conversation to the audience to ask questions.

**Audience member:** So, Janna, you brought up the question of the protagonist. My reading has always been that it's a Gestalt protagonist. Do you think there was any influence of, say, Eugene O'Neill's *Long Day's Journey* and Sean O'Casey, both of whom practice Gestalt protagonists and don't go for that one single protagonist that runs through?

**JS:** Um, I, I'm not really sure how familiar she was—I mean, I'm sure she was familiar with O'Neill and O'Casey, but I don't know how consciously she may have been influenced. I think, um, she's clearly having a conversation with Miller, and the social realism of the day.

**BJJ:** She definitely was influenced by O'Casey. She claims that *Shadow of a Gunman* and *Juno* were significant influences on her composition.

**NN:** Let me just pitch in and say something. One thing that's very important about this play is its timing. Theater is very, very topical and I think that was very important in regards to this play because if you go back to 1953, Louis Peterson had a play called *Take a Giant Step*, which basically is very similar: a black family moves into a white community and so forth. And there was also a movie made of that play, but no one knows of this play. So when Lorraine Hansberry comes around and she writes the play that she does, it takes off and no one, not even Philip Rose, knew that play was going to be as successful as it was. I had a conversation with Arthur Laurents, and Arthur Laurents told me that some producers had come to him and had given him the script and he read the script, and he said the producer asked him, "Do you think this is worthwhile?" And he said he was 100 percent sure that that play would not make any money but he wanted to see a black woman get a production. So he said, "Yes, this is a money-maker." Many of the producers wouldn't invest money in this play. Basically, from my perspective, it was just the timing of the play. If she would have done that play in 1955, I don't think the play would've caught on in the same way.

And another thing that's also important to understand about this play is people are always talking about how huge the black audience was and so forth. And I've talked to Philip Rose [the Broadway producer of *A Raisin in the Sun*] about this, and Philip Rose said at the time only about 10 percent of the Broadway audience was black. And then I've talked to other people who saw the show and they said, there's no way it was 10 percent; it possibly could have been 7 percent. So, that's still a very small black audience that saw the play. So actually in the scheme of things the play was written for a white audience. And I think Lloyd Richards picked up on that and said, how do we sell this to a white audience? Because the truth of the matter is that the play couldn't have survived with just a black audience, and that was true in New Haven and also in Philadelphia.

**BK:** There was another play in 1947 that Canada Lee was in, *On Whitman Avenue*...

**NN:** Ossie Davis was in that also.

**BK:** Yeah, about a black family that moves into a white middle-class neighborhood. It was written by a white female playwright [Maxine Wood]. And the only reason I guess that really got made on Broadway was because of Canada

Lee's name. He was a tremendous star. I don't know how many of you know who he was, but yeah, people forget about that.

**JS:** Well, there's also Alice Childress, who was almost the first African American female playwright to be produced on Broadway, but she refused to change the ending of *Trouble in Mind*. So, um, yeah, we might be having a plenary on Alice Childress if it weren't for the fact that she stuck to her guns.

**BJJ:** I want to say, especially in comparison to *Take a Giant Leap*, there is something unique about the treatment of black femininity in *A Raisin in the Sun* that is, I think, an under-recognized part of its genius and appeal. As ever, I'm sure women far outnumbered the theatergoing audiences, white and black, at this period as well, and I think it's that alchemy of identification that's also helping to create the momentum behind a title.

**JS:** And I think Kenny Leon's revival—the protagonist of Kenny Leon's revival, to me, felt like it was the three women, as opposed to Walter Lee. And not just Mama, but all three of them. And maybe that was also by virtue of the casting, because they were three formidable actresses performing opposite someone who was less experienced.

**NN:** You're speaking of Puff Daddy, right?

**JS:** I am.

**BJJ:** Yeah, which Kenny Leon revival are you talking about? [That in 2004 with Sean "Puff Daddy" Combs; in 2014 with Denzel Washington as Walter Lee.]

**Audience member:** Um, there are two parts to this question. I'd like to have you talk about the theme of belonging in *A Raisin in the Sun*. In a sense, the play is a debate among the variety of characters about how you create a space where you belong in the world: Beneatha's searching for a way in which she belongs; Mama has a sense of I need to buy a home and that's where the family will belong. Walter Lee has this very different vision: he wants to be a space for his family to belong in the world. So could you comment on that idea? And then try to relate it back to Arthur Miller and the way in which Hansberry's working within a thematic arena that O'Neill and Miller created. And the second part [of the question] is—I don't know if you've had a chance, it's only come out recently—*White Noise*, Suzan-Lori Parks's new play, I don't know if you've had a chance to know what that's about, but there is certainly a theme of belonging in that, and if you've had a chance in any way, any familiarity with *White Noise*, if you could talk about that as a continuation.

**TG:** Well, you troubled me in our last session with that question, so I guess I'll just pick up the baton where the trouble remains…

**BJJ:** [*aside*] *Trouble in Mind.*

**TG:** *Trouble in Mind*, yes. So this issue of, of cultural belonging, at least as Hansberry presents it in *Raisin*, I never struggled with it. I've never felt like Beneatha or Walter Jr., or even Travis and Ruth had any question about where they belonged. You raise it as if—the question you asked earlier was about the extent to which Walter Lee struggles with emasculation and not feeling a sense of belonging. And this goes back to the discussion about the trio of women who inform this black femininity. And I think there's a really important connection between the two. And so I mentioned earlier when I read the play for the first time in high school, I hated Walter. I could not make sense of him. I did not understand his rants and, um, his tantrums and I very much identified with Beneatha. But as I got older, and of course when I got married and I had developed a close relationship with my own father and my grandfather, the men in my family, I began to understand him. But I also understood how the women were supporting him. And to a great extent that represents for me this belonging. You know, there was, he's looking for belonging outside of the fold and that was never available to him. He's trying to create something that nobody outside of the black community really ever had created with Walter in mind. And so this idea of what pushes people forward or this, this connection between, I think you asked earlier about belonging, um, masculinity, no, it was belonging. Masculinity and…

**Audience member:** Well, the point was in order to have a sense of belonging, you have to feel you built the space. Walter Lee can't live in a house, if it's his father's money and his mother's bought it, it's not his house.

**TG:** Right. So my point was that any authentic sense of belonging is a mutual one. There are always two parties involved. There has to be some reciprocity. And so Mama recognizes that Walter is not going to find that mutuality outside of their home, which is why she gives him the money and allows him to make the big mistake of investing in Willy Harris's scheme. So I'm eager to read and see Suzan-Lori Parks's *White Noise* because this idea of a black person in the twenty-first century selling himself in order to belong is not what I would define as belonging. It has never been the definition of belonging that has informed African American identity as I know it. That's what I find so troubling: trying to make belonging fit, this idea of selling yourself—literally losing yourself to belong. It's impossible.

**BJJ:** Yeah. I mean, I guess I feel like the reason why Mama takes everyone forward is that the belonging is going to happen in the family. That's what you belong to; and again, that echoes this obsession in American drama with family because it's always about this family kind of moving to wilderness, that outside this apartment is where the wilderness is. And that's somehow the lesson that Walter Lee has to learn: that the belonging isn't going to be pleasant, but this is a family who are belonging and choosing to belong—I mean, as much as Beneatha chooses, you know, to belong, to belong to this home in some ways.

I think *White Noise* needs its own plenary because it really is—I think there are very significant conceptual failures to it and, and I don't know how to, like, I don't really know if it—it's an engagement with realism that oddly doesn't understand realism or something. So it's hard to really talk about. But in terms of the Miller [question], I think a lot about the kind of dime drops in *Death of a Salesman* with, um, what is the woman's name? What is the wife's name? Not Ruth.

**BK:** Linda.

**BJJ:** Oh my gosh—I was thinking Linda Emond, who played her, and thinking that can't possibly be her real name—okay, so yeah, Linda saying, "attention must be paid." I feel like that's the—that oddly, that moment, if you split it in three, that's the rest of the women in *A Raisin* to me: Walter Lee is sort of the Willy Loman who essentially we're watching die a kind of social death. And it's like the family is forcing him to stay alive. That's my read of it.

**NN:** Also, if you extend that to August Wilson's *Fences*, you can see the connection with Arthur Miller. If you go back, there was a point when August Wilson was certainly stating that Miller had an influence on him, and then he got to the point where he discontinued that. But it's very, very interesting because I remember seeing a video when August Wilson is actually on stage with Arthur Miller. When you go through the Arthur Miller Society now you can't find it, no one seems to have it. But you can see when Wilson wrote *Fences*, the premise was that he wanted to prove that he could do what Arthur Miller did in *Death of a Salesman*.

**TG:** But I think in terms of this issue of, of belonging, with Willy Loman at the end of the play, I think it's Linda who says Willy didn't know who he was. He had the wrong dreams. Walter Lee finds out who he is and Lena helps usher him into that when she reminds him of the sacrifices his father made. And she says, I'm waiting for you to be your father's son. I'm waiting for you to stand up and talk to your wife about this baby she's saying that she's going to, to get rid of. This notion of belonging is always informed by self-knowledge and that self-knowledge in the African American community grows from knowledge of your place within the community and your accountability to it.

**WCB:** There was a hand, yes.

**Audience member:** Yeah. I had a question for Branden. So, you mentioned *The Colored Museum* and "Last Mama on the Couch" and uh, it occurs to me that something that I think characterizes your dramaturgy is this taking of pieces or images or ideas from plays that were written before you, and then putting them in service of something new or a new way to look at things. And I wonder specifically about *The Colored Museum* because when I, when I see *The Colored Museum*, I feel a lot of, um, anger toward some of the women playwrights that are being, uh, sent up or quoted. And I wonder how you negotiate that, specifically in terms of Hansberry but maybe even Adrienne Kennedy, maybe even Shange.

**BJJ:** How I negotiate George, sorry, George Wolfe's point of view on these women? Or negotiate...

**Audience member:** His quoting of these moments from these women playwrights, these African American women playwrights that he...

**BJJ:** sends up...

**Audience member:** uses pieces in order to—as you say, he has this thesis [the "Last Mama on the Couch Play"], and I think it is a thesis, and I just wonder how you negotiate those pieces of those African American women's plays in service of what *you* do, which is quite different—how those affect the way that you think about your own conversations.

**BJJ:** Sorry: do you mean the work of women or George's point of view on the women?

**Audience member:** Oh, no, I'm talking about pieces of plays that...

**BJJ:** Oh, that belong.... Yeah, well, I mean I think, the drum I've been tapping on is that I think it's interesting that the history of African American drama is mostly held by women, and that the majority, I mean even right now, two of the like hands-down, just top-of-the-mountain masters are Lynn Nottage and Suzan-Lori. And that's without even thinking about them being black or women, it's just like, you know, that's who's there—and there's two of them. And I always think about tracing their lineage back, and obviously Suzan-Lori was, will say openly that her moment with Adrienne Kennedy and Shange on a panel was this crux, this crucible for her in terms of her calling. And so I feel very hyper-aware of that actually because, um, I think that—you know, Robert O'Hara used to say when he was asked what's the hardest thing about being a black playwright, he'd say August Wilson, because he was truly a monolith. And does he deserve it? Absolutely, I think he deserves it. But people often forget that August died young and tragically, and that he had contemporaries and nobody knows who those contemporaries are. Very sad, you know. But the tradition, for some reason in the theater, our tone has been set by women, black women. And that's the work that's taught more than anyone else, which I find kind of radical. And I think I understand George's bitterness. I mean, he's there, he's a young artist at the time trying to respond to a kind of commercial atmosphere that he feels doesn't include him as a queer voice specifically. I feel like you can't.... I feel like, honestly, the majority of African American drama as it's canonized is female voices. That's just the facts. I don't think it's a political statement to make, for me.

**NN:** It's also interesting that you mentioned George's queerness, but we have to also deal with Lorraine Hansberry's queerness, which is something that's coming up more and more now. Quite a few people are suggesting that Lorraine Hansberry was really out before *A Raisin in the Sun*. That is troubling to me because I just don't think that's true. In an email to me, Margaret Wilkerson writes that her research shows Hansberry "began to write an essay on homosexuality, which is entitled 'Queer Beer,' in about 1955, when she was twenty-five years old" and "although she eventually named herself a lesbian in her journals, she never 'outed' herself beyond her most intimate circles." And I've certainly talked to people about this whole issue of Lorraine Hansberry being out and it seems as if Lorraine Hansberry in some sense was living a double life, a double life in terms of she certainly had white female lovers before *A Raisin in the Sun*. But in terms of the African Americans who knew her, everybody that I've talked to did not know that Lorraine Hansberry was a lesbian, not a single person. This includes Douglas Turner Ward, William Branch, and others. They just said that they had absolutely no idea of that. Now, I didn't talk to Lloyd Richards about that, but among the other people I talked to, they just said they were completely surprised by that. And you can look at the stuff that she's writing for *The Ladder* and other places clearly acknowledging that she is a lesbian. So, that's a very touchy issue right now in reference to how people are highlighting that aspect of Lorraine Hansberry's life.

**BJJ:** I think it's also important to not retrofit ideas of lesbian identity on the past. I think this is a very new moment of even understanding what queer subjecthood was. And I think at the same time she was having queer experiences, James Baldwin was a very dear friend of hers who was certainly an out gay man and he spent lots—so I think that it's not necessarily about her being in the closet or not. I think it's about trying to actually do the work to investigate, well, what was her own subjective experience of this queerness? I mean we have that very famous pro and con list about, you know: her "cons" about being lesbian and "pros." I think she was obviously actively wrestling with it but there's a real profundity to even her committing an idea like that to paper. She's participating in sort of small presses, small literary magazines that were lesbian in bent. I think that there was still something radical about these small choices to identify even when the abyss felt, you know, the risks felt so extreme.

**WCB:** We have time for one more question.

**Audience member:** This is a question I started to talk to Teresa about. It's about teaching *Raisin*, a particular problem I've encountered in recent years with mostly white students (or they're probably all white). And that is when we get to the ending, the overwhelming majority of the class thinks he should have flipped the house. It's a real pedagogical problem to try to make them understand—I'll take any advice for how you might react when the class says, "Yeah, well of course!" And you have to point out that probably everyone in that class is between $10,000 and $50,000 in debt because they're students in college, so I can understand, but that's, you know, yeah. You flip it. Of course. You find another one, do it twice. I mean, that's really... so what do you speak about?

**JS:** Maybe point towards the alternative ending? Maybe say, well, how would the play be different if it had the ending where, um, they actually face terror when they move into that new space, which would make it very hard to flip the house if there had been an act of terrorism, uh, enacted in it. Uh, potentially. I mean, it's, if there's a crime in, on a property, it's harder to sell. I don't know.

**NN:** In reference to the alternative ending, that's another issue I wanted to bring up. Now, the alternative ending is that there's an ending for *A Raisin in the Sun* where the family goes to the white community and the Mama is walking around with a weapon protecting the family. This is the most interesting thing to me because I talked to Lloyd Richards and Philip Rose about that ending, and both of them told me that they knew they'd never seen this ending. So I wondered how did this notion of an alternative ending get started? Most people now are assuming that it was actually part of the play, but Margaret Wilkerson is saying that the alternative ending actually came from the screenplay when they made the movie; it was never in the play. [See Wilkerson's introduction to *A Raisin in the Sun: The Unfilmed Original Screenplay*.]

**JS:** Maybe give them Robert O'Hara's *Etiquette of Vigilance* where Travis is in the house with the shotgun?

**BJJ:** Maybe it's also worth bringing in the biographical material from her life. Her father was a huge real estate developer and yet they were living in fear in their own home. And I guess it's about trying to communicate the reality— I mean, that just tells me people don't understand the stakes of what is happening, so it's about communicating or educating the students to the actual context in which it is truly life or death for these families to make this choice. That they're working within an economy that is systemically dispossessing them. I feel like that is the hot topic today: there's that Matthew Desmond book, *Evicted*; there's a whole interest right now in the world in terms of race and real estate and the disparities there. So it's shocking that a student would come in and treat an old text as if it needed a new idea, you know?

**TG:** But even that, that suggestion that they parody whiteness. Yeah. I mean you would have to have enough money to flip the house. You have to get the house in a certain condition...

**Audience member:** The person's who's going to buy the property [will fix it up]. They don't have to do anything.

**TG:** But it doesn't change the family's blackness. It doesn't change their identity and the fact that they are going to continue to be targeted in a racist, violent country.

**BK:** One of the most beloved entertainers in the United States, Nat King Cole's house was terrorized in Beverly Hills, or Holmby Hills, where the family lived, for them to get the hell out of the neighborhood. And that was a high-rent district—same period, just about the same period, actually.

**BJJ:** It also makes me think the students aren't reading the depra—not depravity, but the actual stakes of what it is for this family to be living in a one-bedroom. You know, they're missing the signs of poverty that are actually being broadcast by Hansberry in the work and kind of misinterpreting it, I guess, as like a nice apartment in New York. But you know, I think it's about how do you educate students down to the economic realities of the past? That's one of the hardest tasks, I think, especially in arts programs, to do for people.

## Works Cited

Brown, Lenora Inez. *The Art of Active Dramaturgy: Transforming Critical Thought into Dramatic Action*. Focus, 2010.
Chemers, Michael Mark. *Ghost Light: An Introductory Handbook for Dramaturgy*. Southern Illinois University Press, 2010.
Coates, Ta-Nehisi. *Between the World and Me*. Random House, 2015.
Jacobs-Jenkins, Branden. *Neighbors*. In *Reimagining* A Raisin in the Sun.
Morrison, Toni. *Song of Solomon*. Knopf, 1977.
Norris, Bruce. *Clybourne Park*. In *Reimagining* A Raisin in the Sun.
O'Hara, Robert. *Etiquette of Vigilance*. In *Reimagining* A Raisin in the Sun.
Parks, Suzan-Lori. *White Noise*. Theatre Communications Group, 2019.
Peterson, Louis. *Take a Giant Step*. Samuel French, 1954.
Rugg, Rebecca Ann, and Harvey Young, editors. *Reimagining* A Raisin in the Sun. Northwestern University Press, 2012.
Wilkerson, Margaret B. Introduction. *A Raisin in the Sun: The Unfilmed Original Screenplay*, by Lorraine Hansberry, edited by Robert Nemiroff. Signet, 1994.
_____. "Lorraine Hansberry: Artist, Activist, Feminist." *Women in American Theatre*, edited by Helen Krich Chinoy and Linda Walsh Jenkins, Rev. ed., Theatre Communications Group, 2006, pp. 168–73.
_____. "Re: *A Raisin in the Sun*." Received by Nathaniel Nesmith, April 5, 2019.
Williams, Thomas Chatterton. *Losing My Cool: Love, Literature, and a Black Man's Escape from the Crowd*. Penguin, 2011.
Wolfe, George C. *The Colored Museum*. Grove, 1988.
Wood, Maxine. *On Whitman Avenue*. Dramatists Play Service, 1948.

# Radical Resurrections: A Performance History of John Brown's Body

## Victoria Lynn Scrimer

### Abstract

*"John Brown's body lies a'mouldering in the grave, but his soul goes marching on." Or so goes one version of the Civil War–era anthem celebrating the deeds of the (in)famous abolitionist. This ode to the triumph of John Brown's rebellious spirit over his physical body has proved incredibly apt in terms of performance genealogies. It is a testament to the theory that performances "live" like ghosts beyond their original embodiment. And the ghost of John Brown has been busy, hovering over countless revolutionary movements, circulating through the American repertoire for almost two centuries in folk songs, poems, ballads and plays. But John Brown's fictive body has also been a constant site of change and shifting values. It is, therefore, worth investigating why this figure continues to emerge in literature and performance and what we can learn from it in terms of its power to move people to action. This essay traces a performance history of John Brown's body from Brown's execution in 1859 to the Industrial Workers of the World's 1915 adaptation of the 19th-century marching song and finally to a 2002 performance of Stephen Vincent Benét's 1928 epic poem* John Brown's Body *at San Quentin prison. In this brief historiography, I argue that John Brown's absent body serves as an invitation to embodiment, engaging our moral imaginations and drawing audiences and actors alike into a variety of subversive performances.*

---

*2019 Winner of the Anthony Ellis Prize  
for Best Paper by a Graduate Student*

John Brown was a white, American abolitionist who is best known for leading a raid on the federal armory at Harpers Ferry in what was then Virginia in October of 1859. Frustrated with the pacifist approach to abolition, it was Brown's intention that the raid at Harpers Ferry would provide firepower for a slave liberation movement, but it ultimately resulted in the death of twenty people including two of Brown's own sons and Heyward Shepherd, a free African American working as a baggage handler at the train station in Harpers Ferry. Brown was captured, tried for treason and murder, found guilty, and hanged in December of 1859. In espousing violent means to stop violent wrongs, both John Brown and the justice system that saw to his execution dramatize a moral crossroads, revealing discomfiting contradictions woven into the fabric of American history. The same government that denounced Brown's bloody tactics did so by means of state-sanctioned violence against Brown himself in defense of the violence daily enacted on black bodies. As Eldrid Herrington notes in her introduction to *The Afterlife of John Brown*, "[W]hat is at issue [in the case of Brown] is what action for what crime" (1). Brown's actions and his execution ask us to consider what role, if any, violence plays in the pursuit of justice—how far is too far to go in the pursuit of right. Perhaps because his actions and his execution evoke these fundamental questions of American morality, the figure of John Brown has experienced a rich afterlife in our poetry, song, and drama.

It would take volumes to give a complete account of the many places in art and politics John Brown has posthumously appeared.[1] It is not, however, simply the historical personage of John Brown that activists and actors continually resurrect in song and performance; rather it is often his *body*—a corpse in all its gruesome mortality—to which these performances repeatedly draw our attention. In the well-known folk song, we sing of John Brown's body "mouldering in the grave" as if the living man posed too many complications, and it is only in his death, when Brown's body is separated from that ferocious spirit, that we dare to possess or let ourselves be possessed.

So, while there are arguably many more notable treatments of Brown in American literary and visual arts (i.e., Henry David Thoreau's essay "A Plea for Captain John Brown" and John Steuart Curry's mural "Tragic Prelude"), this essay focuses on instances of public performance in which the *body* of John Brown is explicitly evoked: Brown's public execution and burial, the eponymous marching tune, and a recent staging at San Quentin Prison of the sadly forgotten epic *John Brown's Body*. What emerges from these examples is an abbreviated performance history not of the subject John Brown but his body, exploring where it has surfaced and how it has been used in performance to process and even reconcile some of America's most deeply engrained contradictions. I suggest John Brown's body, emphatically absent or in various states of disappearance and decay, serves as a performative vehicle—not a mirror but a ghostly and inscrutable double through and against which we are prompted to measure ourselves. Brown's inanimate body acts as a placeholder, inviting performers and audiences alike to step into Brown's shoes, so to speak, resulting in a proliferation of individual performances that, like Brown himself, tend to question or subvert dominant rules, norms, and expectations.

By way of illustration, consider Robert Penn Warren's rumination on Brown during his 1965 listening tour of American Civil Rights activists, *Who Speaks for the Negro*. Warren muses, "[Brown] was arrogant, sometimes unscrupulous, sometimes contemptuous of the truth, ambitious, angry, blood obsessed; but, in the end, he spoke and died nobly. What do we make of a poet who, out of the ruck of a confused and obsessed life, creates the beautiful poem?" (321). Once a Southern Agrarian, in league with Vanderbilt University's "Fugitive Poets," Warren wrote a now-infamous pro-segregation essay in 1930. Though Warren later came to denounce the essay, he was always ambivalent about sanctifying Brown as an American martyr. Nonetheless, Warren remained obsessed with the figure of John Brown for most of his life. Like many, Warren was in equal parts drawn to Brown's uncompromising death and repulsed by the bloody actions that marked his life. What is of particular interest to me is the slippage Warren demonstrates in this quote when he moves from talking about the abolitionist (Brown) to talking about the poet (himself), almost unconsciously laying—like a transparency—the image of himself, the poet, over the image of Brown. In a way, Warren steps into Brown's ghostly shadow, trying it on for size. Despite their arguably irreconcilable differences, Warren saw in the paradox of Brown's life and death a vehicle for understanding the "ruck, confusion, and obsession" of his own life. This, I argue, is the performative power of John Brown's body and the reason we continually summon it forth.

John Brown's body made its stage debut on December 2, 1859, when he tread the boards of the gallows platform in Charles Town, Virginia (today West Virginia). In *Discipline and Punish* Michel Foucault argues that the spectacle of public execution served as a "theatre of punishment," a judicial and political ritual that was intended, among other things, to make manifest a man's crime by reflecting the violence of that crime upon the condemned's body (60). Public executions also served as a ritual of political revenge in which the body of the condemned was literally injured in penance for the injury it had inflicted upon the metaphorical body politic. Foucault, however, also suggests in these executions "there was a whole aspect of the carnival, in which rules were inverted, authority mocked and criminals transformed into heroes" (61). This element of subversion seems to have been in effect on that December day in Charles Town. Despite the state of Virginia's best efforts to avoid it, Brown emerged from his execution as nothing less than a folk hero.

Surrounded by a beefed-up security contingent, Brown's execution was a dramatic, ceremonious, and well-documented performance orchestrated by the state to illustrate its powerful moral authority. One of the founders of the Virginia Military Institute, John T.L. Preston, gave a first-hand account of the execution published in the *Lexington Gazette* in Virginia on December 15, 1859, where he reported the scene to be "most imposing, and at the same time, picturesque." In a letter to his wife, the man who would later be known as Confederate Gen. "Stonewall" Jackson described Brown as behaving with signature "unflinching firmness" (Jackson 130). Walt Whitman described Brown's execution in his poem, "Year of Meteors," which was eventually included in *Leaves of Grass* alongside his American epic "Song of Myself." Of Brown he wrote,

> I would sing how an old man, tall, with white hair, mounted the scaffold in Virginia;
> (I was at hand—silent I stood, with teeth shut close—I watch'd;
> I stood very near you, old man, when cool and indifferent, but trembling with age and your unheal'd wounds, you mounted the scaffold) [191].

Whitman's famous imitation of Virgil's evocation of the muse frames Brown as America's Aeneas—a deeply flawed hero, brave and ingenious but entirely capable, as Aeneas was, of descending into brutality and bloodshed.

This image of Brown as cool, unflinching, and even indifferent is significant to the effects of this particular performance of John Brown's body. Brown was not allowed to speak any final words from the scaffold at his execution for fear he would rouse the rabble, and in the moments preceding his execution his face was covered by a white cap. I propose these measures, designed by the state to neutralize or erase Brown, in fact provided a tabula rasa, a powerful contemplative object upon which the audience could focus its meditation of the complicated moral issues the spectacle of Brown's body on the scaffold unavoidably evoked. Indeed, as Preston notes, Brown was left to stand, hooded and awaiting eternity, for an uncomfortably long time. Brown "stood for some ten or fifteen minutes blindfold [sic], the rope around his neck, and his feet on the treacherous platform, expecting instantly that fatal act" while the audience watched rapt, looking for any signs of weakness, fear, or defiance—for any clue to help them understand how they should feel about this man and this scene. They found none. It was in this inscrutable silence in the moments preceding Brown's death, in the absence of observing Brown's own reaction, that the audience members were forced to engage their moral imaginations. Preston recounts, "It was a moment of deep solemnity, and suggestive of thoughts that make the bosom swell." And while Preston assures his readers that "all felt in the depths of their hearts that [Brown's execution] was right," he also notes "there was not one single word or gesture of exultation or of insult" hurled against Brown. Upon Brown's drop through the trap door, each individual member of the crowd was left to ponder "a wonder, a puzzle, and a mystery" that was the inscrutable John Brown (Preston).

This type of inner dialogue into which the crowd at Brown's execution was drawn is, according to philosopher Hannah Arendt in her study of the Adolf Eichmann trial, a critical activity for avoiding banal or thoughtless evil (the type of evil that allowed Nazis like Eichmann to follow murderous orders untroubled by conscience). The banality of evil, for Arendt, is a failure of imagination, the uncreative inability to picture yourself in someone else's shoes. Eichmann was no "monster," no "clever, calculating liar" (29), "not Iago, not Macbeth" (138) but simply, tragically "thoughtless" (138). Regarding slavery, it was precisely this lack of moral imagination Brown sought to upset in the American conscience during his lifetime. Shortly before his execution, in his final speech to the court in Charles Town, Brown quoted Hebrews 13:3, "remember them that are in bonds, as bound with them," lest his white public fail to imagine themselves in another's place.

Ironically, it was in death, when his silent body "hanging between heaven and earth" posed more questions than it answered, that Brown's audience was forced to grapple with their own conscience (Preston). Herrington notes, rather than a patriotic celebration of law and order "[Brown's] hanging pictured out exactly the failure of the United States, dead in its aspirations for human freedom, daily murdering those who, excluded by others from humanity, required rights to citizenship" (1). In flux somewhere between these two possible performances, without a statement or gesture from Brown to guide their interpretation, the audience was faced for those long anticipatory minutes with the many difficult questions surrounding Brown's actions: What is the worth of a human life? What must it feel like to face death and heavenly judgment? What is worth killing for? What is worth dying for? Thus, the American political establishment staged one performance for John Brown's body—objective, public, retributive, case-closed—but the audience, via the silent, hooded body of John Brown, actively participated in an alternate performance—subjective, internal, individuated, unresolved. It is in this way that John Brown's body first became the site of a moral and political face-off that would reach its fulfillment less than two years later in the American Civil War.

Remarkably, John Brown's body was immediately booked for a second engagement, so to speak, starring in a bit of morbid political theatre directly after his execution. The December 4, 1859, edition of the *Philadelphia Sunday*

*Dispatch* reported that directly following Brown's trial and execution, rumors that Brown's body was to be embalmed in Philadelphia on its way to its final resting place in North Elba, New York, nearly incited riots between Northern abolitionists and the many Southern-born medical students attending the various Philadelphia colleges. In response, Philadelphia mayor Alexander Henry arranged for a "sham coffin" to be unloaded and carted towards the city wharf in order to lure the crowds away from the train station while the real coffin containing Brown's body was shipped out safely to New York ("John Brown Excitement"). This bait and switch is an apt metaphor for the separation of the real John Brown whose body has long lain moldering in the grave and the *idea* of John Brown's body—the empty coffin into which the abolitionists, free Northern blacks, and offended Southerners who marched after it projected their hopes and fears.

Theatre and performance theorist Peggy Phelan's work on the ontology of performance offers us one way to understand the phenomenon of John Brown's absent body. In her 1993 book *Unmarked: The Politics of Performance*, Phelan provocatively declared, "Performance's only life is in the present," suggesting that the very nature of performance is time-bound and unrepeatable, making it uniquely free from the economy of reproduction (146). The disappearance and literal decomposition of John Brown's body, that makes obvious the impossibility of a repeat performance, seems to belie the frequency with which John Brown's body continues to re-appear on the page and stage. Phelan, however, suggests re-stagings of historical events constitute their own unique performance in their own historical moment, not a reproduction of John Brown's life and death but a "descriptive recovering" in which the missing object (i.e., John Brown's body) is reconstituted through "the subject's own set of personal meanings and associations" (147). In this case, the disappearance of John Brown's body—its very ephemerality—is fundamental to its performative power; in disappearing "it rehearses and repeats the disappearance of the subject who longs always to be remembered" (147). It is only in dying and decomposing in the grave that Brown and his actions enter the realm of the subjective, ponderable, and personal. In its disappearance, John Brown's body becomes discursive, moving fluidly through the American performance repertoire, but like the hooded figure on the scaffold and the empty coffin at the docks, John Brown's body continually serves as a site of contestation and introspection.

This shift from objective to subjective consideration of John Brown's body is perhaps best illustrated in the many adaptations of its most famous resurrection—the one from which this essay takes its name—the song known as "John Brown's Body." What began as a religious camp meeting song in the 1850s was reportedly adapted to tell the story of John Brown shortly after his execution in 1858. In a 1916 letter to historian Florence Howe Hall,[2] Franklin B. Sanborn (one of Brown's many biographers) recounted the first time he heard the "sonorous" air and "rude words of the John Brown Song" in the summer of 1861 as Fletcher Webster's regiment sang it while marching up State Street in Boston. After purchasing a printed handbill with the lyrics, Sanborn noted that it was adapted from a "camp-meeting hymn" into a "marching song" that was practiced often by Union soldiers during training drills (Hall 59–60). The song, in most of its many iterations, generally consists of a single-line verse trice repeated, followed by a chorus of hallelujahs and a reiterative exclamation. A nineteenth-century song sheet, similar to the one Sanborn must have purchased on State Street, is available courtesy of the Library of Congress's special collections. The lyrics documented there are as follows:

> John Brown's body lies a mouldering in the grave (x3)
> His soul's marching on!
> (Chorus)
> Glory Hally, Hallelujah! Glory Hally, Hallelujah! Glory Hally, Hallelujah!
> His soul's marching on!
> He's gone to be a soldier in the army of our Lord (x3)
> His soul's marching on!
> (Chorus)
> John Brown's knapsack is strapped upon his back (x3)
> His soul's marching on!
> (Chorus)
> His pet lamps[3] will meet him on the way (x3)
> As they march along!
> (Chorus)
> They will hang Jeff Davis to a tree! (x3)
> As they march along!
> (Chorus)
> Now three rousing cheers for the Union (x3)
> As we are marching on!
> (Chorus)

The fact that many of these lyrics seem to make little or no obvious sense in the context of the story of John Brown (particularly the references to knapsacks and pet lambs) is evidence of John Stauffer and Benjamin Soskis's claim that the original iteration of the song was not a celebration of the formidable abolitionist John Brown but the result of some friendly ribbing at the expense of a "diminutive, good-natured Scotsman" named John Brown, a Boston soldier in the popular Second Battalion, Light Infantry (50). Stauffer and Soskis's research reveals that men in the battalion passed the time by inventing lyrics that made sport of the incongruities between the severe abolitionist and the jovial soldier who bore his name.

> "This cannot be John Brown," [the Scotsman's] comrades would insist. "John Brown is dead." And then solemnly, with downcast eyes to maximize the comic effect, someone would intone: "His body lies mouldering in the grave" [47].

Though the tone of comic inversion here is unlike that of previous examples, we see once more that John Brown's absent body plays a key role in subject formation—in this case, the identity of the Scotsman John Brown is shaped against the austere intensity of the abolitionist. It is only through the absent (dead and mouldering) body of the abolitionist John Brown that the identity of the Scotsman John Brown is verified. The irony, of course, is that in hyperbolically insisting on the dead-ness of John Brown, the song continually breathes new life into his memory, with the abolitionist eclipsing the Scotsman in historical memory. Like John Brown's silent body on the scaffold and his missing body in the sham coffin, John Brown's body in the camp song does not rest in peace; it invites speculation, projection, and comparison, forming new subjects in its wake. The improvised lyrics, whose comic appeal lies in the comparison of the two Browns, emerges in response to the looming challenge posed by Brown's formidable ghost.

What is worth noting, in terms of performance, is the apparently powerful draw of the doubleness between the living soldier and the dead abolitionist. Like Robert Penn Warren's superimposition of the poet and the abolitionist, this doubling is powerful despite (or perhaps because of) the apparent dissimilarities between the two. While the comic doubling of the name in the original lyrics "bequeathed to future version of the song a predisposition to parody" (Stauffer 50), the doubling of the living subject and the dead body of John Brown allows for all manner of subversion (not just comic) in the resonances and dissonances between the living subject and John Brown. Perhaps this is why the John Brown version of the song persists when other versions fail to take hold. Stauffer and Soskis recount improvised attempts by battalion members to replace John Brown in the song with "some other worthy personage" like Elmer E. Ellsworth, who was shot and killed while pulling down the Confederate flag in Alexandria in 1861, but "in the vast majority of the published versions of the song… John Brown refused to yield pride of place" (49–50).

In addition to several other variations of the lyrics that emerged in the 1860s, in the 1870s, abolitionist author Julia Howe famously rewrote the lyrics of the song to explicitly celebrate the Union cause. Howe removed references to Brown and unseemly references to hangings and increased the religious fervor in what we now recognize as the arguably more popular version of the song

"The Battle Hymn of the Republic." Yet, the version of the song featuring John Brown's body in the title is the one most cited as the inspiration for revised activist anthems despite the fact that it is neither the original nor the latest iteration. Notably, in its online archive, the radical labor organization the Industrial Workers of the World (IWW) gives precedence to John Brown's body, noting "one of Organized Labor's most famous anthems" is "set to the tune of 'John Brown's Body'—better known as the Battle Hymn of the Republic."

This points to an important rhetorical function that John Brown's body has come to serve in American activist performance. By citing "John Brown's Body" as the inspiration for their song, the IWW—often accused of promoting sabotage—is able to ally itself with the morality of Brown's abolitionist stance and gesture to the justification of violent means in righteous revolution. So the song capitalizes rhetorically and emotionally on a vaunted revolutionary past, but it also fundamentally reframes that performance. When Ralph Chaplin, the poet laureate of the IWW, adapted the song as the fighting anthem for organized labor in 1915, he retitled it "Solidarity Forever" instead of "John Brown's Body." This rendition replaces John Brown's singular body with the collective body of the union. The song's first verse, meant to be sung in unison during marches and strikes, emphasizes the insignificance of the individual and the centrality of the union:

> When the union's inspiration through the workers' blood shall run
> There can be no power greater anywhere beneath the sun
> Yet what force on Earth is weaker than the feeble force of one but
> The union makes us strong! ["Solidarity Forever"]

In this version, the song's inspirational quality does not rely on an aspirational hero worship of the revolutionary individual but draws its power from a sense of belonging in the collective. Chaplin's lyrics strongly emphasize the operative presence of a "we" and a "they." For example, "It is *we* who plowed the prairies, build the cities where *they* trade." This grammatical shift that incorporates the singers themselves as integral players in the performance of the song is largely absent from the original "John Brown Song" which revolves around the figure of John Brown. To sing "John Brown" is to sing *about* the absent body and the revolutionary spirit; to sing "Solidarity Forever" is to be interpolated bodily into the revolution.

The power of John Brown's body to activate our moral imaginations and draw us into subversive performance evidenced in these earlier examples is again aptly illustrated in two very different dramatizations of Stephen Vincent Benét's 1928 American epic *John Brown's Body* which were staged nearly fifty years apart. A perennial favorite in high-school classrooms for many years after its initial publication, the Nobel Prize-winning poem (which is truly epic at more than 300 pages long) attempts to tell the story of the Civil War through the sweeping narratives of Connecticut-born Jack Ellyat and Georgia native Clay Wingate. John Brown himself plays only a small part—his execution occurs about fifty pages in—but as the dramatic incident, the portion of the poem that treats the raid on Harpers Ferry, Brown's capture, and his execution sets the tone and provides the imagery that resonates throughout the rest of the eponymous poem.

Though it is an epic poem, *John Brown's Body* invites a dramatic reading as it shifts between first person omniscient narration and character monologues. Indeed, it was adapted for a successful national tour and Broadway run starring Dame Judith Anderson, Tyrone Power, and Raymond Massey in 1952. The two-hour show boasted no set and no costumes. It was performed in evening clothes and the lines were divided between the actors who took turns delivering Benét's narrative passages, shifting from one role to another. From the shadows, a twenty-person chorus performed the songs embedded in Benét's poem.

The operative principle of this original performance was to actively engage the imagination of the audience. In a 1952 interview with *Collier's*, the play's producer, Paul Gregory, characterized the production as "daring" (Harvey).

> It's what we call "panoramic theater" ... it takes you places.... Not having any physical scenery to compete with, the audience paints its own, building far better sets in the mind [Harvey].

Likewise, a feature in the January 26, 1953, issue of *Life* explains the success of the tour by suggesting, "perhaps bored by too much movie and stage realism, [the U.S. public] is delighted to accept a theater that relies heavily on imagination" ("Poetic Platform Drama" 85). Not only did the audience have to imagine the costumes and scenery, they also had to engage their imagination as the actors moved from one radically different role to another. For instance, Tyrone Power played both Northern soldier Jack Ellyat and Southerner Clay Wingate. Massey read the parts of Lincoln, General Lee, John Brown, and Cudjo, an African American servant. Thus, the audience was encouraged to envision a reality in which our most salient national divisions (racial, regional, social) were reconciled in a single body.

Like the exuberantly defiant lyric "I" in Whitman's "Song of Myself," this production seemed to challenge its audience: "Do I contradict myself? Very well then, I contradict myself"; despite its three-person cast, it insisted, "I am large. I contain multitudes." This was, after all, what Brown had asked the courtroom to remember in his final speech when he quoted Hebrews 13:3, "Remember them that are in bonds, as bound with them; and them which suffer adversity, as being yourselves also in the body." The fundamental supposition underlying Brown's radical abolitionist stance was always that we are inextricably bound in our corporeality and that we must work to imagine ourselves in a shared body. Brown asked America to imagine what Whitman would later immortalize in verse, that "every atom belonging to me as good belongs to you." Poetically, the 1952 stage production of *John Brown's Body* is a performative gesture towards realizing that end.

As one might have guessed, however, in spite of its daring potential, the play's arguably naive treatment of the Civil War has not necessarily aged well. As Gary Grieve-Carlson notes, in his poem Benét attempted to honor both sides of the Civil War, and consequently he "emphasizes certain romantic, even sentimental elements and evades certain troubling questions" (127). This, combined with the radically different precedent set by contemporary modernist epics like Eliot's *The Waste Land* (1922), has meant that Benét's poem and its stage adaptation have fallen out of favor over time and are today largely forgotten.

That is, until a rather remarkable three-year effort by director Joseph De Francesco to re-stage *John Brown's Body* at San Quentin prison in 2002. Following several years of reading and rehearsal, the final performance featured nine men, all inmates serving sentences for violent offenses at San Quentin, and one woman, a professional actor whose performance was pre-recorded and projected on stage. The multi-racial cast were dressed alike in blue button downs and work pants and, as in the 1952 performance, they sat in chairs on the stage, standing and walking when they performed their lines, which were divided without regard to established characters.

Entitled *John Brown's Body at San Quentin: Prisoners Heal Through Theater*, the 2013 film De Francesco made documenting the production of the play offers a narrative throughline of theatre as a transformative practice that helps shape inmates into better citizens. The film's promotional summary, presumably written by De Francesco, claims the "effect [of the performance process] on the men is dramatic, even transformative." The summary also quotes one of the participants as having said, "Up until we did the play, I was never forced to be responsible. This is one of those times I was forced to be responsible.… It gives me another dimension of who I am. It gives me another dimension of life, period." The framing of the film suggests the extensive, multi-year workshop and rehearsal process helped the men learn real-world, marketable skills: to show up on time, foster commitment, work through racial tensions, and find purpose. This is, while apparently progressive in its intentions, the very manifestation of Foucault's definition of a prison as an exhaustive omni-disciplinary apparatus "intended to render individuals docile and useful, by means of precise work upon their bodies" (231). Yet, like the first performance of John Brown's body on the scaffold in Virginia, this performance of *John Brown's Body* is also subject to slippage and inversion. As one of the performers, Larry Miller recalls in the film, "[The play] took on a life of its own."

Plays have a way of doing this, perhaps because as Marvin Carlson points out in *The Haunted Stage*, theatre in its uncanny re-presentation of life has an inherently ghostly quality. In *Performing History*, Freddie Rokem argues "performing history contains a 'ghostly' dimension" because "historical figures reappear on the stage through the work of the actors—enabling dead heroes from the past to reappear" (6). In other words, the performance acts as a type of séance that brings together the actor and the ghost-like memory of the historical figure. Indeed, in the performance at San Quentin, Brown is veritably raised from the grave. After a lyrical description of Brown's trial and execution, the poem's narrator offers a hushed, foreboding incantation—like a medium summoning a spirit: "Listen now, Listen, the bearded lips are speaking now, There are no more guerilla-raids to plan, There are no more hard questions to be solved of right and wrong.... Here is the voice already fixed with night" (Benét 48). And the actor playing Brown steps forward to speak Brown's words, voluntarily possessed.

The apocrypha of theatre history is full of examples in which such possessions become all too real. In *Death by Drama*, theatre historian Jody Enders reminds us of the ancient Greek actor playing Ajax who "overleaped himself" and, like the character he was playing, actually lost his mind (43). She reminds us, too, of the actor Porphyrius who pretended to be a convert to Christianity in order to mock Christians but found in going through the theatrical motions he had become a true believer (23). Thus, in performance there is always the double-edged hope/risk that the actor might truly be transformed, that they will cease to act and simply *become* that which they had only intended to mimic. The actors in San Quentin participated in their own transformation the night the play was staged—not into model citizens shaped by a rigorous penal institution but into something much more semiotically complicated.

In the documentary, after their performance, the warden, Jeanne Woodford, reflected hopefully, "I think the audience forgot they were watching inmates." That is, of course, what a warden would want—complete sublimation of the disciplinary apparatus. She hoped that in successfully acting like actors, the inmates were transformed in the eyes of the audience from prisoners to useful citizens, rehabilitated and, if not capable of participating productively in society, at least posing no threat. Against the grain of her intentions, though, the inmates became not just actors; they participated in the doubling that the evocation of John Brown's body so often seems to invite. They were not only inmates acting like actors, they were inmates acting like revolutionaries.

In conjuring the ghost of John Brown, the inmates conjured the memory of a moment when the American justice system was revealed to be fallible or at the very least inadequate for grappling with situations of complex morality. In lending their bodies to the memory of John Brown, his raid, execution, and the subsequent events of the Civil War, the inmates implicitly prompt the audience to question not only the morality of Brown's legal punishment but their own incarceration more than 150 years later, in a for-profit prison system that is often likened to modern-day slavery—a prison system that has always valued some bodies over others. Like Brown's own carefully staged execution which "pictured out exactly the failure of the United States, dead in aspirations for human freedom" (Herrington 1), the various frictions and resonances between the social actors (inmates) and their dramatic roles (radical abolitionist, slave, President, Union soldier, Confederate soldier, slave trader) provide the opportunity for critical reflection on both the part of the performers and the audience. This is the performative power of John Brown's body. The insistent reminder in the folk song that John Brown's corporeal body is absent is an invitation to offer up our own body as a temporary host to his intimidating moral certitude. That his spirit marches on, looking for a host, is both a promise and a threat, and we must ask ourselves if and why that prospect frightens us. When confronted with John Brown's body, like the audience at Brown's execution, we are forced to turn inward to our own moral imagination and ask ourselves just what *our* bodies might be capable of in the face of gross injustice.

## Notes

1. See, for example, Andrew Taylor and Eldrid Herrington's *The Afterlife of John Brown* and John Stauffer and Benajmin Soskis's *The Battle Hymn of the Republic: A Biography of the Song that Marches On.*

2. Hall was the daughter of abolitionist Julia Howe, who refashioned the lyrics of the song to "The Battle Hymn of the Republic."

3. This particular song sheet unambiguously reads "pet lamps" but other accounts around the same time somewhat more sensibly report the lyrics as "pet lambs."

## Works Cited

Arendt, Hannah. *Eichmann in Jerusalem: A Report on the Banality of Evil.* Viking, 1963.
Benét, Stephen Vincent. *The Selected Works of Stephen Vincent Benét: Volume One.* Farrar & Rinehart, 1942.
Carlson, Marvin. *The Haunted Stage: The Theatre as Memory Machine.* University of Michigan Press, 2002.
Enders, Jody. *Death by Drama and Other Medieval Urban Legends.* University of Chicago Press, 2002.
Foucault, Michel. *Discipline and Punish.* Translated by Alan Sheridan. Vintage, 1995.
Grieve-Carlson, Gary. "*John Brown's Body* and the Meaning of the Civil War." *Stephen Vincent Benét:*

*Essays on His Life and Work.* Edited by David Garrett Izzo and Lincoln Konkle, McFarland, 2003.

Hall, Florence Howe. *The Story of the Battle Hymn of the Republic.* Harper, 1916.

Harvey, Evelyn. "John Brown's Body Hits the Road." *Collier's Magazine.* 6 December 1952.

Jackson, Mary Anna, editor. *Life and Letters of General Thomas J. Jackson (Stonewall Jackson).* Harper and Brothers, 1892.

"John Brown Excitement... Arrival Here of the Body. A Sham Coffin." *Philadelphia Sunday Dispatch.* 4 December 1859.

"John Brown Song." *Library of Congress Rare Books and Special Collections.* Accessed 1 May 2019.

*John Brown's Body at San Quentin: Prisoners Heal Through Theatre.* Directed by Joseph De Francesco, 2013. Kanopy.

Phelan, Peggy. *Unmarked: The Politics of Performance.* Routledge, 1993.

"Poetic Platform Drama." *Life.* 26 January 1953, pp. 85–90.

Preston, John T. L. "Eyewitness Account." *John Brown Execution: VMI Participation John Brown Hanging.* Virginia Military Institute Archives, www.vmi.edu/archives/civil-war-and-new-market/john-brown-execution/. Accessed 1 May 2019.

Rokem, Freddie. *Performing History: Theatrical Representations of the Past in Contemporary Theatre.* University of Iowa Press, 2000.

"Solidarity Forever." *Industrial Workers of the World Historical Archives.* https://www.iww.org/history/icons/solidarityforever. Accessed 1 May 2019.

Stauffer, John, and Benajmin Soskis. *The Battle Hymn of the Republic: A Biography of the Song that Marches On.* Oxford University Press, 2013.

Taylor, Andrew, and Eldrid Herrington, editors. *The Afterlife of John Brown.* Palgrave Macmillan, 2005.

Warren, Robert Penn. *Who Speaks for the Negro?* Yale University Press, 2014.

Whitman, Walt. *Leaves of Grass,* 150th anniversary ed. Oxford University Press, 2005.

# Deep When: A Basic Design Philosophy for Addressing Holidays in Historical Dramas

## Michael Schweikardt

### Abstract

*Script analysis for the scenic designer is often taught as little more than an exercise in reporting given circumstances. While popular introductory design texts invite the student designer to ask useful questions like "When is the play set?" these texts are unfortunately content with overly simple answers—answers that are insufficient for the scenic designer who aspires not merely to be a provider of scenery, but a builder of worlds. When creating a scenic environment, it is insufficient for student designers simply to know when a play is set; they must first understand the meaning of a play's When. To make this distinction graspable, instructional demonstrations that are more ideational than any that are currently available will be required. This essay provides three examples of how a deeper investigation of the question of When can help the student to create meaningful stage designs.*

### When are they?

After spending many years as a scenic designer working in the trenches of regional theater, I find myself making the transition into academia. One of my first assignments has been to teach an undergraduate seminar titled "Script Analysis for the Designer"—a curious title, for it implies that script analysis

*2019 Winner of the Joel Tansey Memorial Award for Graduate Student Travel to the CDC*

for the designer is somehow different from that of the actor, or the director, or the dramaturg. While all theatre artists engage in some form of script analysis, it is the unique task of the scenic designer to spin her analysis of the text into a scenic environment that the play can ultimately inhabit. The job of the scenic designer is that of a world-builder. Therefore, teaching "Script Analysis for the *Designer*" requires one to instruct students how they can transform their text-based analysis into material ideas for the stage in order that they, too, might become world-builders.

It has been some thirty years since I first studied script analysis, and in that time, for me, the process of investigating a text through design has become intuitive and largely unconscious. Imagine you have been challenged to teach something you do so often that the act has become second nature—walking, for example. If asked to describe how one walks, you might simply say, "I put one foot in front of the other." But, of course, much more occurs: a whole series of unnoticed calculations and decisions add up to the act of walking. To teach one how to walk would require that you articulate a seemingly automatic process before systemizing that process into a practice you could impart to others. More importantly, no one learns to walk without examples. Telling isn't enough; *showing* is necessary. Similarly, in order to teach script analysis for designers, I need to articulate the basics of my own process, turn that articulation into a method that can be communicated to students, and then provide examples to show them how it is done. Herein lies my challenge.

To prepare for teaching, I consulted some popular texts on the design process, such as J. Michael Gillette's *Theatrical Design and Production* (1987), Kaoime E. Malloy's *The Art of Theatrical Design* (2014), and Lynn Pecktal's *Designing and Painting for the Theatre* (1975), to glean what they have to say about script analysis. While these texts invite the student designer to ask some useful questions about when and where a play is set, they seem unfortunately content with overly simple answers—answers that are inadequate for the student designer who aspires to be not merely a provider of scenery, but a builder of worlds.

For instance, in her 1998 guide to the design process *From Page to Stage*, Rosemary Ingham asks if there is any special significance to when a play is set. She phrases the question: "When are they?" But the answers she suggests do not reach beyond the basic given circumstances found in the script. Although creating design solely from given circumstances is a useful exercise for student designers, this exercise does not go deeper than teaching them how to decorate the stage for a specific event. This is a recipe for creating surface design, not scenic environments. Ingham uses Tennessee Williams's 1955 play *Cat on a Hot Tin Roof* as an instructional example. "Is there any special significance to when they are?" she asks, "Is it, for instance, a national holiday" (55)? She determines that it "is Big Daddy's birthday and a celebration is in progress" (62). Having identified the When, Ingham adds it to a list of the play's given circumstances and moves on, leaving the student to wonder how to make use of this information beyond, perhaps, simply decorating the stage for a birthday party?

If a student's interrogation of a play's When ends with the given circumstances, how could the analysis prove to be anything more than superficial? And superficial analysis leads to superficial design. All of the introductory design texts I have vetted fail to provide the student designer with the tools needed to go deeper to create scenic environments because they stop short of instructing designers to ask the next, more significant question: Why has Williams made this choice? Playwrights are makers of plays. Their scripts are blueprints for the drama. Every choice is purposeful. It is insufficient for the student designer who aspires towards world-building simply to know When a play is set; she must first understand the meaning of a play's When. Where is the text on script analysis that will help me introduce this concept to student designers?

Although it is not overtly an essay about play analysis for designers, scholar Elinor Fuchs's 2004 essay "EF's Visit to a Small Planet: Some Questions to Ask a Play" offers a refreshing alternative to given-circumstance-based script analysis. She suggests that "a play is not a flat work of literature, not a description in poetry of another world, but is in itself another world passing before you in time and space" (6). Fuchs instructs students to visualize this world as a planet by molding it into a ball and setting it at a distance. Then she advises them to ask the planet questions. For example, in relation to my theme of When, Fuchs asks:

> How does time behave on this planet? Does "time stand still"? Is time frantic and staccato on this planet? Is it leisurely, easy-going time? How is time marked on this planet? By clock? By the sun? By the sound of footsteps? What kind of time are we in? Cyclical time? Eternal time? Linear time? What kind of line? One day? One lifetime? [6].

Fuchs's questions are not concerned with when the play is set, they are concerned with revealing the sensory details that create a picture of how When is characteristic of the entire planet. For Fuchs, the meaning of a play's When is explicable only by reference to the whole.

Although this holistic approach to script analysis is more in line with my own theoretical thinking, Fuchs makes the world of the play discrete by characterizing it as is its own, unique "planet" where "nothing else is possible besides what is there." This suggests that all meaning of When in a play is internally defined. While I teach my students that every play is sovereign in the sense that it is governed by its own particular set of rules, I would have them understand that a play is also a product of the time in which it was written, and of the time in which it is performed. Students must remain aware of how the play relates to a wide spectrum of time. Moreover, since Fuchs's essay comes specifically from teaching dramaturgs, it does not instruct the student in what is the most important and enigmatic moment in the scenic designer's process of world-building—the transformation of meaning into material design.

To fully understand the meaning of a play's When, students must identify the When, articulate how the When means for the play, and then add to it by materializing the When into a scenic environment that transforms their text-based analysis into a physical idea for the stage. This is what is meant by the Deep When of my title; it is given circumstances, plus insight, plus materialization. Deep When provides inspiration for original and nuanced designs for a production, and it is what the examples that constitute the body of this essay are meant to demonstrate.

## The Project

Recently, for a class on dramatic literature, we were considering three plays from the late nineteenth century: Alexandre Dumas *fils'* *Camille* (1852), Henrik Ibsen's *A Doll's House* (1879), and August Strindberg's *Miss Julie* (1888). When connected chronologically, these works represent a tidy evolution of theatrical style. The melodrama of Dumas's *Camille* yields to the realism of Ibsen's *A Doll's House*, which, in turn, yields to the naturalism of Strindberg's *Miss Julie*. I, however, wanted to connect the plays using design as my lens. So I decided to ask, "When are they?" As it happens, all three plays are set during holidays: New Year's Day, Christmas, and Midsummer, respectively. Here was an opportunity to demonstrate Deep When for the students in the class—an opportunity to identify the holidays, articulate how the holiday means for each play, and materialize those meanings.

Ultimately, I decided to use Deep When as inspiration for design schemes for each of the three plays that would honor the playwrights' choice of holidays while staying relevant for modern audiences and, more importantly, serving as examples for scenic design students. This essay grew from the results of that project.

## Reflecting on New Year's Day in *Camille*

Well-made-plays such as Dumas's *Camille* are characterized by tightly constructed, contrived plots featuring secrets, reversals of fortune, and an obligatory revelation scene followed by a rapid dénouement. But mostly, well-made plays are sentimental. The sentimentality in *Camille* is manifest in the idealized transformation of its main character, Marguerite Gauthier, from worldly wise courtesan to quasi-virginal saint. As a scenic designer I dutifully ask this 1852 play "When are they?" As it turns out, the year in which the play is set is open to some debate. Dumas's own novel, *La Dame aux Camélias*, from which his play is adapted, was published in 1848. France was in a state of political unrest from 1848 to 1852; it experienced both a revolution and coup d'état in that short span of time. In a period of such sudden change, the difference between 1848 and 1852 matters. So, which is it?

Perhaps it is neither. I consider that Dumas had an affair with a courtesan named Marie Duplessis and *Camille* is a semi-autobiographical moral tale based on her life, career, and death in 1847 from consumption (tuberculosis).[1] This means Dumas's play is built on past, not future, events. And, being a well-made-play, *Camille* is not considered to be avant-garde. Because *Camille* looks backward to the past, not forward to the future, I decide that the When of the play must be 1847, the year of Marie Duplessis's death. What is much more important, though, is the fact that Dumas has chosen to set the last act of his play in the morning on New Year's Day. Dumas clearly identifies this by having the dying Marguerite's devoted friend, Gaston, wake her and say, "I have brought a heap of silly presents for New Year's Day" (156). This is a given circumstance, and I make note of it, but to what end? To adorn the stage in some way that signifies the holiday? No. Since Dumas has made the choice to set his play against the backdrop of New Year's Day, this When must be meant to convey something significant. I deepen it by asking "Why?" In pursuit of a nuanced design, I strive to connect with why Dumas made this choice. How does the holiday of New Year's Day mean for his play?

Consider the action. On this day, the dying Marguerite awaits the return of her long-absent lover, Armand. Though barely able to rise from her bed, the holiday has stirred in her a nostalgic mood:

> MARGUERITE. Oh, yes, it is New Year's Day. How much can happen in a year…. A year ago, today, at this time we were still sitting around the table singing and laughing…. Where are the days, Doctor, when we still laughed? [158].

As Marguerite wistfully longs for the past, she also optimistically looks to the future:

> MARGUERITE. The first day in the New Year! It is a day to hope and to look forward in. I think clearly. What happiness there is everywhere today! [161].

Taken together this suggests that, for Dumas, New Year's Day means as "reflection"—reflection on moments past mixed with reflection on the potential of the future. The author is using the holiday to open a space for reflection for both Marguerite and his audience. Having had an insight into how When means for *Camille*, I come to the pivotal moment in any design process: I must now go about materializing When into a physical idea for the stage. How do I do this?

With both the given circumstances of When (Ingham), and the meaning of When (Fuchs) in mind, I turn off my observing self and engage in a process of free association. I stay open and alert to what is conjured. Then, I tease out a way I might physically deploy what occurs to me, and I connect it back to the play. This mysterious process is intuitive—it requires a leap of faith, but student designers can put it into practice by asking themselves a series of questions (thank you, Elinor Fuchs). For instance, when dwelling on When, does the color red occur to me? Should I set the play in a red box? How does a red box speak to how When means for the play? Do arches appear in my imagination? Might I create a labyrinth of arches on stage? How does a labyrinth of arches help to express how When means for the play? Does water cross my mind? What if my stage floor was a shallow pool of water? How does a floor made of water relate to how When means for the play?[2] These are all potential metaphors for the play's action, but metaphors that express themselves in material ways. Here I would emphasize the difficulty in articulating a scientific method for this process. The moment of transformation from When to a physical manifestation thereof remains stubbornly enigmatic. Nonetheless, it is the most important step in the process of scene design and for teaching students. Let's look at how the process of transforming a play's temporal "meaning" into a material expression for the stage works in *Camille*.

I allow the words that characterize *Camille's* When—nostalgia, reflection, and sentimentality—to become a ground-zero for my design inspiration. I dwell on the words for a long time before turning off my observing self and engaging in a quick and spontaneous process of free association. The images I conjure send me hurtling through time and space: Caravaggio's painting *Narcissus* (1598), Lotte Stam-Beese's photograph *Albert Braun with Mirror* (1928), the Roxie Sequence from Rob Marshall's film version of the musical *Chicago* (2002), Yayoi Kusama's immersive art installation *Infinity Room* (2013), and a few other works of this nature.[3] In these images, I am able to spot a trend—mirror—and mirror is an idea that I can materialize on stage. Eureka! The most vital step in the design process has been taken.

Now, imagine for *Camille* a basic required setting, one free of overwrought fuss and detail, where only the minimum necessary, period-appropriate furniture is arranged in front of an architectural wall made of antique mirror. With a lack of distraction around her, would Marguerite now be forced to regard herself, to consider her own reflection in the mirror? And, what if, during the

Deep When *(Schweikardt)* 69

**Figure 1:** Scene design for the final act of *Camille* (sketch by Michael Schweikardt).

final act of *Camille*, the left and right thirds of the mirror wall could pivot, causing Marguerite's single reflection to multiply? Marguerite would fracture into three "selves," perhaps representing her past, present, and future simultaneously. Moreover, the design idea is sentimental, like the play itself. The multiple images floating in the silver of the mirror serve to raise Marguerite to the status of icon, so that perhaps, like so many New Year's resolutions, she will not be forgotten by Valentine's Day. (See Figure 1.)

It is important to clarify that "mirror" is merely *an* answer to the question of how to materialize When in *Camille*, not *the* answer. It is, however, *my* answer, which makes it unique. The key to connecting meaning to a material world is found in one's own subconscious search for imagery. When student designers locate their own association to When, the material solution that follows will be uniquely theirs.

## Signifying Christmas in *A Doll's House*

When I ask, "When are they?" of *A Doll's House*, the simple answer is Christmas. Ibsen makes this clear in his opening stage directions by literally marching the holiday in through the front door of the Helmer home in the form of a Christmas tree:

> Enter Nora, humming a tune and in high spirits.... She leaves the outer door open after her, and through it is seen a Porter who is carrying a Christmas tree and a basket which he gives to the Maid, who has opened the door [250].

But an investigation of Deep When reveals that for Ibsen, Christmas has (at least) two different, but connected meanigs. What is fascinating from the point of view of scenic world-building is how Ibsen expresses this duality through the use of a single icon—the Christmas tree.

The first meaning of this holiday's When is romanticized domesticity. In Ibsen's Norway, winters were long and brutal. During Christmas, extended families would escape the cold by gathering close together around the Christmas tree. Presents would be wrapped in beautiful gold paper and hung on the tree— gifts like those that the protagonist, Nora Helmer, a doting middle-class wife and mother, has bought for her own children: "a new suit for Ivar, and a sword; and a horse and trumpet for Bob; and a doll and doll's bed for Emmy" (251). In Act One of *A Doll's House*, Ibsen uses his audience's associations with the Christmas tree to signify a holiday that means children and family. Ultimately, this serves to create an environment that contributes to the infantilizing of his main character, Helmer's "little lark," (his "little squirrel," his "little featherhead"), Nora. But once Christmas, the holiday of children, is over, Ibsen does a very canny thing—he alters the signifier by stripping it of the varnish of sentimentality, thus changing the meaning of what the Christmas tree represents.

In his stage directions for Act Two, Ibsen paints a very different picture of the Christmas tree:

> The Christmas tree is in the corner by the piano, stripped of its ornaments and with burnt-down candle-ends on its disheveled branches [268].

This post-sentimental Christmas tree suggests a second, darker meaning— unvarnished reality. In this post–Christmas environment, Helmer makes the switch from benignly controlling Nora to trying to possess her physically. This is manifested most memorably in the short scene between them following the Christmas party upstairs, in which Helmer clumsily tries to seduce her:

> You have still got the Tarantella in your blood, I see. And it makes you more captivating than ever.... All this evening I have longed for nothing but you. When I watched the seductive figures of the Tarantella, my blood was on fire; I could endure it no longer, and that was why I brought you down so early [285–286].

Having identified When (Christmas), and articulated its meanings (children and family on the one hand, and unvarnished reality on the other), I arrive

Deep When *(Schweikardt)* 71

again at the mysterious liminal space between meaning and materialization, only this time I must endeavor to demonstrate for students how to materialize two meanings of When in a single physical gesture.

As I consider how to guide my students toward manifesting this double meaning of Christmas on the stage, the notion of dual realities calls to my mind scrying—the art of gazing into a black mirror in order to open the inner, psychic eye to hidden knowledge and other planes of existence (the very skill I am trying to find a way to teach). Could the idea of the black mirror be used to describe a portal between the two realities of the Christmas tree? What if, in Act One, the Helmer parlor was fully realized: an environment of idealized domesticity with all of the stuff of life? Into that comfortable nest would come the Christmas tree. Taking a place of prominence in the center of the room, it would be festively decorated for the celebration of the Christmas holiday, adding light and warmth to an already cozy room. When the play shifts to Act Two, the stage would be stripped of all the sentimental fuss of domesticity. The architecture of the set that was present in Act One would glide away, disappearing into the wings at left and right, to reveal a wall of black glass dividing the space, upstage from downstage. Only the Christmas tree and its resplendent image reflected

Figure 2: Scene design for Act Two of *A Doll's House* (sketch by Michael Schweikardt).

in the glass would remain. Then, through the use of lighting, the glass wall would *bleed-through* like a gauze curtain—the glass wall would become transparent, revealing what is being lit upstage of it: a post-sacred Christmas tree. In effect, the resplendent tree's reflection would disappear, being replaced by the lit image of the sullied tree through the glass. The audience would see as Nora sees. Nora's eyes see the sentimental Christmas tree of children, while her inner, psychic eye reveals the unvarnished Christmas tree of adulthood and isolation. Is this the true magic of Christmas? (See Figure 2.)

I would remind student designers here that the black mirror is only one potential material metaphor for the play's action. This solution creates its own problems of practicality, but those are unimportant for what I am trying to teach. When students connect meaning to material, their own associations will yield unique solutions.

## Midsummer Madness in *Miss Julie*

Strindberg's 1888 play focuses on the struggle between a pair of social opposites—a valet named Jean, and the play's title character Miss Julie, the daughter of a Swedish Count—each born into their particular class and shackled to it by heredity. Strindberg wrote *Miss Julie* as a contemporary play in a contemporary style. He meant for it to take place in or around the year it was written. This choice of year is evidenced by an early production photo that shows actors dressed in what would have been late nineteenth-century Swedish clothing.[4] Again there is a holiday in the play, and Strindberg wastes no time in setting it up. *Miss Julie* begins with supper being served to Jean in his master's kitchen. On the second page of Strindberg's text, he complains, "Beer on Midsummer Eve! No thank you" (221). In that line of text lies the answer to "When are they?": it is Midsummer, a festival coinciding with the summer solstice. Armed with just this information, a student might create a design where festoons of flowers and greenery decorate the kitchen. But this is only decorative. Because I seek to teach students how to create a scenic environment for *Miss Julie*, they must go further: Deep When must be illuminated.

Midsummer is a holiday of misrule. Social norms are inverted and chaos reigns. Its traditions embrace all four of the major characteristics of the carnivalesque as defined in 1965 by the Russian literary theorist Mikhail Bakhtin: free and familiar contact among people, eccentricity, carnivalistic mésalliances, and profanation.[5] Of these, the most important to the situation is carnivalistic mésalliances in that the familiar attitude of Carnival renders the hierarchy that normally separates social classes invisible. All of the characteristics of the carnivalesque are present in *Miss Julie*. Intoxicated by the Midsummer holiday, Jean and Miss Julie, a taboo pair of social opposites, find themselves alone together, in the sun-lit middle of the night, in the kitchen of the Count (her father, his master), acting upon the latent desire they feel for one another. A heady combination of wine, lust, and opportunity confuse the traditional hierarchies and weaken the barrier between the conscious and the subconscious. In this state, Miss Julie shares with Jean the ambivalence she feels about being atop the social ladder:

> MISS JULIE. There's a dream I have every now and then. It's coming back to me now. I'm sitting on top of a pillar. I've climbed up it somehow and I don't know how to get back down. When I look down, I get dizzy. I have to get down, but I don't have the courage to jump. I can't hold on much longer and I want to fall. I know I won't have any peace until I get down; no rest until I get down, down on the ground. And if I ever got down on the ground, I'd want to go further, right into the earth [230].

And Jean reveals to Miss Julie his yearning to rise socially:

> JEAN. I used to dream that I'm lying under a tall tree in the dark woods. I want to get up, up to the very top, to look out over the bright landscape with the sun shining on it, to rob the bird's nest up there with the golden eggs in it. And I climb, and I climb, but the trunk is so thick, and so smooth, and it's such a long way to that first branch. I'd go right to the top as if on a ladder. I've never reached it yet, but someday I will—even if only in my dreams [231].

Jean and Miss Julie are dreaming of inverting the social order, and that is precisely what the carnivalesque, and the holiday, is about.[6]

Given circumstances plus intended meaning helps me see that, for Strindberg, Midsummer is madness. He uses the free-for-all, carnivalesque nature of the holiday to create for his audience a space where the normal rules of society do not apply. This anything-goes environment directly influences the actions of his characters. They behave in ways they never could on a normal day, on a day not influenced by the madness of Midsummer. I make note of this strange condition for use in the scenic environment, and I find myself again at that mystical threshold between meaning and materialization—the threshold I am trying to teach students how to cross.

When I think about a world where up is down and down is up, where right is wrong and wrong is right, and where traditional hierarchies are made unrecognizable, once again art involving a mirror comes to my mind, this time in the form of Leandro Erlich's 2013 East London public art installation *Welcome to the Dalston House*. Here we see a full-scale image of a Victorian house façade lying upside-down on the ground and reflected back to the viewer in a mirror, measuring approximately 33 feet tall and 23 feet wide, positioned at a 45-degree angle above it. What if the kitchen of Strindberg's play was depicted

Figure 3: Scene design for *Miss Julie* (sketch by Michael Schweikardt).

on the floor and reflected back to the audience in this way? Would the topsy-turvy world that it creates capture all the characteristics of the play's carnival When? In a world that can never again turn right-side-up, the unlikely pair of Jean and Miss Julie will remain perpetually trapped in the mirror, between two reflections, with no sense of what is real and what is fiction. With the rules of perspective so upset, Jean's and Miss Julie's dreams would be confounded; they could never know which way is up and which way is down. In a space so unrecognizable, all things might have equal footing—men and women, aristocrats and servants; no rules of social order could possibly apply in the chaos of this carnival mirror. (See Figure 3.)

The upside-down mirror is but one material manifestation, among many, that a student designer might find to reflect the upset social order of Midsummer that characterizes *Miss Julie*.

## Deep When

Throughout this essay my project has been to develop instructional examples for student designers that demonstrate how a deep investigation of When leads to nuanced stage design. Surface When is concerned only with decoration. Deep When, by contrast, is concerned with meaning, and it is on meaning that student designers can build worlds. To investigate Deep When, student designers can engage in the formulaic process exhibited in this essay:

(1) Identify the play's When.
(2) Articulate how When means for the play in question.
(3) Engage in an intuitive search for imagery that connects meaning to When.
(4) Materialize the play's When in the scenic environment.

The defining attribute of scenic designers is their ability to transform meaning into material environment, so understanding the third step is critical for students.

This moment of transformation may seem mystical, and the alchemy by which it happens elusive, but it can be made to be less mysterious. Connecting meaning to design requires one to quiet the mind and use instinct based on the foundation of work done in identifying When and articulating its meaning. The subconscious mind will make connections between the meaning of the play and metaphors that express that meaning. Look for where the metaphors can become material.

All three plays examined in this essay, *Camille*, *A Doll's House*, and *Miss Julie*, were written in the second half of the nineteenth century, and as the reader may have noted, all three of the design ideas presented have to do with mirrors. This is due, in part, to my penchant for going down rabbit holes—for becoming fascinated by an object or idea and pursuing it wherever it may lead (I am currently obsessed with mirrors). While the use of the mirror as a material response to an age concerned with beauty and light seems like a valid approach to the design of these late nineteenth-century plays, the use of mirrors is just one solution among many possibilities.

The design ideas explored in this essay are conceptual. Being narrowly focused on materializing a specific idea for the stage, they do not take into account all of the needs of the script, nor do they deal with specificity of period, architecture, or furniture, all of which are of paramount importance to the craft of scenic design. But those needs are not important to what I am trying to convey in this essay. Ultimately, I would encourage student designers to beware of such high-concept designs. To paraphrase a colleague, "avoid trying to shove the vastness of a play through the needle's eye of your narrow concept." But Deep When thinking is not concerned with finished designs. Deep When is a first step on the journey to teaching scenic design that serves to demystify the connection between script analysis and material design, while introducing students to the notion that a scenic designer is a world-builder. What matters here is encouraging the student designer to live for a while in the kind of thinking demonstrated in these case studies. Taking journeys with the text, like the ones launched by Deep When, can clarify how When means for a play and inspire original ideas for how to communicate that meaning to a modern audience. Later in the process, meaningful inspiration can be shaped into responsible and relevantly detailed design for the stage. Until then, anything remains possible.

## Notes

1. In her book *Grandes Horizontales: The Lives and Legends of Marie Duplessis, Cora Pearl, and La Présidente*, Virginia Rounding suggests that tuberculosis was the "right disease" for a courtesan to die of. The disease was thought to be accelerated by the patterns of breathing observed during sexual intercourse. These "venereal excesses" were thought to be harmful to the respiratory system and therefore a cause of consumption.

2. For students who find the practice of free association daunting, I recommend starting with an image search. While thinking about how When means for the play you are designing, simply collect images that appeal to you, but do this quickly and spontaneously—don't think, simply react. Allow some time to pass. Then, objectively examine the images that you have collected. Try to spot a trend (the thing that occurs multiple times). The trend will reveal something that is subconsciously of interest to you. Once you identify that thing, ask the questions I posed earlier.

3. Caravaggio's oil painting *Narcissus* depicts Narcissus fixated on his own reflection in a pool of water. Charlotte (Lotte) Stam-Besse's photo *Albert Braun with Mirror* depicts a man holding a mirror to the centerline of his face so that the reflection completes the image. In the Roxie sequence of *Chicago*, the character Roxie Hart (played by Renée Zellweger), reveling in her

overnight stardom, dances in front of a wall of mirrors, yielding multiple images of her reflection. Yayoi Kusama (born 1929) has designed more than twenty unique *Infinity Mirror Rooms*; casting the viewer as the subject of the work, her rooms offer the opportunity to step into an illusion of infinite space. Other mirroring images include *All is Vanity* (1892) by Charles Allan Gilbert; the figure depicted in this illustration can be seen in two ways—as a woman looking at her reflection in a mirror, or as a skull—which reminds viewers of both beauty and death. The final image of *All About Eve*, the 1950 film written and directed by Joseph Mankiewicz, is of a young woman admiring her own reflection multiplied in a triptych dressing room mirror as she fantasizes about her own stardom.

4. The photograph of the first *Miss Julie* production, November 1906, The People's Theatre, Stockholm appears in *Strindberg and the Five Senses* by Hans-Goran Ekman.

5. The Carnivalesque tradition might be most familiar to the modern-day design student in the form of Shakespeare's play *A Midsummer Night's Dream*, in which young lovers flee the societal structure of the Court for the chaos and abandon of the woods. Once there and freed from all of the rules of social norms, confusion leads to lust and folly.

6. The inversion of social order that is characteristic of Midsummer is vividly illustrated in Ari Aster's 2019 folk horror film *Midsommer*. As the film's main characters approach a commune in Sweden where they will participate in Midsummer rituals that will alter the course of their lives forever, the camera shot of their vehicle traveling along a rural road rotates to disorienting effect, signaling that they have crossed a threshold into a topsy-turvy reality.

## WORKS CITED

Bakhtin, Mikhail. *Problems of Dostoevsky's Poetics*. Edited and translated by Caryl Emerson. University of Minnesota Press, 1984.

Dumas, Alexander, *fils*. *Camille*. Translated by Edith Reynolds and Nigel Playfair. Ernest Benn, 1930.

Fuchs, Elinor. "EF's Visit to a Small Planet: Some Questions to Ask a Play." *Theater*, vol. 34, no. 2, 2004, pp. 4–9.

Ibsen, Henrik. *A Doll's House*. Translated by William Archer, edited by Oscar Brockett and Robert Ball. Thompson Wadsworth, 2004, pp. 249–294.

Ingham, Rosemary. *From Page to Stage*. Heineman, 1998.

Strindberg, August. *Miss Julie*. *August Strindberg: Selected Plays,* translated by Evert Sprinchorn. University of Minnesota Press, 1986, pp. 218–267.

# Uncanniness and Alienation in Lisa D'Amour's *Detroit* and *Airline Highway*

## M. Scott Phillips

### Abstract

*In* Being and Time, *Martin Heidegger defines the "uncanny" as the "peculiar indefiniteness" that beings in the world experience in the midst of anxiety. This "indefiniteness," Heidegger writes, can be said to be "the nothing and nowhere. But here 'uncanniness' also means 'not-being-at-home.'" In both* Detroit *(2010) and* Airline Highway *(2014), two plays written in the aftermath of the 2008 financial crisis, playwright Lisa D'Amour captures the structure of feeling produced by this uncanniness and sense of unrootedness, as well as the existential anxiety and yearning for a putative lost authenticity that comes with it. Along with Heidegger, the essay draws on political scientist Engin F. Isin's notion of the "Neurotic Citizen" and Fredric Jameson's dialectic between the utopic and the dystopic to discuss the ways in which these two plays explore the challenges of maintaining community amidst the dystopic conditions of our social, political, and post-recessionary landscape.*

When Steppenwolf Theatre Company opened the world premiere of Lisa D'Amour's *Detroit* in 2010, *Chicago Theater Beat* praised the ensemble cast, most especially Laurie Metcalf's "feral" performance, while taking the play to task for its putative weak plot and lack of structure. "We get memorable scenes of memorable people talking," wrote critic Catey Sullivan, "and eventually yelling and dirty dancing and recklessly playing with matches—but there is never anything much at stake.... *Detroit*, in the end, feels both static and incomplete." Hedy Weiss, of *The Chicago Sun-Times*, was even more dismissive. D'Amour's play was "infantile," she wrote, "a latter day, anti-intellectual, 'sex, drugs and rock 'n' roll generation' take on 'Who's Afraid of Virginia Woolf?'" ("A Goofy Woolf").

It is true that *Detroit* is largely driven by desperate and talkative characters who behave erratically and irrationally, but Sullivan and Weiss largely missed the point of D'Amour's play, which would soon be in contention for a Pulitzer. The country was still reeling from the effects of the collapse of Lehman Brothers in 2008, followed by the worst economic crisis since the Great Depression, a crisis that obliterated six million jobs and 6.1 percent of all payroll employment in 2009 (Economic Policy Institute). *Detroit*, coming at the advent of a particularly dystopic American moment, was, in the words of Charles Isherwood regarding the 2012 Off-Broadway production, a "sharp X-ray of the embattled American psyche" ("Desperately"). But it was the *Chicago Tribune*'s Chris Jones who best captured the significance of *Detroit* within the context of the economic wreckage, citing "the sense of unease we all feel … some would call it anger." That anger, he went on to say, was "the most important thing for us to ponder in the theater at this particular moment." For Jones, it was "a play that simply could not have been written before 2008" ("At Steppenwolf").

*Detroit* opened at a particularly anxious moment for the United States (and the world), amidst an economic and political landscape that has, in the intervening years since 2010, only engendered more intense anxieties about income inequality, technological overreach, and distortions in the polity that would have seemed unimaginable even at the onset of the financial crisis. In his book *The Plot of the Future*, the late theatre scholar Dragan Klaic wrote that the utopian impulse is an imagining of the redemptive possibility of that which is yet to come: "the subtle interaction of social ideas about the future and the functioning of the future in drama … [culminated] in the full-fledged utopian dramaturgy at the beginning of the twentieth century" (11). These playwrights (Klaic mentions Shaw and Mayakovsky in particular) were, in turn, followed by a wave of dystopic dramaturgy catalyzed by the early twentieth-century European and American disillusionment with technology, and the failure of political, social, and economic order in the lead-up to and aftermath of World War I. Dystopian drama, too, may focus on an imagined future, "predictive" drama as Klaic puts it in his introduction (1–7), but it is a future greatly informed by the present:

> Dystopian drama is more than the mere effort of a pessimistic imagination to conceive of a possible and dreadful future and then put this scary vision in a dramatic form…, a spectacular scarecrow packaged for the stage, such drama cannot avoid referring to the issues and conditions of the present—invoked as the starting point of the coming horror or as a reassuring, familiar experience to which one can slip back after an uneasy journey into the future [70].

Klaic refers to the type of narrative we find in the science fiction anthology television show *Black Mirror*—a series in which the neuroses and pathologies of the high-tech future are firmly grounded in present-day concerns with, and ambivalence toward, technology. *Black Mirror* is of course satire, which always reorients us toward our present predicaments by making the familiar strange. D'Amour's work, however, does not take us to an imagined future, but is firmly rooted in the dystopic present. Her naturalism, graced by certain surreal touches, re-orients us to the grim realities of our current dilemma, while refusing to foreclose on the possibility of agency and hope for the future. Anthony Barilla of Houston's Infernal Bridegroom Productions has described D'Amour's work as "inexplicably familiar," and it is this "strange" familiarity that provides, in the words of Loretta Greco of New York's Women's Project, a "mysterious clarity" (Apple 46). In an interview with Steppenwolf dramaturg Polly Carl, D'Amour indirectly affirmed this, calling *Detroit* "more recognizable" (in its naturalism) than some of her earlier pieces, but "[m]y hope—perhaps a naïve hope—is that the theatre I make invites people to shake off any unwanted thought patterns that may be ruling them, and move toward something new in themselves and in the world" ("Interview").

In this essay, I offer a reading of both *Detroit* and D'Amour's more recently produced *Airline Highway*, which opened at Steppenwolf in 2014 and on Broadway in 2015, garnering four Tony Award nominations. These two plays serve as companion pieces inasmuch as they may be read as responses to a crisis of neoliberalism, the problems of late capitalism and its attendant social neuroses. "Late Capitalism" is a term that has historically been deployed in a variety of ways, and with varying degrees of rigor. My use of the term comports with Fredric Jameson's, that is as a phenomenon closely associated with the postmodern, and the postmodern as a phenomenon that transcends, as Jameson points out, the "purely cultural." For Jameson, writing in 1991, "theories of the postmodern ... bring us the news and the arrival and inauguration of a whole new type of society, most famously baptized 'postindustrial society' (Daniel Bell) but often also designated consumer society, media society, information society, electronic society or high tech, and the like" (3). These overdetermined forces comprise a "new social formation" that "no longer obeys the laws of classical capitalism, namely the primacy of industrial production and the omnipresence of class struggle" (Jameson, "Postmodernism" 3).

Of more significance to the argument concerning D'Amour's plays is the structure of feeling that Jameson associates with late capital: that is, conveying "the sense that something has changed, that things are different, that we have gone through a transformation of the life world which is somehow decisive but incomparable with the older convulsions of modernization and industrialization, less perceptible and dramatic, somehow, but more permanent precisely because more thoroughgoing and all-pervasive" (xxi). It is this sense of unease, of incomparable change and concomitant feelings of unrootedness that permeate the characters in both *Detroit* and *Airline Highway*, albeit in somewhat different ways. In *Detroit*, the characters are unable to successfully cope with their alienation; in *Airline Highway*, D'Amour shows us a community that creates a space for itself and its essential humanity within the confines of its dystopic predicament.

In a key sense, the crisis that animates both of these plays is one of authenticity and the quest for an authentic life, which are concepts as fraught as they are difficult to define. But authenticity, as the musicologist Carl Dahlhaus once wrote, "is a reflexive term; its nature is to be deceptive about its nature" (qtd. in Bendix 3), and Theodor Adorno, ever suspicious of the logic of identity, described it as being "bought at the price of the decimation of others" (qtd. in Mufti 89). In our current political moment in the United States and in Europe, we see how the debate over who may claim to be an "authentic" American or European works its way into the discourse of far-right politics in efforts aimed at the validation of nativism, authoritarianism, and white supremacy. For racial supremacists, authenticity is seen as ontological, as a thing that exists objectively in the world, and therefore is knowable and measurable. In this essay, authenticity (or its absence) is viewed phenomenologically, and therefore experientially. This is not to say that there is no dialogue with the ontic; subjective experience must be based upon interaction with the noumenal world. I do not intend to suggest a reductionist or totalizing view of the term, but rather a triangulation between materialism and perception.[1] From the phenomenological perspective, authenticity is something to be yearned for as a quality of experience but eludes attempts at absolute quantification.

In *Detroit*, the central metaphor for the authentic is the post-war housing subdivision. The play focuses on two couples, Mary and Ben and Sharon and Kenny, who struggle to cope with their depressed economic circumstances, addictions, and dysfunctional marital relationships. The setting, as stated in D'Amour's notes, does not necessarily take place in the titular city, but rather in the anywhere and nowhere of the generic, homogenized, post-war, "first ring" American suburb, the type of community that once held out the promise of comfort and stability for the rising aspirations of a growing American middle class. These were the communities of the "Suburban Dream," a vision that, according to Christopher Leinberger, was first introduced via the "Futurama" exhibit at the New York World's Fair of 1939–40, a putative micro-utopia which became a reality after the post-war return of American GIs. But in the aftermath of the financial crisis, D'Amour's subdivision represents a now almost unattainable American Dream, or perhaps the American Dream as a fallen utopia, a landscape of foreclosures and decay, a kind of "Slumburbia," as one commentator on CNN's *Open House* characterized the phenomenon of suburban "blight" in 2008 (Schafran 133–34).[2] The elderly Frank, a former resident who makes an appearance in *Detroit*'s final scene, bemoans the mix of dilapidation and ostentation in the neighborhood. "I mean," he says, indicating one of the more "fancified" homes across the street, "how are you going to ask for a cup of sugar from someone who lives in *that* place? ... This is not what the developers intended. They wanted you to have neighbors. They wanted you to be in it together" (D'Amour, *Detroit* 94–95).

While the two couples desperately try to bond, to be "in it together," to embrace the comforting rituals of middle-class normalcy, they are consistently undermined by pathologies and neuroses that bind them up in a web of lies and self-delusion. In the end, the entire edifice, both figuratively and literally, goes up in flames. Sharon, a drug addict whose co-dependent relationship with her equally addicted partner Kenny has entailed a transient life across multiple cities and short-term rentals, yearns for something more. "Neighbors. I mean why is that word still in the dictionary?" she laments. "It's archaic—am I saying the right word? Because you don't need to talk to your neighbors anymore" (17).

In this neighborhood, there are neighbors, but no neighborliness. Sharon's sense of isolation is exacerbated by her relationship with a woman in a pink jogging suit who accuses her of allowing her dog to defecate on her lawn. Sharon does not own a dog, but the woman threatens to call the police. "Are you kidding?" she asks in relating the incident to Kenny, Mary, and Ben. "'The police are going to fucking LAUGH IN YOUR FACE if you call them about some dogshit.' And she said, 'AHA! So you DO have a DOG!' And I said, 'No, no, no, no, no fucking NO there is no dog here, lady!' And she just shook her head and kind of kicked our plant and said, 'Ha, I thought it was fake'" (55).

The fake plant is an illusion of a real plant, just as the neighborhood itself is, in a larger sense, a Potemkin Village. Here the American suburb is a community-in-name-only where no one really knows each other, and where neighborliness has given way to suffocating anonymity, inchoate anxiety, and alienation. The Potemkin theme is further magnified by physical rot—the shabby cement work on the patio, which Kenny says "looks like a do-it-yourself job" (15); Ben's defective sliding glass door (16); and a collapsing patio umbrella, which injures Kenny (18). In a later scene, Mary and Ben attend Sharon and Kenny's cookout, and Ben falls through the shattered floorboard of Kenny's unfinished deck (52). The rot, both social and physical, runs deep.

The broken doors and other inconveniences and chores of suburban life are also signifiers of middle-class identity. Here is another illusion, a bourgeois pretense that both couples perpetuate to mask the real conditions of their existence. This performance of respectability is nowhere more apparent than in the first scene, when Mary gives Sharon and Kenny a coffee table, a charitable gesture which we later learn she cannot afford, and in a subsequent scene, when she and Ben host Kenny and Sharon for a backyard cookout. Mary's choice of hors d'oeuvres—bacon drizzled with chili oil, Danish Havarti with basil served with a specialty olive oil—projects a level of discretionary income necessary to be considered a connoisseur of trendy foods. Of the heirloom tomatoes she serves, she tells Sharon, "I drove all the way to Whole Foods to get them," allowing as only a foodie might, that "they've been grown from the same seed for hundreds of years" (34). So too for Ben, who adopts the pretense that he is a freelance financial consultant, busy during the day with building his website. Ben projects the confidence of the entrepreneurial and creative class, expounding to Kenny the importance of pursuing one's passions, a luxury in which those who live on the fringes of the economy can rarely afford to indulge. "If you follow your passions," he explains, ever the expert, "you're halfway there" (13).

Sharon and Kenny's pretensions are somewhat different—they are transient substance abusers, less concerned about an appearance of faux prosperity than in maintaining self-respect through a narrative of rehabilitation. Their narrative is of hardship overcome, the victory of twelve-step willpower over addictions now squarely in the rearview mirror, and the redemption of the prodigal. To prove this, they too need to compete in ways that challenge their means, inviting Mary and Ben to a cookout of their own, this time with "Cheetos, saltines, a canned bean dip, and Cheez Whiz" (49). It is a pathetic and self-defeating competition, but what both couples share is an estrangement from normalcy, the disjunction between reality and that which they must believe about themselves in order to maintain their sense of self, in order to cope with the brutalizing reality of the post-recessionary world. While written and produced six years before the 2016 elections, D'Amour's characters reflect a kind of pre–Donald Trump Trumpian dystopic funk, a nihilistic surrender to something they cannot fully articulate. As Sharon puts it in a conversation about the technological mysteries of the "next internet," but which could just as well reflect the structure of feeling surrounding late capital, "I can't explain it, and it's outside of our understanding at this time" (51).

It is tempting, but not wholly satisfying, to attribute this disjunction between life and well-being in terms of Karl Marx's concept of labor estrangement. For Marx, human beings become alienated from their labor when labor itself becomes a thing external and alien to workers and their sense of their own humanity. When labor ceases to be a part of the "species being," the activities of life that contribute to a holistic sense of human happiness, it no longer is part of "life-engendering life," but rather "a mere means to existence" (Marx). All four of D'Amour's principal characters are alienated—from each other in their delusions and deceptions, and from their labor. Mary, a paralegal, resents Ben because he stays home all day supposedly building his business, while Ben, the would-be financial advisor with no income, withholds from Mary that he, in fact, has no website at all. Paralyzed and devoid of agency, he eventually confesses, telling his wife, simply, "I think I don't want to" (86). Kenny is fired from his warehouse job, perhaps because of his drug habit, but ostensibly for leaving the floor to retrieve a back brace from his car (56). Sharon, who works in a call center, takes a sick day to get high in a parking lot and have a brief and potentially dangerous flirtation with a stranger in a pickup truck (60).

For each of these characters, "life itself appears only as a *means to life*" (Marx), but there is something more at work here. Engin F. Isin has argued that the past several decades have produced an entirely new type of subject, the "neoliberal subject," not a free subject driven by rationality, but rather a neurotic subject. Isin draws on Foucault's concept of "biopower," that is the state's response to the rise of enlightenment liberalism, of the free and self-determined individual, and the strategies of containment necessary to preserve state power that can no longer be exercised with absolute sovereignty. For the neoliberal government, Foucault argues, "the problem is not whether there are things that you cannot touch and others that you are entitled to touch. The problem is how you touch them. The problem is the way of doing things, the problem, if you like, of governmental style" (133).

Isin surveys scholarship on the sociology of risk, that is, that the neoliberal state (referring to the Anglophone world, including the United States), has become a "risk society," in which "subjects govern their conduct through risk and governments primarily constitute themselves as safeguarding their subjects from risks" (218). Risk societies promote a "culture of fear," in which governments, but also corporations and other special interests, a whole range of ideological state apparatuses, find it profitable and useful to manufacture and perpetuate perceptions of danger and the "commodification of fear," exemplified by "the emergence of panics, gated communities, security industries, and an overall trend toward isolation and insularity" (219). For Isin, the result is a citizen/subject "governed through its affects," a neurotic subject that replaces the "self-sufficient, self-regarding" subject of the Enlightenment, "governed in and through its freedom" (222). This has led to a type of "neuropolitics," and in conjunction with the stresses of life in the neoliberal state, a "neuroliberalism" (223).

The world of the neurotic citizen is one in which government and other social, political, and corporate entities act to manage risk for individuals, encouraging the formation of subjects whose neuroses manifest as a byproduct of the perceived need for security. It is important to note that such management rarely involves direct intervention. Security in any sense is markedly more difficult in a political and social environment that promotes the unfettered, unregulated freedom of capital, devalues the social safety net, and dismantles the welfare state, all while perpetuating a narrative of personal responsibility and self-sufficiency. In short, the neoliberal state retreats from direct intervention and turns instead to exhortation. In other words, we are on our own, and so are Mary, Ben, Kenny, and Sharon.

Their neuroses play out in a number of ways. Mary's economic anxiety manifests in a dream in which her bank is represented by a man sitting behind a rickety card table depositing Mary's money into a shoe box, a dream that links both the bank and her economic circumstances to an image of precariousness and, since the card table is located on an abandoned boardwalk, desolation (7). Sharon dreams that she is grocery shopping with Ben. As she places groceries in her cart, the amount of money in her purse changes, and she must constantly recalculate how much she will be able to buy, even as Ben, sitting in the cart's children's seat, shrinks and withers away. In this dream, food insecurity and an emasculated, infantilized Ben are the dominant images (44). In waking hours, the two couples discuss television, at which point Ben admits to watching NASCAR, but avers that it is only to "decompress," presumably after a long day working on his consulting business. Sharon watches reality television, specifically a show in which women vie for millions of dollars by competing to see who will go "farthest [sexually] for her man." When Mary speaks of her preferred reality program, however, there is a sense that the veil of inauthenticity in both reality TV and in her own life can be penetrated:

> MARY. One time I watched a whole episode of *Fit to be Tied*, and when it got to the end, I realized that I hadn't really seen any of it.
> SHARON. Yes!
> MARY. I was thinking about something else the whole time ... stewing about something ... and so to Ben it looked like I was watching the show, but really I was on another planet ... a really angry planet.
> KENNY. That sounds like the last five years of my life [36–7].

Whenever the veil is penetrated, even slightly, we get a glimpse of the atavistic rage and distress that bubbles beneath, epitomized by Mary stumbling drunkenly into Sharon's yard after fleeing her home in an episode of marital panic and claustrophobia, grabbing Sharon, and screaming "I JUST NEEDED SOME AIR" (29).

D'Amour brings the collective anxiety of the two couples to a nihilistic, almost exorcistic, head in the play's penultimate scene. Ben and Sharon make out spontaneously, Sharon kisses Mary, and furniture is destroyed as they dance around a fire that shortly rages out of control. It is a scene in which the pretense of social order dissolves as the veil falls away completely, even if only for a short time (77–90). In the end, D'Amour leaves her audience to survey the burnt landscape of human lives and property, offering only the faintest of hope for her protagonists. Ben promises to take another look at his website, and Mary tells the elderly Frank that she would like to move to Britain and live on a farm, but both declarations have the air of a pipe dream and the hint of continued self-delusion. In talking with Frank, Mary refers to her husband by an assumed name, and we learn that both she and Ben have been reduced to living at a Super 8, while Kenny and Sharon, revealed to be squatters living under aliases, are simply erased, having fled the neighborhood in the middle of the night. If D'Amour's penultimate scene is indeed meant as an exorcism, it is a failed one.

At the end of *Detroit*, we are left with a disconcerting lack of closure, of tentativeness, uncertainty, and, perhaps most importantly, uncanniness, meant in both a general and very specific way. Certainly there is uncanniness in the sense that the world and the characters seem off-kilter, or, as Collette Conroy has said of the uncanny, that "something is not quite right" (26), but the uncanny also presents more specifically, in the way that Martin Heidegger intended the term: as a feeling of no longer being at home in the world. Heidegger distinguishes between fear—the wariness of and desire to avoid discrete and localized circumstances which may or may not come into being (e.g., losing a job, contracting a disease)—and anxiety, which is a much more inchoate and existential phenomenon. For Heidegger, "[that] in the face of which one has anxiety is not an entity within-the-world" (231); it is an alienation from the world itself, and "uncanniness" is that feeling that the world, which appears superficially familiar, is somehow not as it was or should be. In Heidegger's words, "here the peculiar indefiniteness of that which Dasein [meaning the being who is present in the world] finds itself alongside in anxiety, comes proximally to expression: the 'nothing and nowhere.' But here 'uncanniness' also means 'not-being-at-home'" (233).

Heidegger's "uncanniness," the state of "not-being-at-home" in the world, is to a large extent the thread that binds Isin's neurotic citizen to Jameson's late capital. For Isin, the citizen is governed by her "affects" while lacking the agency to make free choices, and therefore lacking the tools for redress. Jameson's description of the sensibility of late capital as that of a sense of an altered "life world" which is "thoroughgoing and all-pervasive" also evokes the uncanny in a Heideggerian sense. Indeed, Jameson himself has grappled with Heidegger's philosophy of being in his own work.[3]

It is this state of a fallen world, the fact of living in an "uncanny" home that afflicts the characters in *Detroit*, and it is a prison from which they apparently cannot escape. Social theorist Paolo Virno sees the "uncanny" as a "fusion" of both Heidegger's fear and anxiety (Virno substitutes the term "anguish" for "anxiety"), in which fear of identifiable and discrete dangers automatically evokes existential angst. One of the reasons for this, Virno states, is "that one cannot speak reasonably of substantial communities," and this lack of community leads to "a more general disorientation in the presence of the world in which we live" (33). The dissolution of community impels this fusion, in which "the loss of one's job, or the change which alters the features of the functions of labor, or the loneliness of metropolitan life—all these aspects of our relationship with the world assume many of the traits which formerly belonged to the kind of terror one feels outside the walls of the community" (Virno 33).

In *Airline Highway*, home is replete with characters suffering from the alienation of dispossession and from living in a home that has fundamentally changed. Featuring a much larger ensemble than *Detroit*, *Highway* is set in post–Katrina New Orleans in the parking lot of the Hummingbird, a seedy hotel frequented by druggies, hookers, beat poets, and other denizens of the city's underclass, the collateral damage of poor social policy, benign neglect, and bad breaks. They are human analogs to the detritus left behind in the wake of the hurricane, one of D'Amour's central metaphors. Home in *Airline Highway* is both iconic, in that New Orleans retains associations unique to it as an American city, and generic, in that the Hummingbird's neighborhood is in an area far from Big Easy iconicity, from the French Quarter and Jazz Fest, in a part of the city that sits, as D'Amour—herself a New Orleans native—tells us, on the outskirts right before New Orleans "turns into Metairie" (D'Amour, *Airline Highway* 7).

*Airline Highway* depicts the preparation for a farewell party in honor of Miss Ruby, a dying burlesque stripper and a mother figure to her devotees, and culminates with the party itself. It is a living funeral, a ritualistic send-off to a woman who is central to the lives and survival of a community of outcasts. For most of the play, she is an unseen presence, a somewhat mystical figure whose passing is not only a personal loss for her friends and admirers but almost symbolic of a dying, dystopic New Orleans, a town hollowed out by a hurricane and filled up again, not with revitalized neighborhoods, but with the commodified iconicity of the tourism industry. D'Amour herself writes in her notes of "a growing fear that [New Orleans'] rituals and traditions, created by people of many races and income brackets, will be harder to sustain," due to the influx of "outside money" (ix). The people of the Hummingbird are born-and-bred natives, but they are insiders who have become outsiders. It is on the literal and figurative outskirts, D'Amour suggests, that the "real" New Orleans contends with the alienation and reification of the citizen/subject in a city that is, ironically, awash in the business of "authenticity."

Critical reception for *Airline Highway* was mixed after the production's world premiere in 2014. The *Chicago Sun-Times'* Weiss found it overly sentimental, "terribly naïve and simplistic" in its "belief that the souls of the dispossessed are innately nobler than those of the strivers." It was a return to Steppenwolf's glory days of the 1980s "when it let its 'freak flag' fly to such memorable effect in Lanford Wilson's 'Balm in Gilead' (and later 'The Hot L Baltimore')" (Weiss, "Big Easy"). At the *Tribune*, Jones faulted it for an "unintentional Disney-fication of the dispossessed" ("Airline Highway"). But Isherwood, writing in the *New York Times* about the Manhattan Theatre Club production, contended that it transcended the threat of being "a rosy-hued vision of the lower depths ... a happy-go-lucky 'The Iceman Cometh.' ... Ms. D'Amour," he proclaimed, "allows the darkness to erupt with a thunderclap, as the ... recklessness that the characters cannot keep at bay for long begins to consume them" ("Airline Highway").

*Airline Highway* does indeed lend itself to comparisons with well-worn American dramatic tropes, and as such constitutes risky ground for D'Amour. As Isherwood suggests, its sensibility resonates in many ways with Harry Hope's bar and rooming house, and also Nick's Pacific Street Saloon in Saroyan's *The Time of Your Life*, and in certain moments its poetic quality recalls Tennessee Williams's southern delicacy. But while D'Amour's treatment is unquestionably romantic at times, to call it "Disney-fication," as Jones does, is unfair. *Airline Highway* comments on Disney-fication, certainly, but, as Isherwood maintains, there is also a darkness that speaks to our dystopic moment.

The members of the Hummingbird community are the people of the "real" New Orleans, struggling, forgotten, and eclipsed by market forces and city branding efforts that accelerated greatly after the hurricane. Kevin Fox Gotham has written about the ways in which the corporatist, post–Katrina campaign correlated the health of the city with an increase in commercial, tourism-oriented development. Katrina "exposed to a global audience New Orleans' chronic poverty, strained race relations, and intense inequalities," critical problems which the city largely ignored in favor of image reform and rebranding of the town as a "come-back city" (Gotham 825). Tourism, which purports to provide the outsider with an "inside" or "authentic" experience, is inherently (pseudo) anthropological, ethnographic, and caught up within its own contradictions. As Gotham argues, branding seeks to make the city, which is fundamentally a diverse, irreducible, and overdetermined system of communities and groups into a coherent, comprehensive, and totalizing entity (840). Such a project can only be articulated through a simulacrum. In an iconic city such as New Orleans, tourism becomes Baudrillard's map that precedes the actual territory.

Francis, the fifty-something bike-riding beat poet character in *Airline Highway*, speaks of Jazz Fest, not the commercially sanitized attractions at the core, but the Fest as celebrated on the fringes, outside of the auspices of the Fest itself. For Francis, the tourists want the real thing whether they realize it or not. For him, "the center will not motherfucking hold ... [Tourists] don't want a parade *inside* the convention center, sponsored by Coke. They want some dirty shit to happen, authentic top-shelf shit, the stuff they keep under the counter, ya gotta ask for it. Sip it in the back room with a one-eyed banjo player named Biff—*That's* what people want" (14). Sissy Na Na, a trans Creole woman of color, described by D'Amour as perhaps the most socially functional person within Miss Ruby's circle (4), harbors no illusions about what tourists actually want: they are interlopers and philistines and have no idea what they want. "Fuck all them short-dicked doe-eyed tight-lipped tourists from Minnesota," she says (23). For her, the tourists are a nuisance to be borne, provincials who will never understand the culture that they are purportedly there to observe.

Sissy Na Na's contempt for the stupidity of the out-of-towners is complemented by her distrust of the occupants of the Hummingbird's "problem room," a hang-out hosting a racially mixed group of dealers who come and go, presumably to meet their connections (20), with one stopping off to check with Sissy Na Na's friend Tanya, an aging sex worker and burlesque dancer, to see if she if she has "everything" she needs. (29). Like the tourists and the city's pro-development priorities, the uninvited occupants of the problem room contribute to the alienation, dispossession, and uncanniness that the Hummingbird community experiences within its own city.

Heidegger's "fear" manifests itself in myriad ways in *Airline Highway*—mostly in the contingent economic condition of the characters, but Heidegger's "anxiety" finds its fullest expression in the impending death of Miss Ruby. Miss Ruby's death is existential (for her, of course, but also for her community), as it is her maternal charisma that unites the outcasts, endowing them with a sense of purpose and existential foundation. The challenges to this foundation come not only from without—through encroaching commercialization and thralldom to outsiders—but also from within. This occurs most clearly in the character of Bait Boy, a one-time member of Miss Ruby's circle who left New Orleans, hooked up with a wealthy suburban woman, and now lives in an affluent Atlanta suburb. He has come back to honor Miss Ruby, but brings his bourgeois pretensions with him, as well as a platter of fancy sandwiches for the party purchased at Whole Foods. It is an act of dispossession in and of itself, as Bait Boy compels Tanya to put her more modest, but dearly purchased, offering of luncheon meat back in the fridge (48). His attempts to persuade everyone to call him "Greg" instead of his childhood nickname amuse and annoy his friends. "I come back here, I look around," he tells Krista, an exotic dancer and one of his former lovers, "and I'm like, did I really live here? Did all those things really happen?" For Bait Boy, who now works selling advertising for trade magazines owned by his lover, those questions are less a reflection of nostalgia than a wishful disavowal of his former life (61). Bait Boy's presence is also disorienting for Krista, who feels compelled to disavow her own life by pretending that she now works at a law firm as a paralegal. Bait Boy's transparent inauthenticity even manifests physically, prompting Sissy Na Na to remark "he looks pale. Waxy" (49).

Bait Boy's disavowal is compounded by the behavior of his stepdaughter, Zoe, who has come with him to Miss Ruby's party to gather data for a school sociology project on subcultures. Zoe is both hip to her own privilege as a rich suburban white kid, but also oblivious to the offensive nature of her project and its intrusiveness at a time when the Hummingbird community is about to face its greatest loss. "He talked about her as a kind of mother figure," she says of an article on Miss Ruby published in *Gambit*, "and it got me thinking about … tribes" (54). Zoe offers her analysis of the social dynamic in play. "See, you've created a family, and I'm guessing, a hierarchy inside the family…. And a shared language, rituals and responsibilities, so that you can survive" (55). It is not that she is wrong about these survival mechanisms, but she is like an old-school anthropologist, adopting the pose of the disinterested, neutral observer, unaware of the impact of her own presence on the people she observes.

Dean MacCannell, writing in the 1970s and using Erving Goffman's analysis of "front" and "back" regions in social performance as an analytical tool, posited a touristic "back" region, supposedly closed to outsiders, that putatively offers an experience more authentic than the more culturally curated and staged touristic "front" regions. The "back" regions motivate a "touristic consciousness" which seeks to permeate "false fronts" in order to access "intimate reality." But, as MacCannell points out, the true workings of a given cultural formation are not so easily rendered transparent, or accessible (597).[4] Zoe, who disdains what she refers to as the "cookie-cutter corporate land" of the suburbs, has stumbled into one of New Orleans's "back regions" but, despite the tone-deafness of her questions, retains enough self-awareness to know that she can never be anything more than a cultural tourist. When Terry, the Hummingbird's unofficial handyman, tells her that there is another side to Atlanta other than suburban sprawl, she allows that "there are pockets of cool culture in the city, but you have to be born into that, and I was born on another track, and if I stay there, I'm just going to atrophy" (57). A child of the homogenized, reified world of the upper middle class, she yearns for the sense of belonging that Bait Boy has so casually rejected.

It is noteworthy that both *Detroit* and *Airline Highway* are brought to closure through social gatherings. In *Detroit*, we have not so much a party in the celebratory sense, but a nihilistic release, a catharsis that ends in a state of exhausted despair and lacks efficacy. In Miss Ruby's farewell party, however, we have a bonding in community, and a refusal to submit, to be subsumed and absorbed by the wider world. Both of D'Amour's climactic moments are atavistic and exhausting, but only the latter is redemptive. Throughout the Hummingbird celebration, there are moments that take on a ritual structure, at times musical, but also spontaneous, and that allow the participants, like riffing jazz musicians, an improvisational freedom within the frame. "Bacchanal, man, bacchanal," Francis yells out, at one point. "Boundaries out the window, panoramic bliss—fat man down the street smokes reefer to ease pain.... Bacchanal, man, it's a spiritual thing" (92). The party guests are now in a liminal space, in transition with respect to the imminent loss of Miss Ruby, but also toward a reaffirmation of community and a reclamation of agency.

It is Sissy Na Na who serves as the High Priestess and calls the group to order. "We are gathered here today to honor the angel who looks down upon you all with an utterly unjudgmental eye," she intones, almost as an invocation, a call to worship. "If you need to repent," she declares, "she will show you how. If you need a good spanking, well she can take care of that too" (94). The call to repentance and promise of absolution crystalizes in the characters of Bait Boy, the prodigal son who does not wish to return to the fold, and Zoe, the outsider who feels that she cannot belong. There are several almost ritualistic confrontations with Bait Boy, in which Sissy Na Na, Krista, and Francis shame, cajole, and mock him as a sellout. They are frank confrontations, but also sincere invitations to repentance and reincorporation, and he rejects them all. In a final act of rejection, he tells his stepdaughter, "Come on, Zoe, we're getting out of this shit hole" (142). In contrast, and despite her reservations as an outsider, Zoe accepts her invitation to join the women in a circle dance and a responsory, improvisational, and communal singing of Nina Simone's "Be My Husband." As one of the women beats a rhythm on a trash can, she joins in and improvs a solo. It is a small ritual, if not of full incorporation, then of acceptance.

The party's climax is the appearance of Miss Ruby, carried down to the parking lot on her bed, drifting in and out of consciousness. The party guests process around Miss Ruby in a circle holding aloft paper ducks (Miss Ruby refers to the members of her ad hoc family as "ducks"), singing a discordant rendition of "Just a Closer Walk with Thee," in which Miss Ruby assumes the role of the deity. "*I am weak but thou art strong / Keep me, Ruby, from all harm*" (133).

When Miss Ruby awakes and addresses the assembly, which she refers to as "the most gorgeous group of fuckups I've ever seen," it is a final exhortation against the darkness and the despair brought on by countless bad breaks and questionable choices, and the yoke of economic marginalization that accrues to the outcast. They have, she tells them, "drawn the short end of the stick" (134), but she enjoins her followers, despite their despair, to fight the uncanniness of their lives in a way that is almost evangelical. It is a message that acknowledges their dispossession while opening up the possibility of reclaiming a sense of being-at-home-again in the world. She exhorts them: "but you are seekers who have been drawn here, to the edges of the world. And you hold the potential to teach the world something about itself. You live in a city that reveres the ecstatic moment. How do you live in this ecstasy and still use it? Carry it with you without being utterly consumed" (135)?

Her answer to these questions begins with an invocation and paean to sex, to sex "as an energy, as energy creating energy" (134). This is not simply sex as a pleasurable act, but as the primal force without which community cannot exist. It is the ecstatic experience of communion, spoken into existence by "this lonely God, sitting on a solitary cloud, desperately desiring the feeling of being *with*. In the burlesque club of my dreams, there's no *he* paying for *she* performing for *him* who is mad at *her*—we are all in the room *with* each other, open and unafraid, reveling in the present moment together" (134).

Here is where *Airline Highway* is most vulnerable to the charges of its critics. It is a moment that threatens to devolve into the "Disney-fication" to which Jones refers in his *Tribune* review. But Miss Ruby's words are not magic; they do not offer facile resolution. It is not that this ritual brings closure to suffering or quells the self-destructive impulses that we see in *Detroit*; Bait Boy holds fast in his inauthenticity, and Tanya downs some of Miss Ruby's sleeping pills and attempts to strip naked in a nihilistic act of self-degradation. Their lives surely will continue to be messy, incoherent, chaotic. Like Sharon, Kenny, Mary, and Ben, they will continue to be challenged, and possibly governed, by their affects and their neuroses.

But unlike the people in *Detroit*, there is the hope of a way out. Miss Ruby's exhortation offers an epistemological break of sorts, offering the possibility of communitas. Victor Turner, writing almost fifty years ago (and in the gendered language of the time), maintained that communitas "has an existential quality; it involves the whole man in his relation to other whole men" (127). "Don't run from your ragged self," Miss Ruby tells Tanya when she swallows the dying matriarch's pain pills. "Be *with* it. Be *with* each other. Be *with* this moment that is slipping through our fingers as I speak" (135). Miss Ruby's words recall Heidegger's *Mitsein*, the "being-with-others," an obligatory condition of existence. But while Heidegger saw our social relation to others as potentially problematic—as we could, after all, through the influence of others, be distracted from the authentic life (Heidegger 149–168)—Miss Ruby sees it as a consciously chosen, prerequisite condition for the reclamation of subjectivity.

In his work, Jameson has long noted the dialectic between the utopic and the dystopic. Jameson notes that the promises of free market globalism and the "rebaptizing [of] the freedom of the market as the freedom of democracy" may be all that remains, in the context of postmodernism, of the grand utopian impulse (23). But he also acknowledges that the utopian impulse need not always be seen as totalizing:

> The interpretation of the utopian impulse, however, necessarily deals with fragments. It is not symbolic but allegorical; it does not correspond to a plan or to a utopian praxis; and it expresses utopian desire and invests it in a variety of unexpected and disguised, concealed, distorted ways. The utopian impulse, therefore, calls for a hermeneutic, for the detective work of a decipherment and a reading of utopian clues and traces in the landscape of the real; a theorization and interpretation of unconscious utopian investments in realities large or small, which may be far from utopian. The premise here is that the most noxious phenomena can serve as the repository and hiding place for all kinds of unsuspected wish fulfillments and utopian gratifications [25–26].

Miss Ruby's call for her people to embrace communitas, to represent themselves as whole people in relation to other whole people, in spite of the raw power of the reifying, homogenizing conditions in which they find themselves, is not a naïve call to remake the world; it is a call to create one of Jameson's utopic fragments, to create, one might say, a micro-utopia in the midst of a landscape of despair. In the years since the opening of both *Detroit* and *Airline Highway*, that landscape has arguably become even more dystopic, as the economic crisis has receded and been supplanted with a wave of reactionary politics, racial and ethnic resentment, and appeals to irrational fears and anxieties that increasingly govern the national consciousness. D'Amour's work suggests that our hope lies within community, and that community is still possible even within the confines of our fragmented and uncanny home.

## Notes

1. See Maurice Merleau-Ponty, *Phenomenology of Perception*, translated by Donald A. Landes (Routledge, 2012). James Miller has noted that while Merleau-Ponty identified with Marxism's critique of capital and attendant theories of alienation, he eventually lost faith in the ability of the proletariat to bring into being "a rational end of history" and instead "minimized the distance between perception and [the Marxist conception of] history." Miller writes, "what the Hegelian presumed, albeit with doubts—a conceivably univocal coherence governing all of human history—the phenomenologist undermined, by anchoring history and meaning in the ineluctable amphiboles of human existence: equivocations and ambiguities perpetually clarified, but never surmounted" (111).

2. Schafran explores the historical urban/suburban dialectic and the discourse of "decline" and "blight." While acknowledging the emergent problems of suburbia he is actually highly critical of the term "slumburbia," and advocates a new way of framing the issue "in ways that do not define whole communities as the problem" (143).

3. Heidegger is a controversial figure given his membership in the Nazi Party, which he joined upon his election as rector of the University of Freiburg in 1933. His work, however, has long been of interest to Marxists such as Lucien Goldman, Herbert Marcuse, and Georg Lukács. There is considerable scholarly debate as to whether Heidegger joined the party out of convenience or commitment, but in a 2009 interview, Jameson stated, "if Marx's object of study is taken to be *bürgerliche Gessellschaft* [bourgeois civil society] in the most general sense, as the dynamics of capital on all its levels, then Marxism has an obligation to include that phenomenology, to which the 'pragmatic' Heidegger certainly made fundamental contribution" ("Sandblasting Marx"). Christopher Pawling notes that Jameson has been criticized for praising Heidegger's commitment to deploying philosophy in the service of politics, even as he attempts to isolate his admiration for that commitment from any endorsement of Heidegger's Nazism, however nominal (Pawling).

4. For Goffman's formulation of front and back space, see Goffman, *The Presentation of Self in Everyday Life* (Doubleday, 1959).

## Works Cited

Apple, Krista. "Lisa D'Amour: Magic Places." *American Theatre*, November 2006, pp. 46–49.
Bendix, Regina. *In Search of Authenticity: The Formation of Folklore Studies*. University of Wisconsin Press, 1997.
Conroy, Collette. *Theatre and the Body*. Palgrave Macmillan, 2010.
D'Amour, Lisa. *Airline Highway*. Northwestern University Press, 2015.
_____. *Detroit*. Faber & Faber, 2011.
_____. Interview by Polly Carl. *American Theatre*, February 2011, pp. 64–65.
Economic Policy Institute. stateofworkingmerica.org. www.stateofworkingamerica.org/great-recession/. Accessed 19 July 2018.
Foucault, Michel. *The Birth of Biopolitics*. Translated by Graham Burchell. Palgrave, 2008.
Gotham, Kevin Fox. "(Re)branding the Big Easy: Tourism Rebuilding in Post-Katrina New Orleans." *Urban Affairs Review*, vol. 42, no. 6, 2007, pp. 823–850.
Heidegger, Martin. *Being and Time*. Translated by John Macquarrie and Edward Robinson. 1962. Blackwell, 2001.
Isin, Engin F. "The Neurotic Citizen." *Citizenship Studies*, vol. 8, no. 3, 2004, pp. 217–235.
Isherwood, Charles. "*Airline Highway* is a Portrait of the Underclass of New Orleans." Review of Manhattan Theatre Club's Production of *Airline Highway*, by Lisa D'Amour, *New York Times*, 23 April 2015, www.nytimes.com/2015/04/24/theater/review-airline-highway-is-a-portrait-of-the-underclass-of-new-orleans.html. Accessed 27 August 2018.
_____. "Desperately Trying to Stay Stuck in the Middle." Review of Playwrights Horizons' production of *Detroit*, by Lisa D'Amour, *New York Times*, 18 September 2012, www.nytimes.com/2012/09/19/theater/reviews/detroit-with-amy-ryan-and-david-schwimmer.html. Accessed 11 July 2018.
Jameson, Frederic. *Postmodernism, or, The Cultural Logic of Late Capitalism*. Verso, 1991.

_____. "Sandblasting Marx." Review of *Philosophie nach Marx: 100 Jahre Marxrezeption und die normative Socialphilosophie der Gegenwart in der Kritik*, by Christoph Henning, *New Left Review* vol. 55, 2009, www.newleftreview-org.spot.lib.auburn.edu/II/55/fredric-jameson-sandblasting-marx. Accessed 26 August 2018.

_____. "Utopia as Method, or the Uses of the Future." *Utopia/Dystopia: Conditions of Historical Possibility*. Edited by Michael D. Gordon, Helen Tilley, and Gyan Prakash, Princeton University Press, 2010. pp. 21–44.

Jones, Chris. "*Airline Highway* at Steppenwolf Theatre." Review of Steppenwolf Theatre's Production of *Airline Highway*, by Lisa D'Amour, *Chicago Tribune*, 14 December 2014, www.chicagotribune.com/entertainment/theater/reviews/ct-airline-highway-play-review-20141214-column.html. Accessed 27 August 2018.

_____. "At Steppenwolf Theatre, in Touch with our Tense Times." Review of Steppenwolf Theatre's *Detroit*, by Lisa D'Amour, *Chicago Tribune*, 24 September 2010, www.chicagotribune.com/entertainment/theater/news/ct-in-touch-with-our-tense-times-20170421-column.html. Accessed 11 Jul. 2018.

Klaic, Dragan. *The Plot of the Future*. University of Michigan Press, 1991.

Leinberger, Christopher. "The Next Slum?" *The Atlantic*, March 2008. www.theatlantic.com/magazine/archive/2008/03/the-next-slum/306653/. Accessed 30 July 2018.

MacCannell, Dean. "Staged Authenticity: Arrangements of Social Space in Tourist Settings." *American Journal of Sociology*, vol. 79, no. 3, 1973, pp. 589–603.

Marx, Karl. Economic and Philosophical Manuscripts of 1844. 1932. Translated by Martin Milligan. marxists.org. www.marxists.org/archive/marx/works/download/pdf/Economic-Philosophic-Manuscripts-1844.pdf. Accessed 30 July 2018.

Miller, James. "Merleau-Ponty's Marxism: Between Phenomenology and the Hegelian Absolute." *History and Theory*, vol. 15, no. 2, 1976, pp. 109–132.

Mufti, Aamir. "The Aura of Authenticity." *Social Text*, vol. 18, no. 3, 2000, pp. 87–103.

Pawling, Christopher. "Rethinking Heideggerrian Marxism." *Rethinking Marxism*, vol. 22, no. 4. 2010, DOI: 10.1080/08935696.2010.510306. Accessed 26 August 2018.

Schafran, Alex. "Discourse and Dystopia, American Style." *City*, vol. 17, no. 2, 2013, pp. 130–148.

Sullivan, Catey. "Great Characters and a Plot that Fails to Ignite." Review of Steppenwolf Theatre's production of *Detroit*, by Lisa D'Amour. chicagotheaterbeat.com, 19 September 2010. www.chicagotheaterbeat.com/2010/09/19/detroit-steppenwolf-theatre-chicago-review/. Accessed 11 July 2018.

Turner, Victor. *The Ritual Process: Structure and Anti-Structure*. Aldine, 1969.

Virno, Paulo. *A Grammar of the Multitude*. Translated by Isabella Bertoletti, James Cascaito, and Andrea Casson, Semiotext[e], 2004. Semiotext[e] Foreign Agents.

Weiss, Hedy. "A Goofy 'Woolf' in Cheap Clothing; Neighbors Wage a Backyard-Battle in '*Detroit*.'" Review of Steppenwolf Theatre's production of *Detroit*, by Lisa D'Amour. *Chicago Sun-Times*, 20 Sep 2010, *NewsBank*. www.infoweb.newsbank.com/resources/doc/nb/news/1325E142E70FF830?p=AWNB. Accessed 18 July 2018.

_____. "Big Easy Tale Is Big, Easy to Enjoy." Review of Steppenwolf Theatre's Production of *Airline Highway*, by Lisa D'Amour. *Chicago Sun-Times*, 16 December 2014. *NewsBank*. www.infoweb.newsbank.com/resources/doc/nb/news/15241B0DD0309B88?p=AWNB. Accessed 27 August 2018.

# Precious Resources: Cultural Archiving in the Post-Apocalyptic Worlds of *Mr. Burns* and *Station Eleven*

PAUL D. REICH

**Abstract**

*The process of recollection and record is a constant feature in narratives of the apocalypse. Those who successfully transition from one world to the next often feel this call to preserve and share their history before it is lost forever. While preservation of a historical record has long been a feature of civilized society, the post-apocalyptic worlds of Anne Washburn's* Mr. Burns, A Post-Electric Play *(2012) and Emily St. John Mandel's* Station Eleven: A Novel *(2014) challenge our notions of which artifacts are most worthy of preservation. In so doing, they argue for archives more egalitarian and miscellaneous. These collections can help survivors process their grief, form new communities, and craft new artistic productions informed by the cultural artifacts of the past and the experiences of the present.*

Preceding her breakthrough performance alongside Keanu Reeves in the 1994 film *Speed*, Sandra Bullock shared the screen with two other male acting luminaries, Sylvester Stallone and Wesley Snipes. Lest we think her talents were wasted in Marco Brambilla's *Demolition Man* (1993), Bullock not only serves as a potential romantic partner for Stallone but also interprets the film's utopian world for viewers, explaining its distinguishing features to the male lead. San Angeles is a sprawling metropolis that arose from the ashes of a world not far removed from the audience's, one filled with violence, corruption, and rampant injustice. Bullock's utopia has eliminated these features—at the expense of physical contact and freedom of expression—but has retained two curious remnants of our world: Taco Bell, which is now the sole surviving chain restaurant and an established place of fine dining; and advertising jingles from the pre–San Angeles era, now the most popular form of auditory entertainment.

Those familiar with Anne Washburn's 2012 play *Mr. Burns* can see similarities in the privileging of low cultural artifacts in these two texts. While Brambilla employs both Taco Bell and advertising jingles as comedic devices in the interludes between Stallone and Snipes trying to kill each other, Washburn's use of both the American television series *The Simpsons* and the commercials aired with them proves to be much more purposeful. Most narratives of the apocalypse, however, work to salvage or mourn traditional objects that have national and/or historical significance. Consider Roland Emmerich's 1996 film *Independence Day* and those funereal images of the leveled United States Capitol or the shot of the Statue of Liberty encased almost completely in snow and ice in Emmerich's 2004 film *The Day After Tomorrow*. This latter film of a climate change apocalypse provides occupants of the White House time to salvage art and additional articles of established significance, but for those trapped in the New York Public Library, the rapidly falling temperatures rend books necessary fuel for the sole fireplace (fret not, English majors: the copious volumes of U.S. and New York tax codes are the first to burn). High cultural artifacts are preserved; those unable to be saved are appropriately mourned by both actors and audience alike.

A quick review of critical reactions to the 2014 staged production of *Mr. Burns* at London's Almeida Theatre reveals just how much life imitates art; cultural privileging is an accepted standard of measure in the world of theatre as well. Tim Walker's assessment of the play for *The Telegraph* focuses on the temperature of the performance space—he calls his experience "three hours of utter hell"—and laments that the opportunity for theatre "to connect with an audience … [had been] so willfully squandered." Henry Hitchings called Washburn's play "bewildering and overwrought"; fans of *The Simpsons*, he argues, might see it as "irresistible," but others will "find it impenetrable and pretentious." In *The Guardian*, Michael Billington acknowledges the accuracy of Washburn's premise—"in the event of some future catastrophe, people would cling to their recollections of TV shows rather than Shakespeare or the Bible"—but argues that her work suffers from "its reliance on one particular episode of a cartoon comedy." Like Emmerich's characters, Billington also mourns what would be lost and preserved in Washburn's post-apocalyptic world: "I find it a melancholy thought that art, architecture and literature may perish in the collective memory but a popular TV show will be the last relic of western civilisation."

Only Billington's colleague at *The Guardian*, Mark Lawson, seems capable of appreciating the critique Washburn is levying against cultural privileging and preservation. In referencing the negative reviews levied against *Mr. Burns*, he writes:

> What fascinates me about these reactions is that Washburn stands accused of writing a play with a narrow frame of reference, although the American cartoon she invokes has been seen by hundreds of millions of viewers, rather than the average thousands who attend a new play at a small theatre. Drawing on some of the most popular images and stories of our time, the dramatist is paradoxically charged with a sort of elitism by reviewers who either don't recognise or don't respect her references. So, inadvertently, the reviewers are raising the question that *Mr Burns* itself asks: what constitutes a common culture?

Like Washburn, Lawson pushes against the limited definitions of culture which reviewers like Billington, Hitchings, and Walker would provide. Instead, he argues, Washburn's play works *because of* its inclusion of a low cultural artifact that has mass appeal. *Mr. Burns* appeals both to fans of *The Simpsons* and those who have felt its influence seep into the vestiges of everyday life. One need not watch an episode of the show to know the antagonist's singular catch phrase—"excellent"—and use it in an appropriate context. Moreover, Lawson contends, *Mr. Burns* "subtly dramatises the process of cultural transmission in a mass media era." The works of Joseph Conrad, William Shakespeare, and Tennessee Williams may only survive in the post-apocalyptic world of *Mr. Burns* through the recreation of *The Simpsons* episodes; the continued cultural recognition of these authors in our world may owe a similar debt to the show.

While most apocalyptic texts mirror their contemporaneous societies' privileging of high cultural objects, one almost universal feature of these narratives is the desire of the survivors to preserve elements from the past. In Stephen King's *The Stand* (1978), for example, one of its principal characters keeps a written record of her journey across the continental United States that includes in her daily entry a list of things she misses from the time before. In Emily St. John Mandel's 2014 novel *Station Eleven*—shortlisted for the National Book Award—the author herself devotes an entire chapter to "an incomplete list" of what has been lost (31). This chapter concludes with those things that have assumed excessive importance in the last decade. We do not mourn the loss of our devices but the loss of our access to the communities and connections they foster:

> No more Internet. No more social media, no more scrolling through litanies of dreams and nervous hopes and photographs of lunches, cries for help and expressions of contentment and relationship-status updates with heart icons whole or broken, plans to meet up later, pleas, complaints, desires…. No more reading and commenting on the lives of others, and in so doing, feeling slightly less alone in the room [Mandel 32].

This process of recollection and record is a constant feature in these texts, and those who transition from one world to the next often feel this call to preserve and share their history before they lose it forever.

While preservation of a historical record has long been a feature of civilized society, the post-apocalyptic worlds of Washburn's *Mr. Burns* and Mandel's *Station Eleven* challenge our notions of which artifacts are most worthy of preservation. Traditional cultural hierarchies are disrupted; value and values are rewritten. Both Washburn and Mandel critique the worlds in which this privileging occurs and argue instead for one that is both egalitarian and miscellaneous. These acts of cultural preservation, when they are inclusive, can aid in the formation of new communities and the processing of grief for the old ones, including the inhabitants of those worlds left behind.

*Mr. Burns* follows a group of survivors as they attempt to recount the "Cape Feare" episode of *The Simpsons*, and then follows that same group several years later as they rehearse the episode, commercials included. The final act of the play occurs 75 years in the future where this episode is reworked into a musical pageant, transforming this Simpsonian society in compelling ways. In her notes on the play, Washburn describes the genesis of *Mr. Burns* as an exercise into "what would happen to a pop culture narrative pushed past the fall of the civilization." Much of the dialogue in "The First Act," Washburn recounts, sprung "largely verbatim" from tasking a group of actors with trying to recall a single episode of the show. And in this act, the audience is immediately struck with the disconnect between this attempt at recollection and the dangerous environment in which these characters find themselves. While there may be tangential overlap between this *Simpsons* world and their own—Springfield's proximity to Mr. Burns's nuclear power plant and the three-eyed fish created from its waste could connect to the play's characters' concerns over their world's nuclear fallout, for example—there appears to be no reason for this exercise that relates to their survival.

We see, however, that remembering the lines and plot points of "Cape Feare" allows these survivors to process their grief and strengthen their relationships with each other. "The First Act" opens with four characters sitting around a campfire, engaged in a simple recall activity. Matt and Jenny play off each other, affirming and reaffirming their recollections of plot and dialogue from "Cape Feare"; although less vocal, Maria is an active member of the conversation. In their affirmations to each other, the survivors are building trust; in their recall, they are revealing a shared cultural heritage that strengthens those bonds even more. Matt, Jenny, and Maria also speak lines together *"simultaneously"* and laugh in unison at remembered anecdotes from the show (Washburn 15).

As these three characters continue to play off each other, Washburn demonstrates the power of this exercise by introducing other characters into the act. Colleen, who the stage directions identify as *"a woman huddled a slight distance away, in relation to the group around the fire but not part of it"* (Washburn 13), laughs at a Sideshow Bob joke before *"she shrinks into herself again"* (18). And Sam, who alerts the group to a possible danger beyond their shared space, calms and reorients the characters by providing the next line of "Cape Feare" dialogue. For the traumatized apocalypse survivors like Colleen, *The Simpsons* provides a moment of levity, possible only through its mass cultural appeal and recognition. For Sam, the show offers him and his fellow survivors a much-needed distraction from the risks present in a post-apocalyptic environment.

Even as Matt makes a *"conscious effort to rally"* from the attention Sam has turned to the world beyond their campfire, we soon learn that his fears are not unfounded (19). The group again hears a sound and works in unison to determine its origin. Washburn's stage directions here are clear; these survivors are experienced in dealing with external threats and have an unspoken practice through which to meet them. A sixth survivor, Gibson, is soon brought into the act, and after checking through his possessions and divesting him of his weapons, the newcomer and the group begin to cautiously interact with one another. This process has become ritualized. Each character retrieves a notebook from their pack and reviews with the newcomer their list of lost family members and friends, hoping Gibson will have come into contact with them. Part historical record and part memorialization of the dead, these notebooks will become a new cultural artifact, one that is random and egalitarian.

In this ritualized reading of names, Washburn provides her characters with opportunities to show compassion as they begin the difficult process of grieving for their dead. These characters are unfailingly polite to each other— "Thank you," "I'm sorry" (Washburn 25)—and stage directions like *"gently"* (27) suggest a careful tone. As this moment transitions to a more general discussion of Gibson's experiences travelling to the camp, Washburn shows her audience how extended conversations on the present and the myriad of dangers in this changed world are neither helpful nor restorative. Maria's concerns about the long-term effects of radiation poisoning lead the group to *"a rather. Long. Pause"* (36). This silence is broken by Gibson's recall of a single line of dialogue from "Cape Feare," which leads to more *"laughter"* (36) as the group moves from a place of tension and individualized worry to one powered by a shared communal activity. Gibson's line prompts further recall and allows both him and Matt to bring forth another bit of dialogue *"simultaneously"* (36). With this one line, in this short space, Washburn shows us how group acceptance and integration can work. It depends on a shared cultural history, which *The Simpsons* and its ubiquitous presence in American society provides. Even Gibson, who admits that he has "actually never watched an episode of *The Simpsons*," supplied that line because his ex-girlfriend was "a *Simpsons fiend*" (37).

As Matt, Jenny, and Maria work to reconstruct the rest of "Cape Feare," Gibson contributes once more to the group's collective retelling: a stirring production of "Three Little Maids" from Gilbert and Sullivan's *The Mikado*, inspired by Bart Simpson and Sideshow Bob's performance of the *H.M.S. Pinafore*'s score at the episode's conclusion. Maria and Matt encourage him, and Washburn inserts a stage direction to remind us of the performance's context: *"Let's just pause to note parenthetically that these are none of them people who, in their previous life, would have enjoyed the idea of an impromptu Gilbert & Sullivan recital"* (40). But in this time, in this place, Gilbert and Sullivan have transcended their cultural boundaries; Gibson's rendition is a hit. Sam's enthusiastic "Bring it!" (40) is only underscored by Washburn's final stage direction of this first act: *"COLLEEN has crept back, and watches from the margin of the woods"* (41). Here, in these final moments, a clear community has formed.

*Mr. Burns*'s opening act relies on what Sarah Bay-Cheng calls "the shared ritual of collective storytelling" to "lift the mood of the group" (694). I would argue that it does much more than that. In the characters who speak lines together "simultaneously," affirm each other's recall of Simpsonian dialogue, and laugh in unison at a remembered anecdote from the show, we see relationships strengthened and a community created. In the notebooks each survivor carries, we also see the beginnings of a cultural archiving that rests not on recalling a privileged few but on the collective memory and work of all those left behind. Washburn shows us this act of recall and preservation is a universally human one, necessary as the survivors process what was lost and what they hope to build in this new world.

In "The Second Act" of *Mr. Burns*, this community has become a travelling troupe, who perform episodes of *The Simpsons* and are renowned—by their own admission—for their commercial reenactments. We see in the rehearsal space setting of this act a further strengthening of the relationships begun in the previous one, and Colleen has emerged from the periphery to direct the group. Colleen's transition from marginal figure to leader shows the continued positive impact this communal activity has on its members. Washburn is also quick to remind her audience of theatre's contributory nature. As cast members rehearse their commercials, we see problems identified and solved, good ideas valued and affirmed. And in these reenactments of the least valued cultural artifacts, we see this society process their nostalgia for their previous lives as they reconcile themselves to their new ones.

The six survivors of the first act have been joined by a seventh: Quincy. She and Gibson are leads in the company's "Commercial," a feature of their performance. The second act opens with a rehearsal of this staged production, and it continues throughout the act. Although our survivors are less than a decade removed from their own experiences with advertisements, it is soon clear that their interpretation of this form cares little for the selling of a particular product and the run-time restrictions imposed on this media. Instead, these interludes present a snapshot of once-lived lives and all the joy and pain found in them.

Washburn's stage directions have Gibson entering the stage *"wearing an office suit, blouse, the heels, the leather purse, the earrings"* (42). Her repeated use of "the" here is telling; directors and audiences can picture the costuming of a professional woman that the definite article describes. The play on recognized standards continues as Quincy complains of her day to Gibson, who absently listens to her as he watches television. Her quick complaint at his lack of greeting is as familiar to us as his inaction, his attempts to make it up to her with *"a wee bit of fondling"* (48), and her rejection of those advances to get him to once again listen to the anecdotes of her day. The latter involves humor as Quincy describes a string of food robberies from the communal office space. It also provides her the opportunity to describe specific foods no longer available in this post-apocalyptic world. Nostalgia over even the more mundane leftovers—"tuna noodle casserole," "cold pizza," "pineapple fried rice" (49)—add texture and longing to this scene.

As Quincy transitions from this story to an offstage "bath"—complete with "steam," "bath salts," and "a glass of Chablis" (53–54)—it soon becomes clear that this act of recreation is for an audience still grieving a world whose remnants they find all around them. In one telling moment, Jenny and Gibson discuss the point of these interludes as they argue over whether or not he should provide Quincy with Chablis or Shiraz. Jenny dismisses his suggestion of the latter because it is not familiar enough, and says, "The point of a Commercial is to create a reality which is *welcoming*, not challenging" (Washburn 53). Gibson, though, wants these advertisements to be something more: "it's not just about feeling cozy, and bounty, there was that whole other thing commercials used to do, like there always used to be that question of identity. Like, it's not just what is the desire, it's *who has* the desire" (53). Jenny's quick retort—"You're joking" (54)—ends their argument, but Washburn's inclusion of this debate, and the commercial itself, shows the influence these low cultural artifacts continue to exert in a post-apocalyptic world. It also forces her audience to consider how representative they are of our daily lives. While a 21st century audience might consider themselves "woke" to how advertisements establish and reinforce often unattainable and reductive standards, Washburn's use of the medium reminds us again of the power found in popular culture.

"The Second Act" also reinforces the symbiotic nature of commercials and their companion shows. As these survivors' retelling of "Cape Feare" has evolved into a staged production of various episodes from *The Simpsons* that also include commercial interludes so, too, has the economy of this post-apocalyptic society moved from one focused on survival to one that allows for compensated performances and opportunities for the public to participate in them. While Washburn focuses on a select troupe, we understand through their dialogue that this world allows for many such groups, providing a range of entertainment to survivors, from episodes of *The Simpsons* and *The West Wing* to the plays of Shakespeare. For the members of our troupe, the value of these productions is clear; as Washburn does in the previous act, she reveals how the work done in this rehearsal space provides purpose and community for these individuals as they continue to reset their post-apocalyptic lives.

Just as the commercials provide nostalgic value for the survivors of *Mr. Burns*'s world so, too, do the episodes of *The Simpsons* performed with them. The pre-apocalyptic appeal of the show ensures familiarity with its main characters and their personal quirks, comforting to an audience placed in a constant state of disruption. *The Simpsons*'s own predilection for parody and satire also assures that their text need not be the only one memorialized. Survivors will still get glimpses of Joseph Conrad through "Heart of Bartness," William Shakespeare through "Much Apu About Nothing," and Tennessee Williams through "A Streetcar Named Marge" (Washburn 62, 64). While these distillations may not please the critics of *Mr. Burns*'s Almeida Theatre run, they provide one avenue for cultural preservation in Washburn's world. The playwright's use of this show is not accidental; it works, Ariel Watson argues, because the "intertextual weaving and viral reproduction" of *The Simpsons* "serve society, preserving a text and the history it carries even through the process of mutation" (21). As the site for what Lawson calls "cultural transmission in mass media era," *The Simpsons* provides a compelling case for the value of low cultural artifacts. At the very least, it serves as a vehicle to preserve high cultural ones.

This tension between low and high culture is not ignored in Washburn's work, and it is most explicitly expressed in Quincy and Maria's argument during the second act over truth and meaning in their performance. While Maria wishes to add more verisimilitude to their show, Quincy pushes back, reminding her of *The Simpsons*'s original form: "This is a cartoon. That's what we're doing. A cartoon. You keep trying to turn it into a Drama" (Washburn 70). Even as we ignore the essential fallacy in Quincy's argument—they are not doing "a cartoon"; they are recreating a cartoon in live action—Maria clarifies her position as seeing their work as "an opportunity ... to provide ... *meaning*" (70). Quincy retorts: "Things aren't funny when they're true they're awful. Meaning is everywhere. We get *Meaning* for free, whether we like it or not. Meaningless Entertainment, on the other hand, is actually really hard" (70). This place, this space, Quincy argues, is where an audience comes to see "no motivation, no consequence" because "where else do we get to experience that, *nowhere*" (70). This didactic interlude provides Washburn's audience with yet another moment of reflection. Some, we can imagine, will see *The Simpsons* as "Meaningless Entertainment" and enjoy it for the reprieve it brings them from their daily lives. Others might use these performances—both *Mr. Burns* and its referent—to reflect on their lives and the human condition, contradicting Walker's lamentation over the play's "squandered" opportunity to connect with its audience. The act's conclusion shows that Quincy was partially correct— "things aren't funny when they're true they're awful"—and as armed assailants enter the rehearsal space to rob the troupe, Maria is the first to fall.

Washburn's final act, however, provides the meaning Maria desired, and in the intervening 75 years between acts two and three, this society's performance of *The Simpsons* has evolved into a curious mixture of both high and low art tropes. It is, as Ian Farnell writes, "a stunning act of community storytelling that preserves cultural expression from the ashes of the apocalypse while simultaneously restructuring it for the purposes of the new world" (43). In her chapter on *Mr. Burns* and adaptation, Julie Grossman concurs, arguing "Washburn's characters use stories to define their new community" (186), and by the third act, use "'performance' to bind communities together" (185). Washburn is careful to show us how much "The Third Act" depends on the work by the survivors in "The First Act" and the troupe in "The Second Act." The former begins the process of cultural preservation with their retelling of a *Simpsons* episode as they learn to trust each other and process their grief in the wake of a societal collapse; the latter extends that work into a formalized rehearsal space where we see how nostalgia and the tensions of preservation are affecting a society still in its infancy. Although the players have changed, the third act presents us with the performance of this *Simpsons* episode, and as we so often do with our own cultural productions, reading it can tell us much about how this society has remembered its own past and the lessons learned from it.

Careful readers of this play within a play can see nods at the anxieties preoccupying the characters in the previous acts. The performance opens in *The*

*Simpsons*'s hometown of Springfield as several citizens react to warning sirens from a civil alert system. The town's nuclear power plant has experienced a catastrophic event, and it will soon kill most of the community in the destructive aftermath. This concern over just such an event occupied the attention of the survivors in acts one and two, with both Maria and Gibson discussing the long-term effects of radiation poisoning. The chorus of characters in the play then reads off a list of names, an act we assume is in memory of their passing because of the nuclear accident. None of the names, however, are from *The Simpsons*'s world. These names—a clear connection to the notebooks used in "The First Act"—are a memorial to the victims of *Mr. Burns*'s apocalyptic event, and this play is, in part, an artistic interpretation of that time by this society.

One family, the titular characters of the show, escapes the area only to find themselves in a reimagined version of the concluding scene of the "Cape Feare" episode. Mr. Burns has replaced Sideshow Bob; "Three Little Maids" has been dropped for a swordfight between Burns and Bart. No longer a cartoon without consequence, we see Burns kill Bart's father, mother, and sister. Like all the survivors of *Mr. Burns*'s apocalypse—and therefore the immediate ancestors of this play's audience—Bart must decide to live: "And now that I've lost everything / Now that everyone I love is gone / All I have left is everything" (Washburn 94). And in a clear message of hope delivered to an audience that has navigated the remnants of post-apocalyptic world, Bart sings, "I'm running forward anyway / I'm not afraid to meet the day / The world is filled with everything ... / I run to meet it hopefully / Love never dies in memory / and I will meet life gloriously" (94–5). Lest we forget Washburn's argument over the power of this text in building community, her stage directions show us that "*the rest of the cast has come out on stage during the latter half of this ... [and] everyone joins on the last line*" (95). Washburn has shown us in this third act how a low cultural artifact like *The Simpsons* can transform a society. In an essay on *Playwrights' Perspectives*, about her play Washburn writes, "Our culture—national, family, peer, personal—is defined, not so much by what has happened to us, but by how we remember it, and the story we create from that memory." That this society's inhabitants need "meaning" so explicitly says something about their vulnerability and the requirements of a world desperate to preserve their own history as they see reminders of a past world all around them. While one may read that desire as a cynical commentary on our own world—Sue-Ellen Case, for example, interprets those final lines as "a chorus of 'being American' as if promising and happy, but actually presenting the end of nationalist optimism" (46)—I read it as something different. America ceased the moment the apocalypse began; these survivors have created a new society in its place. This is their story, one that may borrow from our culture, but is singular in its origin and drives. Perhaps in another 75 years we would see a parody of this performance—a Simpsonian examination of national impulses—where Maria's desired meanings are implicit, waiting for the critical reader to parse out. For now, this amalgamation of cultural artifacts, refined into a living history of these people, is their artistic contribution to the world.

As the chorus sings those final lines of hope with Bart, the stage is illuminated by a variety of fixtures, and when the actors are taking their bows, "*a trap rises with the actor playing MR BURNS frantically pedaling a bicycle connected to a treadmill*" (Washburn 95). The mechanism breaks and the stage slowly dims to black, but for some time, the world of electricity has returned. The present action of Mandel's *Station Eleven* ends similarly. After two main characters meet one evening, Clark Thompson takes Kirsten Raymonde to the control tower of an abandoned airport he has lived in since their society's collapse. Through a telescope, he shows her an impossible sight: "In the distance, pinpricks of light arranged into a grid. There, plainly visible on the side of a hill some miles distant: a town, or a village, whose streets were lit up with electricity" (Mandel 311). Twenty years after electric light left the world of Mandel's novel, it, too, has been restored.

Published two years after the first staging of *Mr. Burns*, *Station Eleven* shares much more with Washburn's play than their post-apocalyptic settings. Like *Burns*, much of the novel focuses on the acts of rehearsal and performance. The narrative opens in Toronto, on the stage of a production of *King Lear*, just as the ravages of a deadly flu are about to overwhelm the city. While we spend a few chapters on those early days of survival in the wake of an apocalyptic event, Mandel, like Washburn, is less concerned with the tropes of graphic violence amid a post-societal breakdown and moves the story forward twenty years to focus on two primary groups of survivors. One of the narrative threads follows a troupe of travelling actors and musicians as they perform Shakespeare and classical music for the inhabitants of their world. Like their *Mr. Burns* counterparts, these performers derive many of the same communal benefits from their professional lives. The value and affirmation they receive from their work helps them to grieve and find purpose in a transformed society, the strong relationships within the troupe provide them emotional support, and the plays and music they produce keep alive cultural artifacts from the pre-apocalyptic world.

The Symphony performs "music—classical, jazz, orchestral arrangements of pre-collapse pop songs—and Shakespeare" (Mandel 37); they staged "more modern plays sometimes in the first few years, but ... audiences seemed to prefer Shakespeare to their other theatrical offerings" (38). One of the company attributed this to survivors' desire to see "what was best about the world" and avoid thinking about the societal challenges of a still too-immediate past (38). This desire to distance one's self from the immediacy of the past calls to mind the argument between Quincy and Maria in the second act of *Mr. Burns*. Although the Symphony's audience is not viewing a performance bereft of meaning, the contextual remove of Shakespearian theatre still provides them escape from the grind of their daily lives.

While Shakespeare's plays have always drawn a mix of audiences and adaptations—*The Simpsons*, for example, has used the Bard repeatedly, including a satirical retelling of *Hamlet* in "Tales from the Public Domain"—I would like to shift attention to a different use of low cultural artifacts by Mandel in *Station Eleven*. An examination of the *Dr. Eleven* comic that weaves its way through the novel is a useful point of comparison. The first issue—titled *Station Eleven*—serves as the titular influence for Mandel's novel. In "Negative Strategies and World Disruption in Postapocalyptic Fiction," Marco Caracciolo writes about Mandel's use of intertextuality: although the comic "connects all the major characters in the novel," most do not become "fully aware of one another's lives; only the reader has a complete picture of the comic book's history. The plot is thus 'object-oriented' in the sense that it is driven by a material object (see Caracciolo, 'Object-Oriented Plotting')" (230). He goes on to say, "Remarkably, that plotting strategy builds on and integrates the thematic significance of the object, its being located at the intersection of pre- and post-worlds, of human lives and the non-human event that disrupted them (i.e., the catastrophic virus outbreak)" (230). The importance of this artifact, therefore, cannot be understated. Mandel privileges it both as a text to be analyzed within the context of the larger narrative and as an influence on the narrative itself. Read that way, it functions similarly to the final performance in *Mr. Burns*.

Mandel introduces readers to this comic early in the narrative through Raymonde, who has carried two issues with her since the apocalypse. Although they are "dog-eared now, worn soft at the edges," Raymonde understands these texts must have "been produced at great expense, all those bright images, that archival paper, so actually not comics at all in the traditionally mass-produced sense, possibly someone's vanity project" (Mandel 42). Our first narrative glimpse at this work focuses, as we would expect, on the image, but we are given one line that feels prescient: "*I stood looking over my damaged home and tried to forget the sweetness of life on Earth*" (42). It requires no great deductive leap to see why the comic "falls open" to this page; Raymonde must often look around her "damaged" world and try to forget "the sweetness of life" it once held (42). It echoes her own thoughts when she considers how to justify her scavenging trips inside abandoned buildings: "Because we are always looking for the former world, before all traces of the former world are gone" (130).

Like *Mr. Burns*, this tension between nostalgia, preservation, and acceptance occupies much of the interior concerns of *Station Eleven*'s characters. Mandel's use of this low cultural artifact—along with the high cultural performances of Shakespeare and orchestral arrangements—shows the continued power of both. As these survivors encounter reminders of a world that no longer exists, they must reconcile themselves to the one they have, the one they are creating with their own productions.

Another of the narrative threads in the novel follows Miranda Carroll in the pre-apocalyptic world, and much of her story chronicles her authorship of the *Dr. Eleven* comics. From Carroll, we learn a basic summation of the story: set thousands of years in the future, Dr. Eleven and his colleagues have stolen a space station—Station Eleven—and used it to escape an Earth taken over by a hostile alien civilization. We also learn the importance the comic has played in her life. She uses it to distract her from the tedium of an unfulfilling job, the dissolution of her marriage, and the eventual recalibration of her professional and personal goals. As evidenced in the line quoted in the preceding paragraph, Mandel also uses it to comment on Raymonde's post-apocalyptic world and provide greater emotional impact at key moments in the narrative. For example, when Carroll is dying from the same disease affecting the rest of the world, Mandel writes: "Miranda opened her eyes in time to see the sunrise. A wash of violent color, pink and streaks of brilliant orange, the container ships on the horizon suspended between the blaze of the sky and the water aflame, the seascape bleeding into confused visions of Station Eleven, its extravagant sunsets and its indigo sea" (228). Here, in this dying woman's final moments, her thoughts are still with the art she created, the artifact she left behind. In the debate over the value of low art, Mandel's "meaning" is clear.

Before her death, Carroll gave two copies of *Dr. Eleven* to her former husband, Arthur Leander. Leander, an actor returning to the theatre after many years in film, was someone Carroll believed would appreciate another artist's work. Her faith in him was misplaced. In response to a question from his girlfriend who expressed appreciation for Carroll's work, Leander says, "I don't read comic books.... I never really understood the point of it, to be honest" (320). As an unsympathetic character whose judgment is often questionable, it is unsurprising that Leander would dismiss Carroll's work because of his disdain for the genre; in that, he is like the many theatre reviewers dismissive of *Mr. Burns*. The expression of this view by Leander suggests Mandel does not want us to share it. By this point, we have seen the influence of *Dr. Eleven* on the survivors of her post-apocalyptic world. Leander re-gifts the comics to a young actor in his play, Kirsten Raymonde, and his son, Tyler. For Raymonde, these comics become a constant referent in her life; throughout the twenty years she has spent surviving this new world, these texts have been persistent companions, stories she returns to time and again. Although we do not follow Tyler closely, in the moments we have with him, his references to *Dr. Eleven* are many. Mandel sets up a final confrontation of sorts between Raymonde and Tyler, and both are surprised to learn that the other knows of Carroll's work. After Tyler's death, Raymonde finds a single page from *Station Eleven* tucked in his copy of the New Testament. For that moment, "Station Eleven is all around them" (107).

Unlike the illustrations of *The Simpsons*, the influence of *Dr. Eleven* has been largely private in Raymonde and Tyler's worlds. By the end of the novel, however, she arrives at the Severn City Airport and encounters an unusual place in her post-apocalyptic world: a museum. Before Raymonde leaves this place, she will do something which would have been unthinkable to her just a few weeks earlier, leaving an issue of *Dr. Eleven* with the museum's curator "to ensure that at least one of the comics would be safe in case of trouble on the road" (Mandel 331). *Dr. Eleven* now becomes a public artifact, available to museum visitors who can read its themes of loss and nostalgia against their own experiences. Raymonde formalizes a practice she has shown repeatedly in the text with her donation. As she looks "through the former world" in her scavenging of abandoned buildings, she collects clippings from celebrity magazines which mention Leander; in other sections of the novel, she provides an interview to a survivor who publishes a newspaper. Philip Smith argues these characters are all "preoccupied with the idea that fundamental to the creation of a meaningful future for humanity, and the potential return to modernity, is the need to recover and maintain a record of the past" (295). Raymonde's concern for preservation and the power the practice has is clear. For those like Carroll who do not survive, this act does something more: it ensures they are not forgotten. *Dr. Eleven*—like the notebooks carried by *Mr. Burns*'s survivors and the final performance that memorializes them on stage—is the recognition of lives lived. Or as Smith writes, the "artefacts, information, and, above all, texts serve as proof of the individual having existed" (296).

Raymonde's arrival at the Severn City Airport also connects her narrative thread to one other in Mandel's post-apocalyptic America. In this storyline, the author follows another group of survivors who were stranded at the airport during the flu's outbreak. Even though this settlement has primarily focused on remaking the space into a sustainable community, its distinguishing feature is the Museum of Civilization. Located in the former Skymiles Lounge in Concourse C, the museum is curated by Clark Thompson. He founded the museum on "Day One Hundred" of their abandonment in the airport; after wandering into the lounge, Thompson thought of his boyfriend: "Robert was a curator—

had been a curator? Yes, probably Robert existed in the past tense along with almost everyone else, try not to think about it" (254). Like *Mr. Burns*'s survivors, Thompson is trying to process his grief and find some purpose, some reason to continue in his collapsed society. Thompson's eyes then fell on a glass case, and he thought, "if Robert were here, he'd fill the shelves with artifacts and start an impromptu museum. [Thompson] placed his useless iPhone on the top shelf. What else?" (254). More objects followed—an Amex card, the driver's license of a deceased survivor, his laptop—and when Thompson returned a few hours later, others had added "another iPhone, a pair of five-inch red stiletto heels, and a snow globe" (255). For Pieter Vermeulen, the museum is an assembly of "random things" that can now function as a "repository of beauty" (18). Their beauty, Vermeulen claims, derives from their uselessness in this post-consumerist, post-electric society. I would argue, however, these artifacts are less random than we recognize, and they serve a specific purpose to the immediate survivors of the apocalypse.

While Mandel allows us to see the genesis of the museum is in part a processing of Thompson's grief over losing his partner, the objects in the museum do much of that same work. When they first arrived in the airport, most of the stranded passengers occupied themselves with the frustrating and heartbreaking task of calling their loved ones; the donation of the two iPhones to the museum may suggest a relinquishment of the owners' former lives and the pain associated with them. The laptop, the five-inch red stiletto heels, and the Amex card are all trappings of professional and personal personas that no longer have relevance. But in their wish to preserve these artifacts, the donors signaled their desire to pass on the history these objects could tell while still preserving their former lives and the experiences that may have led them here. These objects have particular significance when we place them against the stage directions of Gibson's attire during the commercial scene in "The Second Act" of *Mr. Burns*: "*wearing an office suit, blouse, the heels, the leather purse, the earrings*" (42). While these objects no longer have purpose in this new world, they are impregnated with meaning; seeing them—either on stage or in a museum—allows some patrons to remember their value and others to learn it. The audiences of Washburn's and Mandel's works are forced to question the value we place on cultural artifacts and consider the hierarchies we impose on them.

In a poignant moment at the novel's conclusion, Thompson "finishes dusting his beloved objects in the Museum of Civilization" and reads his collection's newest acquisition, one of Raymonde's *Dr. Eleven* comics (Mandel 331). Thompson was friends with Leander and knew Carroll through his relationship with the actor; he is startled by a dinner party scene on Station Eleven that bears striking similarities to one he attended with the author and her husband:

"tears come to his eyes because all at once he recognizes the dinner party, he was *there*" (332). This artifact strikes a chord with Thompson; it evokes in him nostalgia and longing for a world long gone. But as he thinks more about that night, about Carroll's unhappiness at the party, about her career in shipping, about "all these ghosts," he also thinks of the future: "Is it possible that somewhere there are ships setting out? If there are again towns with streetlights, if there are symphonies and newspapers, then what else might this awakening world contain?" (332). Good art—high or low—does that as well: as it might preserve a moment or evoke a feeling for a memory missed, it also lays open the possibility for a future where new moments and new memories can rival ones we have preserved.

By the time Mandel has pushed forward the airport narrative to match the present timeline of the Travelling Symphony, the museum has grown and its curator aged. In a post-apocalyptic world concerned solely with survival, Thompson would have little to offer; but this world, like *Mr. Burns*, has emerged from its catastrophic event with a desire to preserve and share its cultural history. Thompson's value is clear, as are the objects under his care. In privileging the low cultural artifacts found in their texts, both Mandel and Washburn make compelling cases for a reevaluation of the intrinsic worth of such objects. Rather than pass judgment, they argue instead for audiences to consider the contexts of their use, to recognize how shared cultural histories can provide opportunities for emotional rehabilitation and communal bonding. Their works also show the continued value of artistic performance and historical preservation, even in times of complete societal disruption. The Travelling Symphony recognizes this, and their lead caravan has the words "Survival is Insufficient" emblazoned on its side. It should come as little surprise to us that this quote comes not from the playwright whose works they perform, but from a rather different piece of twentieth-century low culture: the television series *Star Trek: Voyager*.

## Works Cited

Bay-Cheng, Sarah. "Virtual Realisms: Dramatic Forays into the Future." *Theatre Journal*, vol. 67, 2015, pp. 687–698.

Billington, Michael. "Mr Burns Review—Rebuilding the US on Fragments of Pop Culture." *The Guardian*, 12 June 2014, https://www.theguardian.com/stage/2014/jun/13/mr-burns-review.

Caracciolo, Marco. "Negative Strategies and World Disruption in Postapocalyptic Fiction." *Style*, vol. 52, no. 3, 2018, pp. 222–241.

Case, Sue-Ellen. "Anguish and Animals in Cosmopolitan Zones." *English Language and Literature*, vol. 61, no. 1, 2015, pp. 41–50. DOI: 10.15794/jell.2015.61.1.003.

Grossman, Julie. "*Cape Fear*, *The Simpsons*, and Anne Washburn's Post-Apocalyptic *Mr. Burns, A Post-Electric Play*." *Literature, Film, and Their Hideous Progeny: Adaptation and ElasTEXTity*. Palgrave Macmillan, 2015, pp. 177–190.

Hitchings, Henry. "Mr Burns, Almeida—Theatre Review." *Evening Standard*, 13 June 2014, https://www.standard.co.uk/go/london/theatre/mr-burns-almeida-theatre-review-9534501.html.

Lawson, Mark. "From the Bard to Bart: How Mr. Burns Challenges Our Common Culture." *The*

*Guardian*, 21 June 2014, https://www.theguardian.com/stage/2014/jun/21/bart-of-darkness-mr-burns-common-culture.
Mandel, Emily St. John. *Station Eleven*. Vintage, 2015.
Smith, Philip. "Shakespeare, Survival, and the Seeds of Civilization in Emily St. John Mandel's *Station Eleven*." *Extrapolation*, vol. 57, no. 3, 2016, pp. 289–303. DOI: 10.3828/extr.2016.16.
Vermeulen, Pieter. "Beauty That Must Die: *Station Eleven*, Climate Change Fiction, and the Life of Form." *Studies of the Novel*, vol. 50, no. 1, 2018, pp. 9–25.
Walker, Tim. "Mr. Burns, Almeida Theatre: 'three hours of hell.'" *The Telegraph*, 15 June 2014, https://www.telegraph.co.uk/culture/theatre/10897824/Mr-Burns-Almeida-Theatre-review-three-hours-of-utter-hell.html.
Washburn, Anne. "Anne Washburn on Mr. Burns." *Playwrights Perspectives*, May 2013, https://www.playwrightshorizons.org/shows/trailers/anne-washburn-mr-burns/.
_____. *Mr Burns: A Post-Electric Play*. Oberon, 2014.
Watson, Ariel. "Apocalypse Masque: Post-Electric Theatricality in *Mr. Burns*." *Canadian Theatre Review*, vol. 175, 2018, pp. 19–24. DOI: 10.3138/ctr.175.004.

# Past the Lyrical: Mythographic Metatheatre in Marina Carr's *Phaedra Backwards*

## Phillip Zapkin

### Abstract

*Marina Carr's 2011 play* Phaedra Backwards *continually exhibits awareness of the mythic and tragic genre conventions governing it. These generic rules simultaneously structure the play and limit the playwright's flexibility to create a new message. This essay argues that Carr's play uses a specific kind of self-referentiality, employing a strategy I am calling mythographic metatheatre. Through its self-awareness as a theatrical representation of a mythological story,* Phaedra Backwards *calls attention to myth's structuring role in our cultural imaginary by performing a deconstruction of the Phaedra myth. Carr raises questions about how and why people tell culturally sanctioned stories. Without offering concrete answers to these queries,* Phaedra Backwards's *mythographic metatheatre urges us to consider possible answers without forgetting that any answer is likely to be rooted in the myths that shape our consciousness.*

THESEUS. *He had everything to live for.*
PHAEDRA. *Unless the bull pucked him off with his horns, but even that wouldn't be an accident. Or maybe, just maybe the sea came up to meet him, the waves caught hold of his hair, but that's the stuff of lyrics. We're past the lyrical, but was he?* [Carr 78–79].

Almost from the opening line, Marina Carr's 2011 play *Phaedra Backwards* announces its metatheatrical and meta-mythic fascinations. In the epigraph above, Phaedra rejects lyricism. She rejects artistic construction as a way of seeing herself in the world. As we shall see, Phaedra's self-referential post-mythic status suffuses Carr's drama. The play, which shuffles the order of events in the myth, is permeated with postmodern self-consciousness about the constructedness of myth—the ways in which narrative structures control, delimit, and ostensibly unify disparate events into one meaningful plot structure. First performed at the McCarter Theatre in Princeton, New Jersey, Carr's play highlights an awareness of the mythic and tragic genre conventions governing it. This essay argues that Carr's play uses a specific kind of self-referentiality, employing a strategy I am calling mythographic metatheatre. Mythographic metatheatre builds on the theoretical foundation laid out by Linda Hutcheon, who theorizes the systemic interrogation of history-as-narrative in postmodern fiction, which she calls historiographic metafiction. In opting instead for the terms *mythographic* and *metatheatre*, I suggest that (1) mythology is constructed through narrativizing techniques comparable to historical narratives, and (2) interrogating this construction through performance introduces a set of epistemological opportunities and problems not present in fiction. *Phaedra Backwards* calls attention to myth's role in our cultural imaginary by performing a self-conscious deconstruction of the Phaedra myth.

The Phaedra myth is recounted in a number of ancient and modern texts, including several ancient plays, Apollodorus's *Library of Greek Mythology*, Ovid's *Heroides*, passing mentions in Homer's *The Odyssey* (11.322) and Virgil's *The Aeneid* (226), and numerous modern plays, novels, films, operas and songs, etc. One of the best-known versions of the myth is Euripides's 428 BCE *Hippolytus*. In Euripides, Hippolytus scorns Aphrodite, so the goddess of love curses Phaedra, his stepmother, to fall madly in love with him. Initially Phaedra is determined to starve to death rather than give in to her passion, but after confessing to her nurse and the chorus, the nurse betrays Phaedra's confidence to Hippolytus. Enraged and disgusted, the young man threatens to reveal Phaedra's secret to Theseus. To prevent this, Phaedra writes a note accusing Hippolytus of trying to rape her, and then hangs herself. When Theseus arrives, he finds Phaedra's body and the note, then exiles Hippolytus and prays to Poseidon to punish his son. A messenger arrives to describe a bull from the ocean attacking and dragging Hippolytus nearly to death. Artemis tells Theseus his son was innocent, and Hippolytus is brought on to forgive his father before dying. This plot is largely followed by Seneca and Jean Racine, who produced the most famous subsequent versions of the play. More will be said about these versions later.

Unlike Seneca and Racine, Carr significantly replots the mythic events. Braided temporal plotlines make a simple plot summary difficult, but this description should help readers unfamiliar with the play to orient themselves.

*Phaedra Backwards* opens with Hippolytus's death, from the end of the myth. The second scene shifts chronologically backwards to show Pasiphae, Phaedra's mother, setting up a mechanical cow scaffold to seduce her husband Minos's divine white bull. Previous tragedies mention Phaedra's family history, but Carr breaks with her predecessors by actually staging Pasiphae's lust for the bull. Immediately afterwards, the Minotaur makes his first appearance, described in the stage directions as "*From a great distance. Ripping through a dimension*" (84). Throughout the first portion of the show he appears on the fringes, mostly unseen by the other characters. Next, an extended, drunken dinner party develops the primary characters—Phaedra, Theseus, Hippolytus, and Aricia—and their various sexual and interpersonal dysfunctions. Back in Pasiphae's plotline, Minos returns and condemns both his wife and the young Minotaur—her child with the bull—as monsters who should be destroyed. As the tension in Carr's play rises, the time/dimension traveling Minotaur evokes happy childhood memories in an effort to convince Phaedra to kill Theseus as revenge for slaying him. When that does not work, he brings on the spirits of Ariadne (Phaedra's sister and Theseus's former lover), Pasiphae, and Minos, who hang Phaedra and bite chunks out of her body. Phaedra finally agrees to avenge the Minotaur when the spirits threaten her daughter. Seeing her wounds, Theseus asks what happened, and Phaedra's vague answer implicates Hippolytus. Theseus banishes Hippolytus, and the play ends up essentially back where it began: the Minotaur carries the dead body of Hippolytus onto the stage.

Carr is not faithful to any particular iteration of the myth and draws from different versions. Her closest dramatic source is Racine's 1677 *Phèdre*, based on Seneca's *Phaedra*, written around 54 CE. One of Seneca's sources was doubtless Euripides's *Hippolytus* (possibly both Euripides's surviving *Hippolytus Stephanephoros* and his now lost *Hippolytos Kalyptomenos*).[1] Additional precursors include modern plays like Sarah Kane's *Phaedra's Love* (1996), Brian Friel's *Living Quarters* (1977), and Edward Albee's *Who's Afraid of Virginia Woolf?* (1962), each of which will be addressed below. Carr also draws on a long history of Irish adaptations from Hellenic drama, myth, and literature. Irish theatre is saturated with Greek adaptations, which has shaped Carr's dramaturgy.[2]

## Metatheatrical and Meta-Mythic Themes

Metatheatrical and meta-mythic references run throughout *Phaedra Backwards*, starting from the opening scene, which begins at the end of the mythic story. Theseus enters, telling Phaedra that his son has died going over a cliff, immediately signaling to the audience that this is going to be a different kind of Phaedra retelling. Theseus learns the news from an unidentified female messenger, whom he says was viscerally excited to tell of the accident. Phaedra replies, "Well, it is sort of dramatic" and notes, "Some women love giving dramatic news" (78). The self-consciousness of these references points to the fact that we are actually seeing the climactic death of Hippolytus dramatized. The mythic structure is inverted, ironically undercutting the tension of Hippolytus' death. Carr foregoes the series of events leading up to his tragic demise (though she can count on many theatre-going audience members to be familiar with the Phaedra myth).[3] Certainly, for Racine, Seneca, and Euripides, Hippolytus' death *is* a dramatic moment, the climax ushering in cathartic release. But announcing his demise in the first scene eliminates any suspense about the youth's fate.

This scene draws attention to the generic conventions of mythology, as seen in the epigraph above. Phaedra's statement/question, "We're past the lyrical, but was he?" raises significant queries about the characters' relationship(s) to their mythic origins and the extent to which those origins continue to shape, guide, and delimit their fates. Phaedra apparently imagines herself as beyond or freed from the lyrical, from the generic conventions of mythology. However, her supposition that Hippolytus could have been killed by a bull—a symbol that will be discussed in more detail—or physically grabbed by the ocean suggests she is still thinking through the symbolic logic of mythology in which supernatural, extraordinary events are treated as everyday occurrences. The question Phaedra asks implies that she and Theseus have, somehow, broken free of the structural constraints of mythology, though in his death, Hippolytus was still bound by those conventions. He died as he was supposed to die, going over a cliff by the ocean. Dying in that prescribed manner becomes evidence that Hippolytus did not escape the strictures of his storyline. Phaedra, on the other hand, in her ironic self-consciousness, is tempted to think herself liberated from the fate mythology has laid out for her.

The play repeatedly returns to the theme of fate, which is fitting for a myth regularly presented as a tragedy. For the Greeks and Romans, myth and tragedy were driven by a sense that human destinies were written by the gods, and there was no escape from fate. In the (post)modern world, however, we no longer take that for granted. In using this theme, Carr echoes Brian Friel's *Living Quarters*, an earlier Irish *Phaedra* adaptation. As Richard Cave argues, the "dreaming back" technique in Friel's play puts his characters in tension with the mythological fate they seem to be trying to escape (106). Particularly the character "Sir"—who shapes the other characters' memories based on an onstage ledger—suggests the tyranny of the mythological/theatrical source. Phaedra raises this very point, longing for the pre-modern capacity to blame the gods for the accidents of one's life:

> PHAEDRA. A few thousand years ago we could blame Aphrodite.
> THESEUS. For what?
> PHAEDRA. For this. For you. I could blame Aphrodite for you or any of those mad medieval saints. The Italians were allowed to whip their statues if they withheld favours.... Now I have to take the blame for everything myself. That's the thing I really cannot abide about being modern [88–89].

In pining for the days when the gods or saints could bear blame, Phaedra voices a deeply modern concern about the psychologically detrimental effects of a world stripped of the supports provided by superstition or religious faith.[4] Whereas in Euripides, Seneca, and Racine, Phaedra continues to be subject to fate, in Carr's version, she has lost that faith in the gods and destiny. She is adrift in a kind of ideological exile from the sources of comfort her previous iterations could draw upon.

Carr's play is ambivalent about the continued power of fate over its characters. On the one hand, Phaedra makes several metatheatrical or metadramatic references, often in talking with Aricia, her rival for Hippolytus's affections. At one point, Phaedra metadramatically critiques Aricia's superficiality: "You have no capacity for suffering. The first wind will blow you away. The only ones who interest me now, who have ever interested me, are those with the scars and still standing" (89–90). The capacity for suffering that Phaedra values so highly is a distinctive trait of tragedy, which runs on an economy of suffering, perseverance, and redemption. For Phaedra, to be a tragic figure is to be worth something. However, to be a tragic hero also means to be governed by fate, a condition toward which Phaedra expresses ambiguity. On the other hand, Theseus maintains faith in the fateful power of the mythic/tragic structure. At one point he describes his marriage to Phaedra as "fascinating bad news, a *doom-eager* pact" (106; emphasis added). In attributing the relationship to *doom*, to fate, Theseus renounces the personal responsibility that weighs so heavily on Phaedra. For him, life is guided by forces beyond his individual control, and the individual choices he makes are not truly free. This may be part of the reason Theseus never expresses any remorse for the brutal killing of the Minotaur, even though he is repeatedly confronted with this guilt throughout the play.

The Minotaur is the other major meta-mythic figure in *Phaedra Backwards*, embodying the symbolic economy of myth. He plays a disruptive role, breaking down temporal boundaries and blurring the lines between identities. The Minotaur is an unconscious archetypal obsession representing suppressed awareness of humanity's animal nature. Ariadne even says, "He was the original nightmare and vision, slipped through eternity's seam" (111). This is essentially how Carl Jung described the archetype. He writes, "The archetype is a tendency to form such representations of a motif—representations that can vary a great deal in detail without losing their basic pattern ... [Instincts] manifest themselves in fantasies and often reveal their presence only by symbolic images" (58). In other words, the image of the bull represents a shared cultural anxiety—a characteristic or trait that is simultaneously seductive and terrifying.

The Minotaur represents an unconscious obsession for many of the characters, shaping their self-perceptions and desires. The most obvious example is Pasiphae, mother of Phaedra and the Minotaur. As punishment for Minos—Phaedra's father—not sacrificing a specific white bull as he had promised Poseidon, the sea god ignited an obsessive desire for the bull in Pasiphae. According to Apollodorus, at her command the Athenian architect Daidalos "built a wooden cow ... [and] made Pasiphae climb inside. The bull came up to it and had intercourse with it as if it were a genuine cow. As a result, she gave birth to Asterios, who was called the Minotaur; he had the face of a bull, but the rest of his body was human" (98). This is depicted in scene two of *Phaedra Backwards*, where we see the Inventor deliver the wooden cow and show Pasiphae how to get inside it. When he questions her motives, Pasiphae tells him, "I'm only doing what women imagine" (82). This dream-like allure and threat of the bull is reiterated in scene six, where the Minotaur encounters the Nanny who cares for Phaedra and Theseus's daughter:

NANNY. Away with you now to the pastures of the unknown.
MINOTAUR. I bet you dream about me.
NANNY. All women dream of the bull.
*Enter Theseus.*
MINOTAUR. Yes, and all men too.
NANNY. I said away with you. There is no place for you here.
MINOTAUR. No, and never was [101–102].

This passage reflects both the unconscious processes undergirding the archetype and the impossibility of actually manifesting the traits represented by the bull figure. The horrific paradox of the Minotaur. Dreams are the terrain of the archetype, which both characters acknowledge. Archetypes occupy the phantasmatic space of desires half-realized by the conscious mind. But, as the end of this conversation implies, the archetype has no place in the conscious world—the Minotaur/bull must remain in the misty space of dreams and myths.

Carr is clearly aware of this paradox at the heart of the Phaedra myth, which dissolves the distinctions between individual identities. As Jungian psychologist Marie-Louise von Franz writes, "The Self is often symbolized as an animal, representing our instinctive nature and its connectedness with one's surroundings.... This relation of the Self to all surrounding nature and even the cosmos probably comes from the fact that the 'nuclear atom' of our psyche is somehow woven into the whole world" (220). In other words, the animal archetype reflects an acknowledgment of our connection to nature as a whole, rather than our existing as atomized individuals. This interconnectedness reflects the illusory nature of psychological boundaries separating the Self from the outside world. For Jung and his disciples, the archetype is rooted in the collective unconscious—a shared set of symbols deeply rooted in "primeval dreams and creative fantasies" (Jung 42)—and so an individual unconscious mind, for all its idiosyncrasies, is interconnected with every other human mind through a common repertoire of symbols and images. The animal identification also reflects awareness of humanity's animal nature—a knowledge human beings often attempt to disavow. Phaedra directly invokes the animal nature of humanity when Theseus denies guilt for murdering the Minotaur because he was an animal. Phaedra challenges him: "And you're not an animal? And I'm not? And are we not surrounded by animals? You call the way you live human? This country human? The passions of the upright two-feeters human? We're animals. We suffer, we die, we're forgotten" (123). Theseus lives with his conscience because he distinguishes himself from the Minotaur. He sees himself as a human and the Minotaur as an animal, and because a human being weighs heavier in Theseus's ethical scheme, he has no compunctions about slaughtering his opponent.

At the same time, Theseus's interactions with Hippolytus hint at the permeability of these boundaries, the instability of identity categories. He shames Hippolytus for not having achieved great feats, saying, "At twenty I had you. At twenty I'd made my first million. At twenty *I wrestled a bull to the ground*" (121; emphasis added). The bull is external here, an obstacle in the world to be conquered so that Theseus can secure his legacy and prove his potency—defeating the bull is paired with other symbols of masculine potency: fathering children and financial success. However, this seeming externality is soon disrupted. He condemns Hippolytus for not having had sex with Phaedra if that was what he wanted: "If you had fucked her and repented I would've forgiven it, but this girly dithering. I need to see some shadow of the *young bull* in you, some shade of the *bull-slayer* that came down from me" (122; emphasis added). The distinction between the *bull* and the *bull-slayer* is elided. The two figures become opposites which are in fact identical. Theseus and the Minotaur become the monstrous double, which René Girard argues is a fundamental principle of tragedy as a form. In a very basic gloss, Girard claims that the fundamental violence of tragedy stems from the community's desire to avoid its own violent tendencies by attributing all tension to a single individual, who can be exiled or sacrificed in a collective cathartic effort (8). However, the struggle to identify a sacrificial victim produces a doubling effect, as characters cast about to find the "guilty" party. Principal characters reveal themselves to be fundamentally similar. We see this with the dissolution of the distinction between Theseus as *bull-slayer* and *bull*, a dissolution bringing him precariously close to the Minotaur. As Girard says, "The unity and reciprocity that the enemy brothers have rejected in the benign form of brotherly love finally impose themselves, both from without and within, in the form of monstrous duality—the most disquieting and grotesque form imaginable" (160). While incidental, Girard's reference to the enemy *brothers* is especially apropos for Theseus and the Minotaur because Theseus is Poseidon's son while the Minotaur's father is the magnificent bull sent by Poseidon to Minos, so in a very literal sense, the conflict between Theseus and the Minotaur is a fratricidal one. Beyond this, however, both characters—Theseus and the Minotaur—mirror one another to the point where they become identical in their callous violence.

Theseus is not the only character with whom the Minotaur is twinned. The bull-faced Minotaur is closely associated with both the white bull who fathered him and especially with the sea bull that kills Hippolytus at the end of the myth cycle. After Phaedra finally confronts Theseus about killing the Minotaur, the stage directions say, "*Enter the Minotaur carrying Hippolytus, both dripping from the sea*" (124). Over the ceremonially laid out body, the Minotaur tells Theseus, "The wounds on his face are from the rocks but the hoof mark on his back is mine" (124). What might seem like a passing reference conflates two very different figures from the Phaedra myth—the Minotaur slain by Theseus, and Poseidon's sea bull that destroyed Hippolytus. In the original myth, after Phaedra accused Hippolytus of raping her, Theseus asked his father Poseidon to destroy Hippolytus. The sea god sent a bull from the ocean—echoing the divine bull he sent to Minos—which panicked Hippolytus's horses, who dragged the young man to death. By emerging from the ocean with the body of Hippolytus and claiming credit for the boy's death, the Minotaur reidentifies himself as the sea bull. Here we have two temporal hiccups. The first is that Theseus killed the Minotaur before Hippolytus was even born, and yet here the Minotaur—in his avatar as Poseidon's sea bull—delivers the corpse of Theseus's son. Another temporal incongruity is that the play both opens and closes with Hippolytus deceased. The ending returns to the moment of the opening, collapsing the distance between the two points to highlight the cyclical and repetitive nature of mythology.

## A Poetics of *Mythographic* Metatheatre

In what sense are the postmodern meta-mythic and metatheatrical references in Carr's play systemic? Adaptation scholars who study mythological revisions often point to the close affinities between myth and adaptation. Julie Sanders claims, "Mythical literature depends upon, incites even, perpetual acts of reinterpretation in new contexts, a process that embodies the very idea of adaptation" (63). Similarly, Miriam Chirico says, "Myth's inherent identity as an oral genre necessitates the act of revision or transformation each time the myth is told; it is as if the narrator tries to present a more accurate or complete view of the story to his or her listeners" (16). Because mythic stories are rooted in oral folk forms, the stories are generically assured to grow, develop, and mutate in response to different socio-cultural contexts. Each story-teller, singer, or artist re-presents the narratives in slightly different ways to suit the tastes of their own audience. In *Phaedra Backwards*, Carr retains significant plot points, including Hippolytus's death, the conflict between Theseus and his son, and sexual tension between Phaedra and Hippolytus (though Hippolytus seems to be as drawn to Phaedra as she is to him, in contrast to the Greek, Roman, and French versions). However, Carr presents these elements with a unique spin. As Elizabeth Scharffenberger points out, while contemporary (feminist) revisions "contest the biases of the mythological tradition inherited from the Greeks, these recent works also arguably participate in the open-ended process of reinvention that characterized this very same tradition from the earliest days of the archaic period" (52).[5] In other words, the fact that Carr parodically revises a mythical story aligns her play with a long history of mythic storytellers. What I claim, however, is that the particular way Carr utilizes self-referentiality is significant.

Self-referentiality is central to Linda Hutcheon's theory of historiographic metafiction, from which I take my cue. In *A Poetics of Postmodernism*, Hutcheon claims that renegotiating the past as a source of knowledge is one of the key tasks of the postmodern. As Hutcheon explains, "What historiographic metafiction challenges is both any naive realist concept of [historical] representation but also any equally naive textualist or formalist assertions of the total separation of art from the world" (125). In other words, these texts self-referentially re-tell historical events to call attention to the narrative structures always at work in any historical account. Historiographic metafiction novels may depict authors telling/writing the history they are part of, as in Salman Rushdie's *Midnight's Children*, or use striking historiographic methodologies, like Martin Amis's *Time's Arrow* where the plot is told backwards. These techniques draw readers' attention to the process of storytelling inherently embedded in writing history. Hutcheon argues that historiographic metafiction, as a postmodern technique, is parodic and self-conscious. Hutcheon gives this simple working definition: "parody as repetition with critical distance that allows ironic signalling of difference at the very heart of similarity" (26).[6] By parodically redeploying the structures of historical writing, what historiographic metafiction "has taught us is that both history and fiction are discourses, that both constitute systems of signification by which we make sense of the past.... This is not a 'dishonest refuge from truth' but an acknowledgement of the meaning-making function of human constructs" (89). Rather than imagining an ontological truth of the past that we can access, historiographic metafiction privileges the meaning-making epistemological practices of discourse, gesturing toward various ways history could be narrativized.

Carr's play uses similar techniques to demonstrate the cultural power of mythology, re-exploring what it means for contemporary authors to use myth as a tool for meaning making. Basically, a myth is a shared story, often with supernatural or divine components, that does not exist in a single primary text. Myths play an explanatory and unifying role within a community. Sanders says simply, "A culture's mythology is its body of traditional narratives" (63). Chirico develops this definition by pointing out that mythic stories do not have a single, recognizable origin point, and that they frequently deal with magic or divine beings and their adventures (16). Because myths are so rarely attributable to a single origin or text (even if there are famous versions, like those by Homer, Euripides, the brothers Grimm, Hans Christian Anderson, and the Walt Disney Corporation, among others) the broad outlines of stories tend to be well-known within their own cultures, even if individual versions vary. This fluidity opens the door for artists to utilize source materials in new ways, particularly because "in the case of sources in mythology there is often no specific source text to be adapted," so there is less impetus for fidelity to an original than in adaptation, which implies a specific source text or texts (Foster, "Introduction" 2). Carr does not rework a particular version of the Phaedra myth, though she is well aware of the contours of the myth she is revising, and self-consciously draws attention to her revisions.

Carr displays a postmodern self-consciousness through the play's indication of its own parodic processes. We have seen how metatheatrical and metamythic references recur throughout *Phaedra Backwards*, repeatedly signaling Carr's awareness that she is molding mythic elements into a distinct narrative structure, while simultaneously signaling that this is not the only possible narrative structure. Carr repeats elements from the mythic tradition, but with critical distance—primarily by abandoning the chronology in which the myth is typically presented. *Phaedra Backwards*, therefore, enacts both halves of

Hutcheon's definition of parody. This self-conscious deconstruction of structure/time/narrative/causality also appeared in the premier performance run. As Patrick Maley writes in a review for *Stage Magazine*, the play's "first image is a projection saying 'The End,' and the next scene opens with a projection labeling it 'The Beginning,' but the play soon progresses to what a projection calls 'The Beginning of the End.'" The labeling—which is not specified in the published script of *Phaedra Backwards*—shows projection designer Peter Nigrini's engagement with the parodic revisioning at work in this play. The labels draw viewers' attention to the non-linear organization. The parodic structure highlights that revisions are simultaneously unique and the same—they share common foundations and yet inspire new drama, literature, or art. As Hutcheon explains it, parody repeats elements from the source while simultaneously emphasizing a critical distance (*Poetics of Postmodernism* 26). For instance, Phaedra's struggle with modernity—with the weight of personal responsibility in an ostensibly post-mythic age—indicates how different *Phaedra Backwards* is from other versions of the tragic myth. In pining for the paradoxically comfortable structures of the tragic or mythic, Phaedra simultaneously signals her differences from other versions as well as her similarity.

A cursory look at the major sources for *Phaedra Backwards* begins to reveal just how open to parodic re-imagining myth is in terms of form. Each author makes changes to the story, whether major or minor. The basic outlines of the Euripides story remain the same in Seneca, except that Phaedra is determined to pursue her love for Hippolytus and the nurse agrees to help. Phaedra herself reveals her feelings to Hippolytus and then publicly makes the rape accusation rather than putting it in a note. There are obvious differences between the Seneca and Euripides tellings, particularly in how Phaedra herself is presented. In the ancient world, stories did not exist in singular authoritative versions; they were flexible and open to re-interpretation through retelling. Even with highly influential versions like Homer's epics, rhapsodes "may also have ad-libbed and riffed off the script. Rhapsodes presumably introduced variations on the texts in performance" (Wilson 15). This openness to variation is a hallmark of ancient myth—establishing the mix of similarity within difference at the heart of Hutcheon's definition of parody.

The next major version of the story comes from Jean Racine. This seventeenth-century French drama primarily followed Seneca, but with significant changes. In his 1677 Preface, Racine claims that he introduced Aricia—Hippolytus's love interest, added to better reflect the sensibilities of seventeenth-century French theatre patrons—following Virgil and other classical sources (20–21). This is a perfect example of parodic engagement with the myth: Racine capitalizes on the similarity of his story, but simultaneously establishes a critical distance appropriate for his own time, place, and audience through the introduction of a romantic arc absent from the ancient Greek and Roman versions. Aricia, who also appears in Carr's version, marks a major departure from Racine's Senecan and Euripidean sources, as both of those authors' plots hinge on Hippolytus's strident devotion to the virgin goddess Diana (or Artemis). In Carr's version, Aricia is a kind of outsider who, in another meta-mythic gesture, looks at the world very differently than Phaedra, Hippolytus, and Theseus. At an alcohol-soaked dinner party—reminiscent of *Who's Afraid of Virginia Woolf?*—Aricia concludes, "Seems I'm the only one here can hold in what she thinks, the only one with a shred of manners" (92). Her difference is further signified when Phaedra asks her, "Why haven't you run screaming from this house?" (96). Aricia stands apart, almost as though she does not belong to the same mythic structure as the other characters. She does not quite fit in *Phaedra Backwards*, signaling a peripheral relationship to Carr's precursors.

Carr adopts the mythic structure of the Phaedra story, but her reworking clearly signals difference from previous versions of the play. The important point is not simply that Carr makes changes from earlier iterations, but that the play specifically gestures to these changes, pointing out their importance in Carr's dramaturgical project. *Phaedra Backwards* is almost a textbook example of Hutcheon's definition of parody—relying on both similarities to the existing story and differences from any previous version to create critical distance.

## A Poetics of Mythographic *Metatheatre*

The metatheatricality of *Phaedra Backwards* is equally crucial to its ideological project. Not only is the play self-conscious about its mythic origins (and the possibility that those myths could have inspired a very different play), it also signals an awareness of itself as performative. Alex Feldman makes the case that historiographic meta*theatre* is a substantially different business than historiographic meta*fiction*. As with Hutcheon's historiographic metafiction, Feldman's theory depends largely on self-referentiality to highlight the processes of artistic construction: "*metatheatrical* rather than simply theatrical indicates the same kind of perspectival displacement. Metatheatre is the self-conscious counterpart to dramatic art—theatre's acknowledgment of its own artifice" (3; original emphasis). The difference is that in theatre, events are acted out by live bodies, rather than described in words. As Feldman puts it, historiographic metatheatrical plays "explore the ways in which history is written, the *emplotment* of the events of the past, but this consideration is always supplemented by a further dimension. The playwright does not transmit an account of events, but the events themselves, re-enacted" (25; original emphasis). Not only is history discursive, historical events are revealed as performative and ephemeral. Tom Stoppard is a consistent practitioner of historiographic metatheatre, with plays like *Arcadia* and *Travesties* exemplifying the genre.[7] In fact, theatre is especially useful for renegotiating historic (and mythic) discourses because, as Marvin Carlson argues, theatre relies on memory and the replication of past performances. He writes, "The retelling of stories already told, the reenactment of events already enacted, the reexperience of emotions already experienced, these are and always have been central concerns of the theatre in all times and places" (3). The fact that theatre is driven by replication makes it especially effective for reassessing events, stories, performances, etc. Performance is always, to some extent, re-performance.[8] Theatre, especially on historical or mythical subjects, "involves the dramatist in the presentation of a narrative that is haunted in almost every aspect—its names, its character relationships, the structure of its action, even small physical or linguistic details" (17).

Memory-as-haunting plays out violently in scene eight of *Phaedra Backwards*, where the ghosts of Phaedra's past return to literally eat her alive. The Minotaur's accusation that Phaedra forgot him and their sister Ariadne introduces memory as a theme (108). The Minotaur then enters with the spirit of Ariadne—who had helped her lover Theseus defeat the Minotaur, and in death blames Phaedra for stealing Theseus from her (110). Phaedra notes the phantasmic apparition and foreshadows future hauntings, asking, "Are all the graves open tonight?" (110). Shortly after, the stage directions tell us that the Minotaur "*taps his hooves on the stones of the terrace. The stones open, like graves, tombs, vaults. Out climb Pasiphae and Minos*" (113). Phaedra is the last surviving member of her family, and they have come back from the dead to demand retribution from her for surviving and from Theseus for murdering the Minotaur and betraying Ariadne. Her parents accuse her: Pasiphae admonishing, "You cannot continue to live with your sister's husband, your brother's killer," and Minos asking, "Why should you live when we don't? Why should you eat when we starve?" (116).

These ghosts have returned with a vicious hunger, literally to consume Phaedra as revenge for the wrongs fate (or tragedy) has dealt them. The stage directions say, "*Arranging themselves around [Phaedra], they surround her, paw and scrape and lunge. Minotaur lifts her up with one arm, suspends her there, whatever way it's done she is hanging in mid-air*" (116). In the original McCarter Theatre run, Stephanie Roth Haberle, who played Phaedra, was hung from a meat hook (see production photos in *American Theatre*'s "Phaedra Backwards"). As Phaedra hangs center stage, the real violence begins. Ariadne tells the Minotaur to strip the flesh from her bones, and Pasiphae and Minos begin biting hunks out of her legs, back, and torso (117). Phaedra hanging in midair echoes earlier dramatic versions, because in both Euripides and Seneca, Phaedra commits suicide by hanging herself. While Carr's Phaedra is less suicidal than her Euripidean, Senecan, or Racinean avatars, this scene stages her inability to escape the structuring characteristics of myth. Although not suicidal and not fatal, Phaedra's inevitable hanging is parodically revised to illustrate the tyranny of the mythic plot elements.

This scene also draws on another Greek mythic element, one not normally associated with the Phaedra cycle—namely, sparagmos and omophagia. Sparagmos is the sacrifice of a living animal or person by ripping it to pieces, and omophagia is the ritualized consumption of the raw flesh. One of the best-known examples is in Euripides's *Bacchae*, where the Maenads murder Pentheus by tearing him apart. In part because of this scene, sparagmos has strong associations with the wild Dionysian mysteries, and of course Dionysus was the patron deity of the theatre. Carr's incorporation of sparagmos into the Phaedra story signifies on two levels: it self-referentially highlights the Dionysian resonances in classical theatre and increases the hybridity of Carr's collage of sources by adding a further mythological element not normally linked to the Phaedra myth. In addition, this scene evokes another intertext: Sarah Kane's *Phaedra's Love*, an In-Yer-Face version of the myth. At the end of Kane's version, a perversely lethargic Hippolytus is brutally killed by an angry mob. He is strangled by one man while a woman emasculates him and barbecues his severed genitals, which are then fed to dogs, before the disguised Theseus disembowels his son and barbecues his guts (38–39). Each play features a hanging/strangulation with the victim physically eaten. But in Carr's play, it is particularly noteworthy that the ghosts of her past consume her, showing the consumptive force of the myth itself, the ability of past mythic and theatrical predecessors to exert their influence over contemporary adapters.

Theatre is haunted by the very fact of live performance, by the replication of a show night after night and by different companies in different contexts. The ephemerality of theatrical production requires a continual re-engagement with the meaning, purpose, ideas, and imaginings of a play, opening the door for continual revision. As Sanders claims, "The dramatic form encourages persistent reworking and imagining. Performance is an inherently adaptive art; each staging is a collaborative interpretation" (48). Performance nods to the changeable potential of narrative because any given performance enacts only one possible potential, only one possible way a show could be put on. This can reflect back on narrative (or myth) as a meaning-making tool by reminding us that any given version is only one potential interpretation of the narrative materials. Or, as Feldman puts it, "theatre is the ideal medium in which to consider the versions of history, in all their instability, because the provisionality of the stage and the ephemeral nature of its representations complement postmodernism's sense of the plurality of historical truths" (25). The same premises apply with myth—that myth is inherently open to re-interpreting, and that performative choices made in theatre reflect the same processes of choosing and shaping that go into any given telling of myth. In the theatre it is done live and in real time. What distinguishes mythographic metatheatre from simple retellings of myth is the postmodern self-referentiality that marks a play like Marina Carr's *Phaedra Backwards*.

In *Phaedra Backwards*, Carr takes a particular approach to mythic repurposing, in which postmodern self-referentiality draws attention to the constructedness of both mythology and theatre. Through this self-awareness, which I am calling mythographic metatheatre, Carr raises questions about what artists can do with culturally sanctioned stories—stories that outline the hopes, aspirations, ethics, and ideals of those cultures. In particular, Carr's revised Phaedra asks us to consciously reconsider the role of mythology and tragedy in shaping our self-conceptions. To what extent do we remain subject to the stories we tell ourselves? To what extent are we subject to our cultural narratives? To what extent can we exercise genuine individual freedom? And does it matter if we do so? Without offering, or seeking to offer, any concrete answers to these queries, mythographic metatheatre and *Phaedra Backwards* urge us to consider possible answers without forgetting that any answer we create for ourselves is likely to be equally rooted in the myths which shape our consciousness.

### Notes

1. There was also a *Phaedra* play by Sophocles that may have been available to Seneca, though both its performance date and content are unknown today (McDermott 241).

2. For more information on Irish adaptations of Greek drama in general, see, for instance, Brian Arkins, Marianne McDonald and J. Michael Walton, Peter McDonald, or Kelly Younger.

3. The difficulty of audience recognition/familiarity is something that any number of adaptation theorists have considered, and I do not propose to wade into the discussion here. For some information on the problem, see Verna Foster's "Introduction" (4–5), Linda Hutcheon's *A Theory of Adaptation* (120–128), or Julia Sanders's *Adaptation and Appropriation* (45).

4. Freud's *Civilization and Its Discontents* provides a famous analysis of modern anxiety (10–21).

5. For an argument on the feminist implications of *Phaedra Backwards*, see Melissa Sihra (517), or for more general feminist analysis of mythic revisions, see Elizabeth Scharffenberger (50–53).

6. Hutcheon's most developed treatment of parody is her aptly named book *A Theory of Parody*.

7. See my essay "Compromised Epistemologies" for more on historiographic metatheatre in these plays (313–322).
8. There is disagreement among theatre and adaptation scholars about whether individual performances are fundamentally adaptive. This is, again, a larger debate I will not enter in this essay. For an argument that individual performances do/can constitute adaptations, see Daniel Fischlin and Mark Fortier (3–4); for the opposite argument, see Margaret Kidnie (32–34).

## WORKS CITED

Apollodorus. *The Library of Greek Mythology*. Translated by Robin Hard. Oxford World Classics, 2008.
Arkins, Brian. *Irish Appropriation of Greek Tragedy*. Carysfort, 2010.
Carr, Marina. *Phaedra Backwards. Marina Carr: Plays 3*. Faber & Faber, 2015, pp. 69–125.
Carlson, Marvin. *The Haunted Stage: The Theatre as Memory Machine*. University of Michigan Press, 2006.
Cave, Richard. "'After Hippolytus': Irish Versions of Phaedra's Story." McDonald and Walton, pp. 101–127.
Chirico, Miriam. "Hellenic Women Revisited: The Aesthetics of Mythic Revision in the Plays of Karen Hartman, Sarah Ruhl and Caridad Svich." Foster, pp. 15–33.
Feldman, Alexander. *Dramas of the Past on the Twentieth-Century Stage: In History's Wings*. Routledge, 2013.
Fischlin, Daniel, and Mark Fortier, editors. *Adaptations of Shakespeare: A Critical Anthology of Plays from the Seventeenth Century to the Present*. Routledge, 2000.
Foster, Verna A., editor. *Dramatic Revisions of Myths, Fairy Tales, and Legends: Essays on Recent Plays*. McFarland, 2012.
_____. "Introduction." Foster, pp. 1–14.
Freud, Sigmund. *Civilization and Its Discontents*. Translated and edited by James Strachey. Norton, 1989.
Girard, René. *Violence and the Sacred*. Translated by Patrick Gregory. Johns Hopkins University Press, 1992.
Homer. *The Odyssey*. Translated by Emily Wilson. Norton, 2018.
Hutcheon, Linda. *A Poetics of Postmodernism: History, Theory, Fiction*. Routledge, 2000.
_____. *A Theory of Adaptation*, 2d ed. Routledge, 2013.
_____. *A Theory of Parody: The Teachings of Twentieth-Century Art Forms*. University of Illinois Press, 2000.
Jung, Carl G. "Approaching the Unconscious." Jung, pp. 1–94.
Jung, Carl G., editor. *Man and His Symbols*. Dell, 1968.
Kane, Sarah. *Phaedra's Love*. Methuen Drama, 2002.
Kidnie, Margaret Jane. *Shakespeare and the Problem of Adaptation*. Routledge, 2009.
Leitch, Thomas. "Vampire Adaptation." *Journal of Adaptation in Film and Performance*, vol. 4, no. 1, 2011, pp. 5–16. DOI: 10.1386/jafp.4.1.5_1.
Maley, Patrick. "Gripping World Premier of PHAEDRA BACKWARDS at McCarter Theatre." *StageMagazine.org*, October 2011, http://www.stagemagazine.org/2011/10/gripping-world-premiere-of-phaedra-backwards-at-mccarter-theatre/.
McDermott, Emily A. "Euripides' Second Thoughts." *Transactions of the American Philological Association*, vol. 130, 2000, pp. 239–259. JSTOR, http://www.jstor.org/stable/284311.
McDonald, Marianne, and J. Michael Walton, editors. *Amid Our Troubles: Irish Versions of Greek Tragedy*. Methuen, 2002.
McDonald, Peter. "The Greeks in Ireland: Irish Poets and Greek Tragedy." *Translation and Literature*, vol. 4, no. 2, 1995, pp. 183–203.
"Phaedra Backwards." *American Theatre*, vol. 29, no. 1, January 2012, pp. 62–63.
Racine, Jean. *Phèdre*. Translated by Margaret Rawlings. Penguin Classics, 1989.
Sanders, Julia. *Adaptation and Appropriation*. Routledge, 2006.
Scharffenberger, Elizabeth W. "'That story is not true': Unmasking Myth in Ellen McLaughlin's *Helen* and Saviana Stanescu and Richard Schechner's *YokastaS*." Foster, pp. 50–65.
Sihra, Melissa. "Circuitous Pathways: Marina Carr's Labyrinth of Feminist Form in the US World

Premier of *Phaedra Backwards*." *The Palgrave Handbook of Contemporary Irish Theatre and Performance*, edited by Eamonn Jordan and Eric Weitz, Palgrave, 2018, pp. 517–525. doi.org/10.1057/978-1-137-585882_36.

Virgil. *The Aeneid*. Translated by John Dryden. P.F. Collier & Son, 1909. *Online Library of Liberty*, https://oll.libertyfund.org/titles/virgil-the-aeneid-dryden-trans.

von Franz, M.-L. "The Process of Individuation." Jung, pp. 157–254.

Younger, Kelly. *Irish Adaptations of Greek Tragedies: Dionysus in Ireland*. Edwin Mellen, 2001.

Zapkin, Phillip. "Compromised Epistemologies: The Ethics of Historiographic Metatheatre in Tom Stoppard's *Travesties* and *Arcadia*." *Modern Drama*, vol. 59, no. 3, Fall 2016, pp. 306–326.

# Infidelity, Adaptation, and Textuality: Approaches to Directing Late Medieval and Early Modern French Farce

## Scott D. Taylor

### Abstract

*What is the nature of the theatrical text? Is there a necessary relationship between the written text and its scenic enunciation, and if so, what are the boundaries of this relationship? Who is the author within the structures of theatre, or is there one? How can theories of textuality and semiotics inform and guide the artistic process, particularly when approaching period pieces? These are just some of the questions that this essay attempts to explore in a discussion of the directorial processes involved in the theatrical production of two French-language comedies from the late medieval and early modern period. The first part discusses theoretical concepts of textual authority and the notion of (in)fidelity, particularly from the perspective of French theatre practitioners and theorists. It also examines how advancements in adaptation theory, in combination with theories of textuality, offer new perspectives on the relationship between text and performance. The second part approaches the question of how these theories can be applied by modern directors to bring new life to historical works. It offers a close analysis with a more concrete, pragmatic examination of how textual theory and adaptation theory were utilized and implemented in realizing two contemporary performances:* La farce de Maître Pathelin *(anonymously authored in the fifteenth century) and Molière's seventeenth-century farcical comedy of manners,* Les précieuses ridicules.

The staging of classic plays presents directors with a crucial choice: should the production be oriented to a so-called *faithful* interpretation of the text, where the artistic focus is based on a process of historical accuracy and recreation in representation, or should it diverge from traditionalism and seek new and inventive ways to read and theatricalize the canonical work in an attempt to render it more pertinent and relevant to modern audiences? This dilemma evokes one of the most historically contentious debates in theatre and performance studies: the question of textual authority. More concretely, the issue concerns the determination of who exercises ultimate control over the text in the act of performance: the playwright or the director? Drawing on post-structuralist theories of textuality and recent advancements in Adaptation Studies, this essay will propose a directorial approach for staging contemporary productions of late medieval and early modern French farce. Specifically, it re-examines discourse on authorship and textual (in)fidelity within the context of adaptation theory and post-structuralist thought, and then discusses the implications that such an understanding of textuality had on the directorial processes of two French farces, the late fifteenth-century French comedy *La farce de Maître Pathelin* and Molière's seventeenth-century satirical comedy of manners, *Les précieuses ridicules*.

Traditionally, textual authority in theatre has ultimately been seen as the right and privilege of the playwright over that of the director, of the written text over performance. This authority granted to the playwright and the written text has been further reinforced and legitimized by the legal system through its creation of copyright laws and production rights, which serve to protect the so-called sanctity of the written text. In this view of textual authority, the dramatic text is seen as a sort of recipe to be followed strictly; it is "a set of instructions given by a writer to actors" (or directors); and at best, the work of the actor, director, and designer might be to "fill in the gaps" of an incomplete written text in performance (Puchner 293–295).

This is a very Anglo-centric view of textuality, and is in direct opposition to French approaches, where directors like Roger Planchon have insisted on the importance of *écriture scénique*, or "stage writing," which, as David Bradby explains, applies the theories of Brecht and "endeavors to develop a performance language sufficiently complex to express truths of both a personal and a political nature ... [L'écriture scénique seeks] to discover new ways of staging the individual's relationship with history" (Bradby 43). This new language of the stage challenged notions about the very nature of theatrical texts and of how and where theatre could be made. It also ushered in a trend in the reinterpretation of classic plays, in which French directors hoped to "restore ... masterpieces of the past that had become obscured or distorted by the passage of time ... to scrape away the accumulated deposits of history" (49). Perhaps this is why, contrary to Anglo-American copyright laws, the Société des Auteurs et Compositeurs Dramatiques (SACD) states that "le metteur en scène est un auteur" ("The director is an author").

Thus, there has long been a pushback from directors, actors, designers, and other practitioners of the stage who have sought to diminish the importance given to the written text and to declare the autonomy of the art of *mise en scène*.

> There exists today the idea that the dramatic text is less important than it used to be, that we live in a 'post-dramatic' age [...]. [This is] a century-long polemic against the dramatic text, launched by actors, directors, and theater visionaries ranging from Edward Gordon Craig to Antonin Artaud. Begun at the turn of the [twentieth] century, it gained steam in the Thirties, and then again in the Sixties, at which time it also entered the critical vocabularies of theater and performance studies [Puchner 292].

Indeed, it was advancements in post-structuralist critical theory that had a huge impact on elevating the status of performance as a fully autonomous discipline and artistic practice in its own right—one that is its own *author*, and that incorporates written texts, occasionally but not always, as just one element in a number of tools and materials at its disposal, which it uses to articulate its own ideas, concerns, questions, solutions, interpretations, and affirmations. "The author is dead!" infamously declared Roland Barthes in 1967, consequently giving birth to performance.

But if the author is dead, as Barthes proclaimed, then why are changes made to the written text in the production process so hotly contested? And why do so many theatre companies still spend their time engaged in pseudo-psychoanalysis of an author whom they usually do not know and have never met nor spoken to? It is commonplace, for example, to hear conversations during the rehearsal process between actors, directors, and designers about what they think the author "meant" by such and such a line, such and such an action, such and such a scenic description. However, in Barthes's model of textual criticism, which was anticipated, to some degree, by New Criticism and its notion of the "intentional fallacy," the goal is to liberate the text, to free it from singularizing and authoritative interpretations. "To give a text an author is to impose a limit on that text" (Barthes 147). For Barthes, the author is not necessarily the text's creator; instead, the author is a "scriptor" who is born simultaneously with the text, which Barthes compares to a "fabric of quotations" drawn from "innumerable centers of culture" (147).

Taking this idea even further, French psychotherapist, philosopher, and semiologist Félix Guattari implies an even more distant and relativistic understanding of textuality and meaning, arguing that "subjectivity" (here understood as "the text") is "the product of individuals, groups, and institutions"; it is plural and polyphonic with "no dominant or determinant guiding instance issuing from some sort of univocal causality" (1). Guattari decenters the Subject (i.e., The Text) and affirms that the "existentialising function [of the text] resides in the reversibility of content and expression" (22). In other words, content manifests itself in expression, but then expression becomes new content that once again seeks form, and so on—a procession. This leads him to offer a new view of semiology based on a machinic rather than linguistic order. It is a model of semiosis that shifts from a scientific to an ethico-esthetic paradigm. Simultaneously, this semiotic model proposes a psychological metamodelization, one which infers that humans are faced with an ethical choice concerning subjectivity, here understood in theatrical terms as textuality: "We can scientificize it, or grasp it in the dimension of its processual creativity" (Guattari 13). To understand subjectivity in the latter dimension is to view it as "the ensemble of conditions which render possible the emergence of individual and/or collective instances as self-referential existential Territories, adjacent, or in a delimiting relation to an alterity that is itself subjective" (9). Such an idea infers that there are not only internal and external factors contributing to the processes of textuality, but that the text is, in fact, machinically produced via various social, psychological, and historical modes that pre- and post-date it. The emergence of the text then becomes a creative process, an act of autopoeisis (i.e., self-creation) where the sensation of unity or integrity is an effect of a crafted "refrain that fixes me in front of the screen" (16). In his psychoanalytic work, Guattari implies a sense of subjectivity/textuality that reflects a chaotic and fluctuating state of affairs where thoughts, words, Self, Text, and Other are not fixed entities, but instead struggle interminably against each other, shifting and quaking, sliding and shaking—an existential state which can only be mediated through an ethico-aesthetics that requires spontaneously generated and intentional engagement combined with active and artistic intervention.

Unfortunately, most theatrical companies are still caught up in fidelity discourse when it comes to questions of text and representation, where success is defined by the extent to which a theatrical production adheres to a supposed understanding of an author's vision and then faithfully renders it on stage. But such a practice is both critically naive and manifestly illusory, and furthermore, it indicates a failure to understand that the art of *mise en scène* is an act of adaptation and that there is a difference between dramatization and theatricalization.

One of the most famous companies to embrace this distinction, particularly the notion of *mise en scène* as an act of adaptation, is the Wooster Group. According to Martin Puchner, "What distinguishes the Wooster group from more traditional companies is their attitude toward the dramatic text: they believe that it has to be taken as an art object needing adaptation to a different medium" (300). Consequently, they work with a variety of techniques and technologies such as distorted voice recordings, the use of flat screens, film footage, hand puppets, and other visual and auditory material in order to make the actor into "a kind of technological operator or vehicle" (Puchner 300). And much to many playwrights' chagrin, most notably Arthur Miller, who once made the company remove his name and the title of his play from a production of *The Crucible* on which they were working, the Wooster Group attempts to develop "an entire theatrical vocabulary" in order to adapt the written text into a stage performance. With such textual experimentation, it is no surprise that the company is most known for "taking classics," which have now become part of the public domain, free from the legalities of copyright laws, "and then doing with such plays what they will" (Puchner 299).

Of course, such an unfaithful approach to the written text, especially classic texts, has not gone without criticism, particularly by textual purists, who prefer what they call "authenticity" in performance. Michael Friedman has done an excellent job laying out the arguments against such liberties with classic texts in his 2002 article, "In Defense of Authenticity." Focusing particularly on productions of Shakespeare, Friedman does not categorically deny the value of experimental productions, but he does not believe that they allow contemporary audiences to learn anything about the original contexts in which the play appeared:

> The more a production adapts the text, the less that production can tell us about the text as an object of study. Adaptations, which can be just as interesting and informative as authentic productions in their own right, nevertheless reveal more about the cultures and eras that produced them than they do about Shakespeare's work [Friedman 56].

However, in light of post-structuralist theory on textuality, the very notion of originality and authenticity so dear to Friedman and textual purists is suspect, given that a text does not have *an* author but rather *many* authors (and arguably, it is its own author); it is the product of social forces that both pre- and post-date it. A text is a living entity, not a fossil; it is engaged in an evolutionary process, shaped by a long genealogical line of ancestors, and reproducing and adapting itself anew in its contact with each new reader who, in turn, adds another mutation to the textual gene pool.

To return specifically to Friedman's criticism of experimental productions' inability to tell audiences anything about the "original" circumstances of classic plays, I would argue that it is only through experimentalism that contemporary audiences can understand anything about the so-called "originality" of classic texts. Truly achieving "authenticity" in a production of a classic work would require the reproduction of its "original" audience. We would have to experience not only the play as that audience did, but the world they experienced as well. We would have to somehow forget all about the history, the knowledge, the scientific advancements, the social changes that have occurred since the time of the "original" production and experience the play from that limited mentality and viewpoint if we really wanted to have an "authentic" experience. Obviously this is neither possible nor desirable. Like it or not, we come to a play with a contemporary consciousness, well aware of things the "original" audience was not, and this makes "authenticity" impossible. Consequently, as theater artists, we can only approximate; we can adapt classic texts and make parallel allusions from our own world that might allow for deeper insight and understanding into a text's history and the way it was experienced by its first audiences, but it is only an approximation, never original. Furthermore, these approximations must continually be renewed, updated, re-contextualized and adapted periodically in order to remain relevant to new and changing audiences.

In more recent years, there have been efforts to rupture the binary of text versus performance, to move beyond fidelity discourse and redefine the language of performance. Advancements in adaptation theory have been particularly fruitful in this endeavor. One of the more interesting proposals to surpass this seemingly unavoidable binary was made by Gary Bortolotti and Linda Hutcheon in their article "On the Origin of Adaptations: Rethinking Fidelity Discourse and 'Success'—Biologically." Echoing back to the evolutionary understanding of textuality to which I alluded earlier, Bortolotti and Hutcheon propose a "homology between biological and cultural adaptation" (444). They see a "similarity in structure that is indicative of a common origin: that is, both kinds of adaptation are understandable as processes of replication. Stories, in a manner parallel to genes, replicate; the adaptations of both evolve with changing environments" (444).

Although their article deals specifically with film adaptations of stories, a parallel with textuality in the theatre is evident since *mise en scène* is adaptation. The crux of their argument is that, biologically speaking, we "do not evaluate the merit of organisms relative to their ancestors; all have equal biological validity. So too do cultural adaptations ... both organisms and stories 'evolve'— that is, replicate and change" (446). In this way, the idea of textual "success" is not defined in terms of fidelity to an original "ancestor," but rather by mutation and selection that allows the text "to thrive." Homologically speaking, we can look at staging as a "vehicle" and the written text as a "replicator." "The replicator's (aka written text) success is measured by its survival in the form of long-lived copies and versions of itself: that is, by its persistence, abundance, and diversity. The vehicle's success (staging) is measured by its capacity to propagate the replicator that rides inside it, so to speak" (452).

Before turning to a discussion of the pragmatic implications that this view of textuality has on directing classic works, I would like to reference a few of Patrice Pavis's thoughts on the subject of fidelity, taken from his article "On Faithfulness: The Difficulties Experienced by the Text/Performance Couple." Pavis argues that he has "always considered mise en scène as a category in itself" (117). For him, the question of textual fidelity in performance is primarily a "Western obsession," and "the old question as to whether theatre is literature or an autonomous art has not been of interest for some time" (118). The bigger question, however, is when we engage in theatrical practices, are we "directing a play" or "making a performance" (118)? To direct a play is to envision the "theatre as text," to "presuppose that the text contains a coherence that must be recovered or established"; it "finds the author at its source" (118).

On the other hand, to "make a performance" is to envision "the theatre as material," as Stéphane Braunschweig termed it; it is to worry less about "reading the text as a whole," and instead focus on assembling, editing, and binding "together these verbal and extra-verbal fragments within a show" (118). Ultimately, it is the "making of a performance" that interests me as both a director and scholar, moving away from *mise en scène* to a *mise en performance,* or *mise en perf,* as Pavis calls it. Such a notion echoes back to what Artaud called for in his seminal work, *Le théâtre et son double,* where he insisted on the existence of a concrete, metaphysical stage language that had an advantage over the written and spoken word of being able to free the signifier from its conventional signified. This did not necessarily negate the importance of the written text, but instead relegated it to the level of just one of many possible sources of signifying systems in the theatre. Pavis hints at this in his notion of *mise en perf,* where the written text is, in many ways, just another prop to be (re)utilized for larger performance goals. "Perhaps it is just a mirage. If it does not materialize, it at least encourages us to go forward, to move our feet and not get stuck in the same position forever. At least then we will not repeat the same simplifications, the same old faithful philanthropic philology" (Pavis 125).

Classic plays are a particularly rich area to apply both Pavis's and Barthes's understanding of textuality and new perspectives from adaptation theory, for both pragmatic and theoretical reasons. The classical canon offers a freedom from the litigiousness that hampers most contemporary theatrical texts, and consequently offers a freedom of interpretation, inviting directors to re-envision how such challenging works can be made to appeal to modern audiences. Falling outside of the cultural constructs of contemporary society, and more importantly, outside the reaches of modern-day copyright laws, plays from the classical canon, such as those of Molière, give theatre artists an extraordinary liberty to experiment with the text—a freedom that cannot be so easily exercised legally with more contemporary material. But to restore a classical work does not necessarily imply to achieve some kind of perfectly rendered realistic representation as it would have been presented in its original context, complete with period style costumes and set design; instead, to restore a classical piece is to utilize the components of scenic language in such a way that allows for contemporary audiences to "access" historical texts via an approximated reinterpretation that defies the cultural, temporal, and linguistic features that separate it from contemporary reality and reference. This is what inspired me when I decided to direct two classic French farces: a production of Molière's 1659 one-act, *Les Précieuses ridicules* and a production of the late fifteenth-century play, *La Farce de Maître Pathelin*. I will first focus on the Molière production and follow this with a discussion of the medieval farce.

Confronted with a 350-year-old play written not only in a foreign language, but also in the exaggerated language of *préciosité*, with characters obsessed with frivolous literary knowledge of the time, I was challenged with figuring out how to make this seventeenth-century farce speak to modern American audiences. Ultimately, my solution involved expanding the notion of textuality and drawing on Planchon's concept of scenic writing in order to present the show in two different languages and in two different staging styles. The first, performed in English, drew parallels between seventeenth-century *préciosité* and contemporary Hollywoodization of American society; the second, performed in the original French, drew upon the work of Jacques LeCoq, in a circus-like, buffoonesque production of the play.

The performance began with the English production of the play, and my first step was to write a new English-language translation of Molière's one-act that would facilitate easier access to the text for modern English speakers, so that the contemporary audience members could hopefully rediscover both the eloquence and the rhythm of Molière's language. Since this is not one of Molière's verse plays, perhaps my task was a bit easier. Luckily, I did not have to worry about using iambic pentameter to reflect the poetics of the French *alexandrin*; however, I did have to reckon with precious language, which by nature is purposefully complicated and pretentious. Additionally, I wanted my translation to capture an element of cruelty expressed in the play because it reflects a fundamental quality of Molière's comedies and of the genre of French farce in general.

In *Les Précieuses ridicules*, the two protagonists, Magdelon and Cathos, are taught a lesson in humility after they ignore and offend two suitors, La Grange and Du Croisy, whom their father/uncle, Gorgibus, had hoped the two girls would marry. This cruel lesson is taught to the girls in the framework of theatre-within-theatre, and the cruel nature of this theatrical lesson is eventually recognized by one of the girls, who claims that they have been witnesses to "une pièce sanglante, literally 'a bloody play'" (Molière, *Les précieuses ridicules*). Ultimately, I believe that it is the extreme measures of cruelty presented by Molière that explain why audiences are able to laugh as well as empathize with all of his scoundrels, misers, misanthropes, and would-be gentlemen. It is a characteristic that I hoped to highlight in my written translation as well as in my staged production.

Perhaps the most obvious difference in my translation of the work, which signals the great departure I take in its scenic enunciation, is in the title itself. Traditionally translated as "Precious Maidens Ridiculed," I decided to rename the play "Princess Butterflies," so as to simultaneously evoke the flightiness and beauty of the play's two protagonists, Magdelon and Cathos, who are portrayed in the English staged production as caricatures of Hollywood starlets in the likes of Paris Hilton and Nicole Richie. To further establish the rapport that I hoped to articulate between the time period and culture in which the text was originally created (seventeenth-century Paris) and that of contemporary America, I also chose to portray the two male protagonists, Mascarille and Jodelet, as over-the-top modern-day metrosexuals, fashionably clad in skinny jeans, vests, bowties, fedoras, scarves, boots, etc. The play's two other male suitors, La Grange and Du Croisy, were cross-gender cast and portrayed as a mix between modern day yuppies and tech geeks—all of this to hopefully restore, not reproduce, the experience, novelty, and genius of Molière's work through the prism of our own time.

Of course, costuming is just one means of articulation in the grammar of scenic language. Other elements of the *mise en scène* obviously also come into play, from lights and sound to props and set. One of the most important elements in my textual expansion of Molière's one-act, however, was the use of visual projections. These served a variety of purposes, but primarily: (1) to function as devices for establishing setting, (2) to better contextualize and illustrate unfamiliar cultural phenomena and linguistic features, (3) to offer a running comedic commentary on the action, characters, and themes of the play, and (4) to maintain the parallel that I was trying to emphasize between seventeenth-century France and twenty-first-century America. This is why, as the curtains rose on my English language production of the play, well before any characters walked onto the stage, audiences were brought into this hybrid world between Paris and Hollywood, between the seventeenth century and the twenty-first century, with a large projection of the Hollywood Hills sign glowing in spotlights. This was followed by another projection of a luxurious

Hollywood mansion with a supertitle that read "Scene 1: The House of Gorgibus in the Hollywood Hills." And as these projections were shown, the 1990s plastic techno hit "Barbie Girl" blasted over the house speakers.

In fact, there were a total of 100 visual projections that were used in the 45-minute English language production of *Princess Butterflies*, which comprised the first act of this two-act bilingual show. Since I have already schematically shown how slides were used to help establish the hybrid setting in which the show took place, I will examine how they also functioned to contextualize and illustrate unfamiliar cultural and linguistic references. One example of this is when Cathos explains to her uncle, Gorgibus, that she and her cousin, Magdelon, his daughter, simply could not welcome the suitors whom Gorgibus had sent, not just because of their vulgarity, but more importantly because "they had never even seen Mademoiselle Scudéry's 'Cartography of Tenderness,' and that the spiritual and emotional territories she maps out are completely unknown to them" (Taylor, *Princess Butterflies* 14). In order to give modern American audiences a better idea as to who Mademoiselle Scudéry was and what she represented in seventeenth-century France, I used a slide that combined a picture of a Danielle Steel romance novel combined with a photo of the American TV pop psychologist Dr. Phil and a superscript that read: "Mademoiselle Scudéry: Sort of a cross between Danielle Steel and Dr. Phil."

Or another example, in scene 9, when Cathos again expresses her admiration for Ms. Scudéry's work by stating that Mascarille, the pretend marquis who has come to visit her and Magdelon, resembles the character of Amilcar in Mlle. Scudéry's novel, *Clélie*, another slide appeared to evoke a more contemporary connotation, as well as to offer a little humorous commentary, and which helps to restore the spirit of the text and scrape off some of the "accumulated deposits of history" (Planchon, qtd. by Bradby 49). This slide included a picture of the two main characters from the *Twilight* movies and had a supertitle that stated: "Mademoiselle Scudéry's *Clélie*: Sort of the *Twilight* of the 17th century, but without all the vampires." In this way, I attempted to approximate the connotations that seventeenth-century French audiences had of Mademoiselle Scudéry and her work with contemporary allusions that had parallel significance. And as for unfamiliar linguistic features, the slides were used as a part of this scenic language to serve as a kind of gloss as well, illustrating vocabulary words as well as certain precious expressions. When, for instance, Magdelon, using precious language, asks Marotte, the maid, to "quickly fetch the commodities of conversation," a slide was cued showing a picture of a chair and a supertitle that addressed the audience directly, stating: "Chair! She means chair."

This leads to the third, and what I consider the most important, function of these projections: to offer a running, self-conscious comedic commentary on the characters, actions, and themes of the play. Although there were many instances of this in the show, I will give only one example in particular that gives a very clear idea of how scenic language can be used to expand the text. In scene 4, Magdelon explains in a monologue to her father the so-called "Rules of the Game," which must be followed when conducting oneself properly in the rituals of courtship and marriage. "To be truly seducing, a lover must know how to express his beautiful sentiments with elegance and grace; he must be sweet, tender and passionate, and he must know the rules of the game" (Taylor, *Princess Butterflies* 13). As Magdelon enumerates the various rules, which involve, among many other things, "affairs, enflamed and menacing rivals, forbidding fathers, unfounded jealousies provoked by false appearances, complaints, episodes of melancholia, kidnappings, and everything else that always follows," slides were once again used to highlight and reinforce each action mentioned with an image to underscore it. Additionally, when she added the part about "and everything else that always follows," this cued an interlude series of sixteen consecutive slides that were used to add comedic commentary on the natural progression of courtship and marriage, to include slides that read: "breaking up, getting back together, breaking up again, swearing off relationships forever, meeting someone new, using that person to stir up jealousy, accidentally running into each other, reconnecting, $500,000 wedding, $5,500,000 mortgage, baby, college tuition, grandchildren, trips to faraway lands, stock market crashes, nuclear war, and death." The slides were underscored by a musical interlude of Haddaway's 1992 hit song, "What Is Love?" The characters stopped the action, watched, and reacted to the slides as they appeared on the screen, all of which were expanded extratextual images and superscripts.

Finally, the last usage of these visual projections was once again to reinforce the parallels between the two time periods and cultural contexts: seventeenth-century Paris and twenty-first-century Hollywood. The examples of this are numerous; suffice it to say that as I went through the script in my original analysis, I looked for places in the text where I could reference contemporary cultural images in order to approximate the connotations implied in Molière's original text. For example, when Magdelon and Cathos ask Gorgibus to not refer to them by the names given to them by birth, but rather by "Polyxène" and 'Aminte," a slide with the new name and an image of Paris Hilton and Nicole Richie appeared. As another example, when Mascarille tells the two precious maidens that he will introduce them to all of Hollywood's "arbiters of good taste and fine living," an image of the drunken reality-TV star "Snookie" and a photo of "the New Jersey tanning mom" were shown. When

Mascarille talks about a certain someone he knows whom he considers "an enlightened spirit," an image of Charlie Sheen making a goofy face popped up with the word "Winning!" written underneath it. The goal, in short, was to bring as many pop culture references into the production as possible so as to give contemporary audiences an approximated understanding of the genius of the text in its original context, taking my cue from adaptation theory. Of course, these references would need continuous updating by a director if they are to remain pertinent. After the English production of the play, there was a fifteen-minute intermission, which was then followed by the French language version. This was presented in a completely different style, a circus-like, or buffonesque, performance inspired by the work of Jacques LeCoq.

Describing "buffoonery" in this sense, the Québecois producer and director Phoebe Greenburg, who was a former student of Le Coq, and who incorporates the techniques she learned from him into her own work, states that:

> Bouffonerie is very vast [ ... ] What is most important is the element of parody. *Les bouffons* make fun of us, and also of our beliefs, our deepest convictions. The element of mockery carries with it a certain mystery. It allows us to look at things from a different angle, to distance ourselves a bit, to talk about things in a new way.... Les bouffons laugh at us, but it's a hollow laugh that borders on the territory of tragedy [Greenberg qtd. in Labrecque 19; my translation].

It was this notion of the tragic associated with mockery in buffonesque representation that drew me to apply it to Molière's work since it, too, shares these same characteristics. Additionally, I appreciated how such a representational style could allow for a sense of distance that gives new perspective, and I hoped that this would be the case for this French language production. Again, I wanted to deconstruct people's notions of Molière with a production that did not try to replicate the original in period style costume and setting; instead, I wanted to find a new mode of representation that would "restore" the original work for contemporary audiences while at the same time challenge conventional notions of textuality in theatre. And by "restoring," again, I must emphasize that this does not imply an attempt to re-create an historically faithful rendition of the play, but rather to give a nod to its history and to demonstrate how this history is connected to contemporaneity. Buffoonery and clowning were, thus, an integral part of the scenic language that allowed for this restoration.

Therefore, as the curtains rose for the second-act French version, Gorgibus's Hollywood mansion had been replaced with a new slide of a circus tent and a clown on a unicycle while circus music blasted through the house. All of the characters in this production wore traditional white face clown makeup and circus-like costumes. In addition to the changes in costumes and music, the French version also incorporated slides that were often more circus-themed, and which were also used to illustrate vocabulary words and expressions. Granted, the French version had a more pedagogical aspect to it than the English version did. When, for instance, the characters talk about the various kinds of parlor games played in the Parisian salons, I created a slide to give definitions of these unfamiliar aspects of seventeenth-century French culture. I also wanted to help audiences comprehend the French by referring back to the English production at times so as to reassure them as to where we were in the French text. Thus, when Magdelon gives her speech about the rules of the game of which I spoke earlier, I grouped the images altogether onto one slide, instead of individually as they were in the English version, so as to remind audiences, many of whom had limited French, of what the character was talking about and of the action that took place.

Other techniques that I used in both productions to experiment with scenic language to restore the text included breaking the fourth wall and talking to the audience directly. I also had certain entrances and exits take place through the house so as to envelop the audience in the action. Furthermore, I chose to integrate dance sequences that momentarily interrupted the action. I included some limited audience-actor interaction and participation. And of course, I continued to use slides to integrate pop cultural references or to highlight certain quotations from the play that I found particularly pertinent to the themes of the show, or to make commentary on them.

The larger directorial goal was to escape the prison of realism, to avoid getting caught up in the no-win game of trying to reproduce some sort of historical accuracy that would basically be meaningless to modern American audiences; nor did I want audiences to escape into some other imaginary world. I wanted to draw specific parallels between two different time periods and two different societies in order to show the continued pertinence of Molière's play. I also wanted audiences to always remain aware that they were in the theatre watching a show, which is why there were many other staging techniques employed in order to render an aspect of self-consciousness in both the English and French productions. In this way, the text, at least in its written form, was just one element among many with which to play and experiment. Perhaps to a playwright's dismay, I as a director do not consider texts holy, sacred, or authoritative; instead, I seek to show the plurality of the text while exploring the limitless territory of theatrical signification, and thus reinforce the autonomy of the art of *mise en scène* and the importance of viewing the relationship between text and performance as a *trans-reading* rather than a *translation*.

This continued to be a guiding principle in my approach to staging a production of the fifteenth-century French play *La farce de Maître Pathelin*, which took the form of a *lecture mise en espace* rather than a traditional *mise en scène*.

The most famous medieval farce in the history of French literature, *La farce de Maître Pathelin* was published for the first time by an anonymous author circa 1464. Written originally in Old French, the play centers on the character of Pathelin, a do-it-yourself, self-taught "lawyer" who has gained a reputation for tricking people. Having fallen on rough times, he sets out to procure some fabric with which to make some new clothes for himself and his wife, Guillemette. The problem is that he does not have a penny with which to buy the fabric, so he devises a plan to trick a local shopkeeper, Guillaume Joceaulme, to "sell" it to him on credit, with the false promise of getting his money back to him that very same day, along with a nice goose dinner and beer. But when Guillaume comes to collect his payment, Pathelin and his wife put on a show for him that leaves him frustrated and confused.

The second part of the play, or "second act," opens with the shopkeeper threatening to take the not-so-innocent shepherd, Thibault L'Agnelet, who tends to his sheep, to court because he has lost thirty of the shopkeeper's sheep in the last three years. The shepherd, who is actually guilty of eating the sheep, seeks Pathelin's help to defend him in court. True to his nature, Pathelin comes up with a sneaky scheme to dupe the shopkeeper and win the favor of the judge. But Pathelin may have just met his match with the shepherd when it comes to the art of trickery.

How might a staging practice grounded in adaptation theory and a critical understanding of textuality enhance a director's ability to better communicate to modern audiences an older, classic text, such as *La Farce de Maître Pathelin*, which was written nearly 600 years ago in several different dialects of Old French as well as Middle French? In order to successfully take this play that is from another culture, from a distant time-period, written in a different language, and even in an earlier version of that culture's language, and make it meaningful to contemporary audiences, I chose to direct it in the form of a *lecture mise en espace*, literally a "reading put into space." In so doing, I sought to define what was *lisible* (readable) and *théâtralisable* (theatricalizable) and what was *illisible* (unreadable) and *nonthéâtralisable* (non-theatricalizable). In directing the play in such a staging style, I, once again, hoped to bridge the temporal, cultural, and linguistic gaps that separate contemporaneity from originality and "read the Middle Ages" on the contemporary stage.

What is a *lecture mise en espace* and how does it differ from other styles of theatrical presentation? Generally, there are at least four different types of staging practices. In French, there is "la lecture à haute voix," (or reading aloud) which is primarily a scholastic practice whose goal is the "the deciphering and functional oralization of the written message"; then there is the "mise en voix" (or voiced reading) which is "a more artistic activity, corresponding to what stage actors simply call a 'reading: it is an esthetic work that researches, in a neutral or non-neutral way, the effects of meaning, by trusting in the language of the text, exhibited, worked, and orally produced"; then there is the "lecture mise en espace"—"adding to the mise en voix, it allows to search for all that the body and the space can generate as possibilities to give shape to the materiality of the text and thus to favor an interpretation"; and finally, there is, of course, the *mise en scène* "which assumes more professional technical means that are not necessarily within reach of" all producing companies (Bernanoce, "A la recherche de cent et une pièces").

With a *lecture mise en espace*, "blocking, gestures, props may accompany the reading, not to retranscribe the fictional situation of the text in a naturalistic way, but to make sense through the image [ ... ] the reader/actor will keep the role of proffering the text, to bring it to the viewer to whom the reading is addressed, to 'push it forward,' but it will also offer an interpretation of the characters" (Bernanoce). As Pavis points out in his article, "Aux frontières de la mise en scène," the *lecture mise en espace* is a contemporary effort "to get back to the simplicity of reading," which he sees as "theatre's most urgent task" (73). He also laments the lack of attention that has been given by scholars to this genre of public reading, as he sees it as "the site of the emergence of meaning, where the poetic voice traces a theatrical path" (74–75); it is a practice that "does not mean that we must return to dramatic literature, but rather that staging should be as discreet as possible in order that the spectator might enter the text" (75). The "task" of the director is therefore "to remain suspended in the world of the written, to listen to the written" (Pavis 75).

To return then to the question of performance and reading the Middle Ages on the contemporary stage within the context of the *mise en espace* of the play that I directed, my first theoretical premise as a director was, again, to eschew notions of authenticity and to forgo the misguided temptation of fidelity. As stated before, a faithful theatricalization is neither possible nor desirable. We come to classic works with a contemporary consciousness, therefore making "authenticity" impossible, and thus, a so-called faithful rendition or faithful reading was not my goal. With this in mind, I will discuss some more of the practical techniques that I used to make this 600-year-old play *lisible* and *théâtralisable* in the form of a *lecture mise en espace*.

The first technique was the use of gender-blind, or rather, gender-inclusive casting. Most notably, the actor in the title role of the play, the role of Pathelin, was played by a woman, an actress from Montreal. She was dressed in yellow trousers and a blue, modern(ish) jacket; her long hair was worn up in a bun or under a hat, and she was the only character in the production to wear a mask. The use of the mask in particular, I hoped, would allow the audience to accept her in the role of Pathelin, setting her apart from the others, and also establishing that in this production, we were not going for any type of realistic or faithful rendition of the text in our staging. The actress also stood out because she was the only one with a Québecois accent, which I felt would give the audience a flavor of some of the original sound of old French. (It should be noted that we used a modern French translation of the text except in the scene where Pathelin speaks in a variety of Old French accents while putting on his show for the shopkeeper).

Another character with which I used gender-inclusive casting was that of the Judge, played by an American actress. Again, not striving for historical accuracy, I merely wanted to communicate to the audience the role of this character and play on notions that they already had of cantankerous judges. I did this by having the actress wear a colonial-style white wig and a modern black judge's robe to indicate her social role. I also once again made use of visual projections. During the entire court scene, a photo of perhaps one of the most famous TV judges of our time, Judge Judy, was projected onto the screen in the background, which served the practical purpose of establishing setting and a directorial purpose of using anachronisms to produce comic effects.

The final character that involved gender-inclusive casting was that of the shepherd, Thibault L'Agnelet, played by a bilingual French-American actress. To show her status as a shepherd, she wore a long white gown beneath a brown, rustic vest, and boots. She carried with her a small, stuffed toy sheep that she used to create a lot of comic business with. During the infamous courtroom scene she sat, mesmerized, watching Pathelin and the shopkeeper dispute with each other in court, while gobbling down handfuls of microwave popcorn as the courtroom drama unfolded. Again, with the projection of Judge Judy in the background, combined with the shepherd's carrying of a stuffed toy sheep and a red-and-white-striped bag of microwave popcorn, I was playing with temporality, situating the action both in the Middle Ages and in modern society. The other two characters, Pathelin's wife, Guillemette, and Guillaume the shopkeeper, utilized traditional gender casting. Their roles were portrayed rather traditionally, although the shopkeeper did also make use of anachronism by using his iPhone to tally up the cost of the fabric that he was supposedly selling to Pathelin.

Keeping true the goal of a *lecture mise en espace,* which is, as I pointed out earlier, to keep the staging as discreet as possible in order to place emphasis on the text, the stage was primarily an empty stage. The actors either kept their scripts in hand or utilized one of the three music stands that we placed on stage, facing outward toward the audience, on which to set their script. The "set" also included a screen upstage-center that I used for projections, and we made use of a black rehearsal box that served various purposes. Much of the action and speech was declamatory and directed outward toward the audience rather than having the actors look at and interact directly with each other, although this was not always the case. In fact, many times, the music stands were pushed to the side and more traditional blocking was used, with greater face-to-face interaction between the actors. Thus, in many ways, this production was a hybrid between a *lecture mise en espace* and a *mise en scène*, making it more akin to a *mise en perf* as coined by Pavis. The projections that I used served many of the same purposes as they did in my Molière production of *Les précieuses ridicules*: (1) to function as devices for establishing setting, (2) to better contextualize and illustrate unfamiliar cultural phenomena and linguistic features, (3) to offer a running comedic commentary on the action, characters, and themes of the play, and (4) to play with temporality, situating the staging in a hybrid space, reflecting certain aspects of the Middle Ages and certain aspects of contemporaneity.

This leads me to the final aspect of this essay that I would like to address: the question of *lisibilité* and *théâtralisabilité*. What can be read and what can be theatricalized? Obviously, with such an old text there are many cultural references, phenomena, and linguistic features that are no longer easily understood by contemporary audiences. For example, the text makes references to certain juridical practices and realities that no longer exist; several types of fabrics, currencies, measurements, and even songs that are no longer known are also mentioned and alluded to, making it challenging for modern audiences to truly understand, and difficult for modern directors to stage. The biggest challenge posed by the text is undoubtedly the sequences in which Pathelin, feigning to be sick and delirious, speaks in several different versions of Old French, including Limousin, Ancien Picardie, Old Flemish, Anglo-Normand, Breton, Lorraine, and even Latin. Had I been doing an English translation of the play, I probably would have opted for the actor playing the role to use a variety of English accents to get the idea across. In this instance, however, since the production was in Modern French, I decided to keep the Old French language intact, let the Québecois actress playing the role experiment with a variety of accents, and project modern French translations of what was being said on screen. Furthermore, the actress played the space as much as possible, doing absurd, funny business and physical comedy on stage during parts of the speeches, and then breaking the fourth wall, exiting into the house and interacting directly with audience members.

In conclusion, when approaching classic works on stage, like these two early French farces, modern directors would do well to take their cues from adaptation theory, where, as Gary Bortolotti and Linda Hutcheon describe it, "success means 'thriving,' figuring out how to thrive in the world"—in the world in which we live now, today, this moment (Bortolotti and Hutcheon 450). In so doing, theatre artists affirm the autonomy of both *mise en scène* and of dramatic texts, where *mise en scène*, or in this case, *mise en performance*, is a process of adaptation, much like the Wooster Group does in their staging of classic works. Or as Pierre Boulez described it within the context of opera:

> One does not have the right to fix the work in a definitive attitude, it continues to evolve. Anyone who claims to be safe-guarding a work within its initial traditions soon finds himself standing guard over a tomb. What is fidelity, in fact? Is it respect for what is transitory? Or is it not the belief that the work is eternally capable of bearing new truths, decipherable according to period, place, and circumstance? … True fidelity is not remembering how people were, but recalling them in order to integrate them into our own lives [qtd. in Ronis 11–12].

## WORKS CITED

Barthes, Roland. "The Death of the Author." *Image / Music / Text*. Translated by Stephen Heath. Hill and Wang, 1977.

Bernanoce, Marie. "A la recherche de cent et une pièces." *Editions Théâtrales*, https://www.editionstheatralesfr/pedagogique/mot/la-mise-en-voix.

Bortolotti, Gary R., and Linda Hutcheon. "On the Origin of Adaptations: Rethinking Fidelity Discourse and 'Success'—Biologically." *New Literary History*, vol. 38, no. 3, Johns Hopkins University Press, 2007.

Bradby, David. *Mise en Scène: French Theatre Now*. Methuen/Random House, 1997.

Friedman, Michael D. "In Defense of Authenticity." *Studies in Philology*, vol. 99, no. 1, Winter 2002, pp. 33–56.

Guattari, Félix. *Chaosmosis: An Ethico-Aesthetic Paradigm*. Indiana University Press, 1995.

Labrecque, Marie. "Le Temps des Bouffons." *Voir* (a weekly arts and culture journal). Montréal. Feb. 10–16, 2000.

Millington, Barry, and Steward Spencer. *Wagner in Performance*. Yale University Press. 1992.

Molière. *Les Précieuses ridicules*. Petits Classiques Larousse. 2008.

Pavis, Patrice. "On Faithfulness: The Difficulties Experienced by the Text/Performance Couple." *Theatre Research International*, vol. 33, no. 2, July 2008, 11–126.

———. "On the Frontiers of Mise en Scène." *Contemporary Mise en Scène: Staging Theatre Today*, Routledge, 2013.

Picot, Guillaume, translator. *La Farce de Maître Pathelin*. Paris: Petits Classiques Larousse, 2008.

Puchner, Martin. "Drama and Performance: Toward a Theory of Adaptation." *Common Knowledge*. vol. 17, no. 2, Spring 2011, pp. 292–305.

Ronis, David. "Wagner, Appia, and 'Authorial Intention.'" *The Opera Journal*, Vol. 45, no. 4, December 2012.

Taylor, Scott. *Princess Butterflies: A New Translation of Molière's "Les Précieuses Ridicules."* Amazon Digital Services LLC, December 3, 2012, https://www.amazon.com/Princess-Butterflies-Scott-Taylorebook/dp/B0.

# Rectories Meet "One-Hour" Rooms: Williams on Summery and Eccentric Loves

## Jeffrey B. Loomis

### Abstract

*Affirmations of sexuality decisively feature as a central focus in Tennessee Williams's dramatic work. Yet issues concerning the nature and practice of love elicit a nuanced variety of responses from him. One early draft of Summer and Smoke (Texas 45.3/81–88; Harvard 49.1/11–1 to 11–12) flaunts the sexual antics chosen by the previously prudish central character, Alma Winemiller, as she seduces a traveling salesman stranger into serving as her evening's paramour. Yet a slightly later "revision" (Texas 45.4/A1-A2) suggests, in all of its three major characters, a conviction that more spiritual and lasting dimensions of love do still exist. Like Alma, his chief protagonist, Williams often, and probably essentially, finds "love" ever to remain an "ordinary human need" (T Thtr of TW2, 93). Granted, both Williams and his fictional figures often find the most fulsome love extremely hard to sustain. Hence, they often come to rely upon, and even to revere, sex's more fitful (yet possibly somewhat loving) pleasures. But meanwhile, Williams does, albeit perhaps accidentally, hint that some highly valuable types of love are not sexual (or at least not principally sexual) at all.*

In the many archives housing Tennessee Williams manuscripts, fairly odd documents often enrich our views of his plays' growth. One such group of pages is the closing scene of *Summer and Smoke*'s "First reading version," from 1946 (Texas 45.3/81–88; Harvard 49.1/11–1 to 11–12). Added onto a full-length manuscript that otherwise resembles most of the eventually published *Summer and Smoke*, this excerpt quite raucously flaunts the new antics chosen by the previously prudish central character, Alma Winemiller, as she now seduces a traveling salesman, a stranger whom she will cajole into becoming her evening's paramour. Quite shockingly, or so it seems, this encounter occurs in the very parlor of the Episcopal Church rectory, where Alma's now-deceased clergyman father had once dwelt.

Ultimately, the 1946 rectory-as-incipient-cathouse scene anticipates the closing moments (although they are significantly more muted in tone) of both *Summer and Smoke*, first performed in 1948 and 1951, and its 1964 rewrite, *The Eccentricities of a Nightingale*. In all these finale episodes, both the unpublished and the published ones, Alma appears to affirm what critic John Clum considers a major Williams theme: "sexual liberation" looked upon as a quasi-"religio[us]" ritual (37).[1]

Such affirmations of sexuality are, unquestionably, key features of Williams's work. Yet issues concerning the widely ranging varieties of love elicit nuanced responses from him. Importantly, for example, there still is extant (Texas 45.4/A1-A2) a variant archived draft, less ribald in its focus, of the original 1946 closing scene. In this quite different document (specifically marked by Williams as a "revision"), key modifications announce a divergent, but apparently still sincere,[2] respect for a more complex, more spiritually resonant, focus upon love. Like Alma Winemiller, his central personage throughout these two dramas, Williams appears to have recognized that even "eccentric" persons find "love" to be an "ordinary human need" (*T Thtr of TW2*, 93). Granted, both he and his fictional figures also often find the most fulsome love extremely hard to sustain. Hence, they often come to rely upon, and even to revere, sex's more fitful (and possibly somewhat loving) pleasures. Yet Williams still hints, albeit perhaps accidentally, that some highly valuable sorts of love are not sexual (or at least not principally sexual) at all.

*Summer and Smoke* focuses on two characters who through most of their stage lives, beginning with a dramatized prologue scene that depicts them as adolescents, cannot stop countering each other's positions on the meaning of existence. Alma Winemiller does not forget, at least through most of the play and its drafts, that her first name means "soul" in Spanish (Texas 46.3/G45; *T Thtr of TW2*, 130). She therefore seeks to present herself to all as a clergyman's celibate, pious, and demure daughter—and also as his loyal assistant in parish events because her mother is too mentally addled to serve (Texas 46.4/A37; *T Thtr of TW2*, 152–153). Alma's neighbor John Buchanan, meanwhile, is a doctor's son and trained physician himself. Yet he for a long while finds disease scarily ugly to deal with,[3] so—behaving much *against* his own father's wishes—he pursues nightly distracting (and far from medical) shenanigans: gambling, sex, and self-soaking in booze (NYPL NCOF+91–293/P-5; Delaware 3.63/8–82; *T Thtr of TW2*, 195).

As a devotee, at least at first, of the idea that the "Chart of Anatomy" explains all of life (Texas 45.3/50–51; *T Thtr of TW2*, 220–221), John frequently opposes Alma's very different credos of absolutely necessary spiritual aspiration (Texas 45.3/50–51; *T Thtr of TW2*, 197). At the end, though, John reacts to his father's sudden shocking murder by committing himself, henceforth, to emulate his late parent's medical service. Declaring himself anxious to find redemption (*T Thtr of TW2*, 240), he now avidly aids in the healing of epidemic fever victims.[4]

Also, in the play's waning but amply ironic moments, Alma finally proves ready to admit, to both herself and John, that she has always desired him as a lover (Texas 46.4/9; *T Thtr of TW2*, 244). Alas, though, he is already engaged to marry another woman: Alma's former music student Nellie (Texas 46.6/13; *T Thtr of TW2*, 248).

Thereafter, as if providing a fitting corollary to Alma's thwarted late pursuit of John, *Summer and Smoke* signs off with her now turned (albeit timidly) into a would-be seductress, randomly flirting with shoe company shill Archie Kramer (*T Thtr of TW2*, 251–256). The "First reading version" manuscript, by contrast, has her seducing, much more flagrantly, one *Floyd* Kramer. Flaunting a mid-century "Eadie Was a Lady" type of theatrical bawdiness,[5] this rectory spree scene begins when Alma returns to her residence from earlier public frolics on a lake and in its adjacent casino. She totes along salesman Kramer, whose shirt has somehow become soaked, and she promises to launder it, dressing him in a mandarin jacket. She then sloshes him with bourbon and delights him with a round of tickling (to his libido's clear stimulation, according to Williams's text). Almost immediately, a burly male policeman, known as Officer "Polly" Parrott, arrives, having been summoned by an irate neighbor (who turns out to be Mrs. John, or Nellie, Buchanan). Nellie hopes to have Parrott quiet the noise level being roused at the Winemiller abode. But any pique that the gendarme feels toward Alma becomes almost immediately quelled after Alma's "delicate wink" at him, aided by alcoholic libations. Alma subsequently dances "coquettishly" for both male visitors before the on-duty policeman departs (although receiving her invitation to return at a later date). Ultimately, she and Kramer watch city fireworks from her window, playfully set off some tiny sparklers that Alma has on hand, and close the scene with a pre-coital, "clumsy, middle-aged" kiss (Texas 45.3/81–88).

This sketch of Alma giddily hosting, in her late father's very rectory space, a rollicking pre-debauchery party is undeniably humorous and hence often entertaining. It may also foreground that tenet which Williams so often hosannaed: his belief that sex is the main constituent of life.[6] Yet its particular depiction of frenzied sex appetite looks overly anxious to erase, swiftly and with great force, the consistent earlier dialogue in *Summer and Smoke* between themes of body and themes of spirit. It is an inescapable fact that the final depicted John of *Summer and Smoke*, without evident regret, decisively appears to reject his earlier sex-frenzied roguishness for a more spiritually guided, vocationally committed, life. And, albeit that Alma in *Summer and Smoke* and *The Eccentricities of a Nightingale* concludes with a decision for her own sexual liberation, she does not do so without still revealing some timidity and self-doubt. She thus does not, as she does in the "First reading version," appear to so radically repudiate her own previously dramatized, much more cautious, personality.

Granted, even as I judge the "First reading version" finale scene to be a bit simplistic and brash, I do not deny the sense of John Clum's central perceptions. He is surely right to find that Williams, quite dominantly and in many plays, lauds "sexual liberation," treating it as a quasi-religious topic (I would propose perhaps doing so by portraying a rectory parlor as a potentially fit venue for sexual assignation).[7] To be sure, in the printed official version of *Summer and Smoke* (*T Thtr of TW2*, 254), Alma shares one of her tranquilizer pills with Archie Kramer, her random evening escort. In a potentially witty send-up of the sacred, she proclaims the pills' prescription number ("96814") to be "the telephone number of God!" Then she quickly accompanies Archie to the bawdy pleasures of Moon Lake Casino.

In *The Eccentricities of a Nightingale*, a somewhat older and "hardened" Alma (Phillips 246) tells one random male escort (*T Thtr of TW2*, 109) that her town of Glorious Hill, despite its Golgotha-reminiscent name, should be regarded quite secularly, as a borough with "population five thousand souls and an equal number of *bodies*" (108; emphasis mine).[8] She also remarks that its "Episcopal church," of which her late "father was [once] rector," is a building now seemingly most distinguished for its "steeple" lacking a "cross," as it instead features "an enormous gilded hand with its index finger pointing straight up, accusingly, at—heaven" (109).[9]

Several sexually antinomian Williams short story manuscripts had already served as predictive advance documents for what became the *Summer and Smoke* dramatization. Written half a decade before the *Summer and Smoke* play, two short tales called "Summer and Smoke" laud poets teaching an anarchic *élan* to their disciples—who become, as a result, happy practitioners of the joy of "copulation" (Texas 46.2/A). In another short story, "The Yellow Bird," an Alma from Arkansas, the daughter of the Rev. Increase Tutweiler, revolts against her father's gabby sermons, smokes in the rectory attic, goes "juke"-ing with multiple men, and eventually drives her papa's auto straight through the garage door and on toward the titillation of frequent New Orleans sex (Texas 52.9; CS 232–239).

Indeed, Alma Winemiller is often close to being compared, in many *Summer and Smoke* and *Eccentricities* drafts, to a figure resembling the "Yellow Bird" narrative's Alma Tutweiler. Alma Winemiller, manuscripts often remind us,[10] had a scandalous aunt named Albertine (sister of Alma's somewhat mentally unwired mother). Albertine was said to have let fierce sexual passion drive her to marry a disreputable gambler (and actual bigamist) named Fordyce, Forsyth, or Schwarzkopf; whatever his name, he died either on the street or in a fire at his New Orleans *musée mécanique* (LOC 1.10/3–58; Texas 46.6/17–18; Texas 46.7/123; *T Thtr of TW2*, 41–44).[11] Alternate scripts propose Albertine turning into a hapless whore, perhaps one hopelessly in love with her pimp, in a New Orleans "good time house" (Texas 46.2/C1-C12; Texas 46.6/18).

Albertine's somber fictive life, in all its variant patterns, keeps emerging within many Williams fragments and fuller scripts. Some of the longer texts, as Williams's friend Donald Windham surmised (ctd. in Clum 35), might even be very early sketchings of what in 1964 became *The Eccentricities of a Nightingale* (Texas 46.1, Texas 46.5, NYPL NCOF+91–294). Even in the official *Summer and Smoke*, Albertine remains somewhat present, although now vaporized into a vague ghost in a speech declared by Alma to John. Without any clear explanation, Alma seems to be hallucinating about herself as a bizarre reincarnation of her late aunt. That character, after all, was regularly portrayed as performing the action Alma references in the following passage—the desperate last-minute snatching of a memorial token from the coat or hands of some beloved man (be he pimp or suitor or husband) who was deserting her, moving on either to a place of his geographical relocation or to death (Texas 46.2/C8; Texas 46.3/G45; Texas 46.6/10):

> [N]ow I have changed my mind, or the girl who said "no" [to you], she doesn't exist anymore, she died last summer—suffocated in smoke from something on fire inside her. No, she doesn't live now, but she left me her ring—You see? The one you admired, the topaz ring set in pearls.... And she said to me when she slipped this ring on my finger—"Remember I died empty-handed, and so make sure that your hands have something in them!" [*T Thtr of TW2*, 243].

The Alma plays, even in these wispy references to a sexually liberated Aunt Albertine, seem amply iconoclastic about standard social attitudes toward sex. Meanwhile, the same dramas typically also question most traditional religious tenets and practices.[12] This is true even as an Eternity fountain statue, which Alma long reverences, is a major set motif. Without much detail but, I think, with wisdom, Thomas Adler finds in the Eternity statue "a severely diminished rite of communion" (119). According to playwright Williams, the statue dominates the vista from a "promontory," appearing as a "fountain in the form of a stone angel, in a gracefully crouching position with wings lifted and her hands held together to form a cup from which water flows, a public drinking fountain" (*T Thtr of TW2*, 120). A few pages later, Alma as a little girl is delineated as having "a habit of holding her hands, one cupped under the other in a way similar to that of receiving the wafer at Holy Communion" (125). The little sometime-communicant at the Christian Eucharist evidently passes her young existence in a constant reverent pose, waiting ever upon the divine for a bestowal of grace. Yet the Eternity fountain, apparently the play's symbol of the grace-giving divine, also has its hands open—as if itself begging some gift from humanity. Perhaps (at least for Williams) this gift may be offered when, in the "Prologue" scene for *Summer and Smoke*, young boy John "*seizes [child Alma's] shoulders and gives her a quick rough kiss. She stands amazed with one hand cupping the other*" (131). Her quasi-eucharistic pose while she is carnally interacting with John appears to declare that human relationships, even sometimes very ephemeral and casual sexual ones, might themselves create at least their own facsimile of sacrament.[13]

Images of sex as incipient sacrament may indeed convey Williams's most central personal conviction about life, especially as that conviction permeates the plots of some of his most ferociously racy short stories (Clum 37–42). Yet he still could, at times, intuit within his imagination a sense that emotionally and even spiritually rich love can enduringly motivate even people who may have moved far past (or existed without) an originating sexual encounter. In the final scene of another primordial 1946 *Summer and Smoke* manuscript (today archived as Texas 45.4), the now-married John Buchanan looks out, through his own house's window, at the visible late evening lust on display within neighbor Alma's living room. He is soon interrupted by his wife, Nellie. Although definitely in a querulous mood, she still appears to love him strongly and lastingly. Meanwhile, Alma apparently still lastingly loves him, too:

NELLIE. Now I know. You come in here every night. You watch her out of this window.
JOHN. (*Hoarsely*) Yes.
NELLIE. How pitiful for you both that you made the mistake of taking me instead.
JOHN.—Yes.
NELLIE. Why didn't you take her?
JOHN. She had—too much of something....
NELLIE. Too much of what?
[*Roman candle flashes.*]
Too much of what, John?
JOHN. Something that I was afraid of!
[*Alma and Mr. Kramer toy with sparkler.*]
NELLIE. (*insistently pulling at John's arm*)—What?

JOHN. (*Breaking away from her with impatient force*) Something a chart of anatomy doesn't show!
[*Alma's and Mr. Kramer's kiss occurs; Alma exclaims "Why, Mr. Kramer!—Floyd!"*]
(*John rushes out of the study. Nellie follows him, calling his name with a childish wail.*)
NELLIE. Johnny! Johnny!
ALMA. (*like an echo*)—Johnny!

This particular sketched final scene (Texas 45.4/A1-A3) could conceivably be argued, I suppose, still to treat sexuality as life's one overriding issue.[14] After all, Alma is hosting a would-be bacchanal, or at least an evening of erotic assignation. But then, too, by definite contrast, John clearly speaks like the convert to spirituality that he becomes at the end of almost all *Summer and Smoke* manuscripts. Hence, an interplay between sensuality and spirituality reverberates as the now-basically carnal Alma appears still to yearn, at least in part, *spiritually* for John, and he certainly longs (in his very own words) spiritually for her. The experiences of both spirit and flesh remain foregrounded.[15] The major trio of characters all seem to aspire (at least in part) to a love consisting of more than mere sex. Meanwhile, though, the most idealized love definitely registers with them as fleeting. Thus only Floyd Kramer, who evidently can accept mere fleetingness as adequate pleasure, may fully be satisfied with this frail evening of frail encounters at or near a rectory parlor.

*The Eccentricities of a Nightingale* revises *Summer and Smoke* quite considerably. In one major change, it removes John's father from the onstage cast—thus no longer featuring what many have deemed his "overdramatized" murder by casino owner Gonzales, whose tempestuous daughter was dating John (Hofler 2 of 3). The elder doctor character (who admittedly is sketched with only inconsistent stabs of detail) surely lacks appeal for us as he himself provokes this murder by earlier insulting the ethnicity of the Hispanic hotelier (*T Thtr of TW2*, 216). Contrarily, though, the dramatized medical man often sounds quite astutely aware of life's complexities. Hence, it seems sad that his voice is absent from *Eccentricities* at such times as when he advises the neurasthenic Alma that she needs to seek more holism in her stances toward life (Texas 46.7/35; Delaware 3.63/2–37). He finds her "self-centered" in all of her diffusive tensions between overwrought stern restraint and inner palpitations of passion (Delaware 3.46B/153: Delaware 3.63/2–37), and so he deems her in need of personality balance, which she can achieve by both letting more passion into her life and showing more activated *spiritual* care—especially for the marginalized poor (Princeton 1.8/2–37 to 2–39).[16]

In *Eccentricities*, the parent who is most seen to influence the Buchanan son is, instead, his mother: a prissy woman, with sycophantic social ambitions, who smothers John and tries to manage his romantic life with a zeal almost matching that of the harridan matriarch in Sidney Howard's *The Silver Cord*. Her ridiculous behaviors include caroling in Mrs. Santa Claus garb and visiting her son's bedroom while wearing a negligée (*T Thtr of TW2*, 36, 55). Her effect on John may have produced in him some level of sexual aberration, since he reports that he fled in a panic from his first planned evening of heterosexual coupling, even though he later could "find ... blindfolded" the "rooms that people engage for an hour" (*T Thtr of TW2*, 95–96).[17] Most significantly, though, the character of John has emerged from his mother's odd style of parenting with an impressive quality of great gentleness; he definitely is more sensitive to Alma than was his roguish namesake in the first two-thirds of *Summer and Smoke*. He may actually realize that in his own way, as critic Hedy Weiss has concluded, he is as "eccentric" as Alma. Such eccentricity, whether consciously or unconsciously accepted by him, seems to help him develop his capacity to be kind—not only to Alma, but at times additionally to her socially alienated, feeble, and mentally rather daft mother (*T Thtr of TW2*, 42–43).

Most notably, the John of *Eccentricities* agrees to share, with Alma, the episode which Foster Hirsch (29) judges "more tender than anything in [*Summer and Smoke*]," and which Walter Meserve (255) thinks makes *Eccentricities* a "better" play than its predecessor, because of this "more direct romantic confrontation." Reviewing the Frank Langella-Blythe Danner television *Eccentricities* transcription of the 1970s, John Leonard in *The New York Times* calls the visualized hotel room tryst between Alma and the ambivalent young Dr. John a sequence toward which "[if] you aren't moved, you need a bulldozer and professional help" (qtd. in Phillips 247). Of course, in the episode John might seem to exist mostly to affirm Alma's "honesty" (*T Thtr of TW2*, 104).[18] After all, she proclaimed clearly to him that she desperately "want[ed] to be in a small room with [him] at midnight when the [New Year's Eve] bells [would] ring!" (*T Thtr of TW2*, 97). Therefore, to her confession "I know that you don't love me," he, in his own honesty, responds, "No. No, I'm not in love with you" (98). Nevertheless, in the tacky little chamber to which they go, a place "cold" and nearly impossible to heat up, a miraculous "*flickering red glow*" suddenly embers forth in the fireplace just as John is offering Alma a beneficent "kiss" (106).

This kiss seems to link up with another touching of amorous lips during *Summer and Smoke*. Alma, in both plays, muses on her past dating life, which was filled with only the stark non-communication of days spent as if in a "desert" or on an "uninhabitable ground" (*T Thtr of TW2*, 91, 198). As evidently a partial response to such expressed sadness, John in both plays suddenly leaps forward to adjust Alma's hat "[s]o that [he] won't get [her] veil in [his] mouth when [he] kiss[es her]" (*T Thtr of TW2*, 106, 200).

Yet that line, and the resultant kiss, originates in *Summer and Smoke* during the fairly early scene when John takes Alma to Moon Lake Casino and randily seeks to lure her reluctant self into "intimate relations" with him (201). This John thus comes across basically as a lecher, while the John who much less aggressively exchanges a kiss in *Eccentricities* seems more complex: he acts, at least on this one occasion, as a gentle giver to Alma of one night's affectionate tenderness, of spiritual kindness—of compassionately filial, more than merely erotic, love.[19] He thus becomes perhaps the most vital realized version we have of the John Buchanan character, as he fuses expressions of sexuality with sensitive giftings of spiritual care. At the same time, though, he does not fit into traditional stereotypes of romantic heroism—for he does not at all believe that he can commit himself to love Alma with such a transcendent *eros* as could last decades (Lewis 117–118). Thus his subsequent disappearance from her life apparently causes lingering depressiveness in Alma. At the play's final curtain, she is only able to declare, with frustrated memories of loving John but also with more immediate reference to a casual later sex partner, "Oh, no, I'm not going to lose you before I've lost you!" (*T Thtr of TW2*, 111).

It appears no likely accident that Williams, in these Alma Winemiller plays, makes the most stirring scene of romantic coupling occur when *Eccentricities*' Alma and John intimately meet in one of those *liberated* chambers that people rent "for [just] an hour" (*T Thtr of TW2*, 95). Williams here, as so typically for him, enshrines even that sex which many would label as illicit, and he seems to judge it as an experience where at least glimmerings of spiritual beauty (and maybe, sometimes, even true love?) can actually (at least briefly) emerge. On the other hand, he cannot escape awareness that primarily sex-motivated encounters do risk ample future disappointment. For example, he suggests, in *Eccentricities*, that Alma suffers, in her later years of abundant sexual promiscuity, from noticeable malaise.[20]

Williams's range of human understanding is what makes him partly, but also more than, an apostle of sexual freedom. Like the Alma of most of *Summer and Smoke*, in her belief that "bodies," "hearts," and "souls" are *all* potentially amorous (*T Thtr of TW2*, 202), Williams truly *could* conceive how the fullest experiences of love at heart contain far more emotional resonance than does frictive touch all by itself. He clearly knew, too, that both casual sex and richer love relationships are vulnerable to the stresses enforced by time's passing. His *Notebooks* therefore abound in laments about amorous happiness not found, or not enduring and satisfying when it was found: "I wish I loved [s]omebody very dearly besides myself" (45); "Nostalgia for an old love—it does strange things" (67); "I want life and love again" (167); "I ache with desires that never are quite satisfied" (187). Even his long-term relationship with Frank Merlo was ever-troubled and eventually basically broken, even before Merlo's premature death (Lahr 417–421, 456–466). Such was true even though he once had declared his love for Frank, in some rather lustrous words, to be "unconditional," "not ... wild, disorderly, [and] terrified" (*Notebooks*, 607).

To be sure, the Alma Winemiller plays do not advertise any idealized views about traditional marriage (or even long-term sexual partnerships) as the sole locale wherein worthy love may be expressed. The Winemiller parents, for example, seem fairly miserably matched. Yet Williams—in the revised "First reading version" dénouement of Texas 45.4, as well as in the "one-hour" hotel room tryst of *Eccentricities*—does suggest that life can meaningfully allow deeply heartfelt love, even if that love proves frustrated and perhaps unrequited. While retaining a sense that romantic involvements are for many folks only extramarital and brief, Williams nonetheless shows all sorts of folks able to express some of that spiritual energy which opens toward what become the eventual widest expanses of love.

## Notes

1. Examining a 2018 production of *Summer and Smoke*, Sara Holdren similarly wrote that Williams in that play was "trying to make a complex argument for an embrace of life that held passion... as sacred as prayer."

2. In examining the many manuscript variants of Williams's writing, I suppose one always should wonder whether any individual draft might just have been a frivolous stab at a different approach to his currently developing plotline. He may potentially sometimes have been merely trying, in a new script, to cajole audience members who had different attitudes than his own. Nonetheless, I doubt that we can ever know for sure that he was simply playing compositional gaming with variant optional texts. I would instead propose that we generally should assume him to be sincere, at least to a degree, with the focus of every draft.

3. These fears on John's part derived from his awareness of his aging and mortality-threatened parents (Texas 46.9/96–97; Texas 45.5/6–7), as well as from the illnesses of patients with whose ailments he as a medical professional was forced to deal (Harvard 50.1/30).

4. Critic Signi Lenea Falk (92) thought John's spiritual sort of conversion to have occurred too suddenly to be credible. Williams himself (*Conversations* 223) claimed that John's character lacked dynamic interest, and he also judged that the "social dimension" of John's eventual medical zeal hindered the play's main intended focus on personal "relationship[s]" (qtd. in Maruéjouls-Koch 25). He opined, too, that he did not wish John to look traditionally holy like Saint Paul (Texas 46.4/B30). Yet multiple Williams draft manuscripts suggest plans for much fuller dramatization of John's intense post-conversion medical service (Texas 46.4/A34-A35, B39; Texas 45.6/2–49). And, indeed, scenarists for the eventual *Summer and Smoke* film did specifically picture that medical stewardship at length (Phillips 233; HNOC 53.980/117–123; HNOC 53.981/112–115; Texas 45.11/103–104; *S&S* DVD).

5. For discussion of "Eadie Was A Lady" and other 1930s Broadway songs (e.g., "Love for Sale") which honor "shady" nighttime dames, see Mordden 44, 62.

6. It does seem telling that Alma is a minister's daughter and singer, as was Tennessee's own mother Edwina, his likely key psychological nemesis because she was so trenchantly puritanical (Hayman 1, 3, 8; Leverich 42, 60, 71, 133).

7. I can understand why some early readers of *Summer and Smoke* labeled Alma's final stance as exemplifying "decadence," "disintegration," "degradation," "a morass of sex," and "tawdr[iness]" (Jackson 137; HHH, in Columbia 18.3; Nelson 129; Tischler 156; Da Ponte 69). Yet these interpreters may run too quickly away from the full range of Williams's dialoguing arguments.

8. It remains worth noting, however, that she still judges the town square's central Eternity statue to be the "loveliest thing" around (*T Thtr of TW2*, 109).

9. Even as Kenneth Holditch and Richard Freeman Leavitt (4) have found a *Presbyterian* church edifice in one of Williams's childhood Mississippi hometowns, which could be said to flaunt a bizarre steeple like the one noted by Alma in *Eccentricities*, the steeple's mention in Williams's drama does appear to make Alma sound blasphemous, or at least sardonic, toward the traditional religion in which she was so sternly raised.

10. One of those manuscripts is the official published edition of *The Eccentricities of a Nightingale*—where the Schwarzkopf version of Albertine's backstory is partially recounted by Alma and her mother, at different junctures in the script (*T Thtr of TW2*, 41–45, 86–88).

11. The textual discussion of this museum and its adulation for mechanical cartoonlike sculptures focuses a minor sub-theme of these Winemiller plays: the debunking of coldly mechanistic social mores, especially those by which men marginalize the concerns of their female mates. Otto Schwarzkopf, for instance, ignores his supposed chosen amorous partner among human beings, Albertine, when he attends much more often to admiring the "bird girl" in his museum collection of artifacts (Clum 48). Meanwhile, the smug Rev. Winemiller seems to have driven his wife to a wedding week collapse into borderline madness by his insensitivity, perhaps including lumbering sexual practice. It thus appears to be quite fitting that his wife mocks him (with likely vituperative sexual innuendo) by comparing him to a "missionary" who lost all possible success with would-be Maori converts because his sermonizing always lacked "punctuation" (Texas 46.6/17).

12. At the same time, however, I am intrigued that in the mid-1940s Williams the notebook-writer was so laudatory of the biblical Good Samaritan (*Notebooks* 431 [December 8, 1944]). He also at times delineated social justice activities, in his characters, that looked directly imitative of Jesus (Loomis 129–130).

13. In *The Eccentricities of a Nightingale*, Alma tells John that she (and, she says, her literary discussion group friends, too) "devoured" him "with [their] eyes," since he was "like holy bread being broken among [them]" (*T Thtr of TW2*, 79).

14. Early and fragmentary compositions picture either Alma or her Aunt Albertine shouting "Johnny!" after an elusive but much-adored New Orleans pimp (Texas 46.2/C9-C10). Maybe, then, this Texas 45.4 scene totally concerns the sex-drive which might make a woman shriek when a lover departs. But Alma and Nellie, in the proposed Texas 45.4 finale, do seem to express ardor for John that is more than merely sexual in nature.

15. Flesh-versus-spirit tension seems especially strong in the painstakingly developed (although eventually rejected) "silent film sequences" of some early drafts. Williams began his toying with the device by proposing to project only one single image at a time (e.g., John lustfully chasing young Nellie around his lab [Texas 46.2/A29]). He gradually began to propose single images that nonetheless conveyed a combination of tones (e.g., Alma writing John a letter apologizing for her annoying prudery, but then dousing the letter with perfume [Texas 46.2/G6]). Eventually, he came around to mixing two opposed images together, apparently so as to emphasize yet more completely his play's spirit-versus-flesh dichotomies (e.g., John shown killing a man in a drunken brawl, but then being almost simultaneously viewed when working as a dedicated physician among indigent rural fever patients [Texas 46.4/A23-A24]).

16. However, in drafts the doctor does voice a rather discordant and sudden situational ethics when (as a mouthpiece for Williams's own greater liberalism, probably) he utters a contention that Alma should go to New Orleans as a sexual rebel, imitating the frantic behavior of her late Aunt Albertine (Texas 45.9/2–27; Princeton 1.8/2–37). At this point the physician actually seems to echo the seemingly hyperbolic carnality of the "First reading version" finale scene.

17. One cannot but wonder, since John ran away from his projected coupling with a "lady of the evening," if his later returns to the rooms-by-the-hour hotel weren't, at least sometimes, same-sex visits. His character thus, as much as Alma's, may support John Clum's argument that *Eccentricities* especially affirms "queer," and often sexually ambiguous, personalities and lifestyles.

18. That "honesty" might best illustrate the existentialist self-determining dimension of Alma's character, as it is delineated by such interpreters as Meserve (255) and Brooking (385).

Actress Mary McDonnell, who played Alma onstage, labeled it a "plus" to watch Alma "take action," and "gain her dark side" (qtd. in Allen 27).

19. On the variant types of love, see C. S. Lewis, *The Four Loves*.

20. Seconding my observation as I watch the made-for-television movie of *The Eccentricities of a Nightingale* (*Ecc* DVD), Gene Phillips (246) notes that Blythe Danner, portraying Alma in the final scene of *Eccentricities*, is at times "smiling wryly and wearily in anticipation of an hour with another [man] in the endless series of anonymous strangers who have replaced John in her life."

## WORKS CITED

*Manuscripts from the many repositories holding Williams's archived drafts and letters are each cited in this study with, first, the encompassing information for the entire collection; then a box number, followed by a period; a folder number, and, after a slash, any subfolder indication (A, B, C, D, for instance, according to the sequence of any subfolders within a larger folder). The various entries ultimately provide (if such are available), manuscript page numbers.*

Adler, Thomas. "Before the Fall—and After: *Summer and Smoke* and *The Night of the Iguana*." *The Cambridge Companion to Tennessee Williams*, edited by Matthew Roudané, Cambridge University Press, 1997, pp. 249–258.

Allen, Norman. "Mary McDonnell: Watch Her Smoke." *Theater Week*, September 30, 1996, pp. 27–29.

Brooking, Jack. "Directing *Summer and Smoke*: An Existentialist Approach." *Modern Drama*, vol. 2, no. 4, Winter 1959, pp. 377–385.

Clum, John. "From *Summer and Smoke* to *Eccentricities of a Nightingale*: The Evolution of the Queer Alma." *Modern Drama*, vol. 39, no. 1, Spring 1996, pp. 31–50.

Da Ponte, Durant. "Tennessee Williams' Gallery of Feminine Characters." *Critical Essays on Tennessee Williams*, edited by Robert Martin, G. K. Hall, 1997, pp. 259–275.

Falk, Signi Lenea. *Tennessee Williams*. Twayne, 1961.

Hayman, Ronald. *Tennessee Williams: Everyone Else Is an Audience*. Yale University Press, 1993.

Hirsch, Foster. *A Portrait of the Artist: The Plays of Tennessee Williams*. National University Publications / Kennikat, 1979.

Hofler, Robert. "'Summer and Smoke' Theater Review: Tennessee Williams Sets Off Sparks Among the Dross." *The Wrap*, May 3, 2018. the wrap.com/2018/Summersmoke theater review—tennessee williams sets off sparks among dross.

Holditch, Kenneth, and Richard Freeman Leavitt. *Tennessee Williams and the South*. University Press of Mississippi, 2002.

Holdren, Sara. "Theatre Review: *Summer and Smoke* Has That 'Immaterial Something.'" *Vulture*, May 3, 2018. vulture.com/2018/05/theater—summer and smoke has that immaterial something.html.

Howard, Sidney. *The Silver Cord*. Samuel French, 1928.

Jackson, Esther Merle. *The Broken World of Tennessee Williams*. University of Wisconsin Press, 1965.

Lahr, John. *Tennessee Williams: Mad Pilgrimage of the Flesh*. W. W. Norton, 2014.

Leverich, Lyle. *Tom: The Unknown Tennessee Williams*. Crown, 1995.

Lewis, C. S. *The Four Loves*. HarperCollins, 1960.

Loomis, Jeffrey B. "'Cassandra, Meet Leadbelly': Tennessee Williams Battles to Become Orpheus." *Text and Presentation*, 2013, edited by Graley Herren, The Comparative Drama Conference Series, vol. 10, McFarland, 2014, pp. 123–139.

Maruéjouls-Koch, Sophie. "The Haunted Stage of *Summer and Smoke*: Tennessee Williams's Forgotten Silent Film Sequences." *Modern Drama*, vol. 57, no. 1, Spring 2014, pp. 19–40.

Meserve, Walter. "Accepted Reality: Survivors and Dreamers in Tennessee Williams." *Critical Essays on Tennessee Williams*, edited by Robert Martin, G. K. Hall, 1997, pp. 249–258.

Mordden, Ethan. *Sing for Your Supper: The Broadway Musical in the 1930s*. Palgrave Macmillan, 2005.

Nelson, Benjamin. *Tennessee Williams: The Man and His Work*. Ivan Obolensky, 1961.

Phillips, Gene. *The Films of Tennessee Williams*. Arts Alliance Press / Associated University Presses, 1980.

Tischler, Nancy. *Tennessee Williams: Rebellious Puritan*. Citadel, 1961.
Weiss, Hedy. "*Eccentricities of a Nightingale*: Chopin Theatre Review." *Chicago Sun Times*, Aug. 3, 1999. chopin theatre/com/event.php? id=1374.
Williams, Tennessee. Columbia University, Butler Library, Rare Books and Manuscripts, Tennessee Williams Papers, Series 2 (Works): Columbia 18.3—*Summer and Smoke*, 1949–1982.
_____. *Collected Stories*. Introduction by Gore Vidal, New Directions, 1997. (*CS*)
_____. *Conversations with Tennessee Williams*, edited by Albert Devlin. University Press of Mississippi, 1986. (*Conversations*)
_____. Delaware Special Collections, Tennessee Williams Papers, Morris Library, University of Delaware: Delaware 3.46B—"*Summer and Smoke*—A Film Play"; Delaware 3.63—*Summer and Smoke* –Playscript, TS.
_____. *Eccentricities of a Nightingale*. DVD, Broadway Theatre Archive. Kultur, 1978. (*Ecc* DVD)
_____. Harvard Theatre Collection, Tennessee Williams Papers, Houghton Library, Harvard University: Harvard 49.1—*Summer and Smoke* or *A Chart of Anatomy*, First reading version, August 1946; Harvard 50.1—*A Chart of Anatomy*, Second Version, November 1946.
_____. Historical Collection of New Orleans [HNOC], Fred W. Todd Tennessee Williams Collection, MS 562: HNOC 53.980—*Summer and Smoke*, Second Temporary Yellow [Script] for the Wallis-Paramount-Hazen Film Version, May 16, 1960; HNOC 53.981—*Summer and Smoke*—Revised Final White Screenplay, Adaptation by James Poe, 12/14/60.
_____. Library of Congress [LOC], Tennessee Williams Manuscripts: LOC 1.10: *Summer and Smoke* by Tennessee Williams, copyright April 16, 1948.
_____. New York Public Library for the Performing Arts [NYPL], Billy Rose Collection: NYPL NCOF+91–293—*Summer and Smoke*, Rome Version (March 1948); NYPL NCOF+91–294—*The Eccentricities of a Nightingale* or *The Sun That Warms the Dark*, Author's Gift, Premiered Tappan Zee Playhouse, Nyack, NY, Summer 1964.
_____. *Notebooks*, edited by Margaret Bradham Thornton. Yale University Press, 2006.
_____. Princeton University Library Rare Books and Special Collections: Princeton 1.8—*Summer and Smoke*, March 1947 [revised].
_____. Texas Tennessee Williams Collection, Harry Ransom Humanities Center, University of Texas, TXRC-C99-A14, Series I (Works): Texas 45.3—*Summer and Smoke* [or *A Chart of Anatomy*], Typescript Draft, First reading version, August 1946; Texas 45.4—*Summer and Smoke*; Revisions, 1946, n.d.; Texas 45.5—*Summer and Smoke*; Typescript Draft, 1947; Texas 45.6—*Summer and Smoke*; Revisions, 1946; Texas 45.9—*Summer and Smoke*; Rome Version—Mimeo Script, 1948; Texas 45.11—*Summer and Smoke*; Motion Picture Script, 1960, n.d.; Texas 46.1—*Summer and Smoke: The Bird Girl in His Arms*; Texas 46.2—*Summer and Smoke*; Draft Frgs, n.d. [1]; Texas 46.3—*Summer and Smoke*, Draft Frgs, n.d. [2]; Texas 46.4—*Summer and Smoke*, Draft Frgs, n.d. [3]; Texas 46.5—*Summer and Smoke*; *Eccentricities of a Nightingale*, n.d. (*The Eccentricities of a Nightingale* or *The Sun That Warms the Dark*); Texas 46.6—*Summer and Smoke*; *Fiddler's Green*, n.d.; Texas 46.7—*Summer and Smoke*; Incomplete Transcript, n.d.; Texas 46.9—*Summer and Smoke*; *The Room Is Cold*, n.d.; Texas 52.9—"The Yellow Bird," 1941–1946, n.d.
_____. *The Theatre of Tennessee Williams*, vol. 2. New Directions, 1971. (*T Thtr of TW2*)
Williams, Tennessee, Meade Roberts, and James Poe. *Summer and Smoke*, DVD, directed by Peter Glenville. Olive Films, 2013. (*S&S* DVD)

# A Portrait of the Krapp as a Young[er] Man: Michael Laurence's *Krapp, 39*

## WILLIAM HUTCHINGS

### Abstract

*Originally performed in 2008, Michael Laurence's one-act play* Krapp, 39 *is a portrait of Samuel Beckett's Krapp as a younger man—thirty years younger, in fact, at 39, the same age as the play's only on-stage character and the age of Michael Laurence the author when the play was written as well as the age of Michael Laurence the actor, all or any of whom may—or may not—be one and the same. Younger Krapp provides perspective and context for what the audience knows will be his fate thirty years later (assuming that they are at least somewhat familiar with Beckett's play). But in a startling metaphysical time-warp, younger Krapp has quite sophisticated twenty-first century technology that older Krapp with his reel-to-reel tape recorder could never have imagined. Clever in its ensuing complications, Laurence's play is both an homage and a postmodern complement to Beckett's original, yet complex and highly original in its autonomy. This essay contains analysis of* Krapp, 39 *by William Hutchings, notes on the development of the play by Michael Laurence, and an interview between the two.*

Originally performed in 2008, Michael Laurence's one-act play *Krapp, 39* is a portrait of Samuel Beckett's Krapp as a younger man. To be precise, Laurence's Krapp is thirty years younger than Beckett's character; yet at 39, he is exactly the same age as (a) the play's only on-stage character *and* (b) the actual Michael Laurence by whom the play was written, as well as (c) the actor Michael Laurence who stars in the play during every performance. All or any of these three may—or may not—be one and the same; accordingly, the play is a remarkably innovative and intriguingly complicated form of metatheatre, in some ways even Stoppard-esque in its layered complexity. Krapp the Younger (Laurence's character) provides an entirely new perspective and context for readers and viewers of *Krapp's Last Tape*. That character may be hereinafter identified as Krapp the Elder, i.e., Beckett's original character in the now earlier-yet-later play.

A juxtaposition of the two plays creates a time-warp all its own: Krapp the Elder, first portrayed on stage in 1958, relies upon his reel-to-reel tape recorder to evoke memories of his earlier life, listening to his own voice as a much younger man—a technological feat that Beckett was among the first to exploit on the stage. Yet, surprisingly, Beckett's first stage direction in the text specifies that the play actually takes place on "*A late night in the future*" (emphasis mine), which complicates still further the play's timeline and creates a mysterious detail that remains too often ignored. Laurence's Krapp, however, is necessarily younger than Beckett's—although he lives unmistakably in the twenty-first century, surrounded by technological innovations that are ostentatiously new: a flat screen monitor, video cameras on tripods, a six-foot "tech" table, and a camcorder on a "quick-release" tripod, all of which "hum and glow in the darkness" of his room (343-A). In contrast to the austerity of Beckett's set, there are thirty-seven listed additional props that are visible on the cluttered set, including numerous books—a well-worn copy of *Krapp's Last Tape* is there, of course—as well as assorted "open journals and composition notebooks," the aforementioned reel-to-reel tape recorder (of course), videocassette tapes, assorted playbills, and a supply of vodka, cigarettes, and pills. Playwright Laurence terms all that "the flotsam and jetsam of a self-archivist's life" (341). As such, actor Laurence "takes the camcorder and films various objects on the 'tech-table' … [so that] his live-cam images appear on the live flat screen monitor" in front of the audience in "real time" (341). Laurence's Krapp the Younger is definitely a man of *our* (as opposed to Beckett's) time.

Despite such explicit details for the set, author Laurence insists that the stage space is to remain "ambiguous. Or maybe dualistic. Or even a contradiction. In one sense, it is a 'personalized space,' sort of an actor's rehearsal space, or laboratory. In another sense, it is 'neutral.' A stage in this very theatre. Wherever 'this very theatre' is" (341).

Furthermore, he also specifies that "the amiable fiction of this play is that every time that it is performed is [the character] Michael's birthday. Therefore, all dates and times need to be adjusted accordingly for each performance" (341).

Shortly thereafter, the play's specific thesis is announced quite forthrightly early in the performance: "I want to record … in front of a live audience …

the 39-year-old Krapp soliloquy that I will use in a conventional production of *Krapp's Last Tape* thirty years from now, in the year 2038, when I'm sixty-nine years old" (343-A).

After a musical interlude that blends The Beatles' "Birthday" and Schubert's "String Quartet in C Minor," Michael the actor, costumed as Krapp, appears eating a banana (of course!) and "look[ing] like a guttersnipe's phantom—wild, [with] unkempt hair, unshaven, [in a] dirty 3-piece gray suit" (343-B). He reads a letter to the Literary Agent for the Samuel Beckett Estate seeking permission for what "might be best characterized as an autobiographical 'documentary' theatre piece" that presents "an investigation of myself, of the famous character Krapp, and the psychological intersection of the two" (344-A).

For a one-act, single-set, single-actor play with a 1¼ hour running time, *Krapp, 39* has a remarkably complex and sophisticated narrative structure; its published script can be found in *Plays and Playwrights 2009*, edited by Martin Denton (n.b., since the text itself is double-columned, quotations are identified by page and column, A and B; prefatory material is single spaced and has only a page number). By my count, *Krapp 39* consists of twenty-three segments of varying lengths, organized associatively rather than chronologically, ranging from August 1975 (when Michael was 4½ years old and declared that he would someday become a writer) to October 2038 (when Michael imagines two alternative responses to the production of his play). Eight segments are interpolated telephone messages or conversations—all of which are *recorded* rather than in-the-present: mechanically captured rather than directly spoken, an absence *and* a presence, a next-best-thing-to-being-there when *not* there (or pretending not to be). All of that furthers isolation instead of making actual human contact, a resonant sign of the times of twenty-first century isolation and anomie amid ostensible technological progress. Three other characters are heard (on recordings) *but not seen* during the play: Michael's mother (who died at age 59 but is voiced during a flashback sequence) and his two friends, George and Jon. George remains skeptical about Michael's Beckett project, "trying to understand ... [and] trying to muster enthusiasm" (343-B), while Jon advises Michael that "at 39, well, there's the iconic bridge to middle age ... looking back at the last moment of a certain kind of possibility in life" (347-B). Yet, a crucial element of Michael's alienation and anomie is related to the technological conveniences that, in effect, isolate him from his friends and associates rather than connect him with them. Every one of Michael's telephone calls is a left (i.e., abandoned) message, a recording to be played later at some convenient moment, but never is there the voice of an actual human being present in person in real time, able to engage in an *interactive* human conversation. Each is thus an absence and a presence simultaneously, there audibly whenever summoned yet never *engaged* in conversation and not making any *live* human contact. Accordingly, the recipient of the call is left with only an infinitely replayable voice—the exact counterpart of Krapp's chosen spool of tape—who nevertheless is *not there* quite literally but audibly *is there* vocally even after death.

Michael's Beckett-based obsession, particularly with Krapp, seems to be a product of his many anxieties and neuroses as the plot unfolds. The details of his life are set forth in associative but non-linear order, spanning not only more than a decade of recorded reflections, each birthday, but paired flashforwards beyond the above as well, wherein Michael foretells his life thirty years into the future, when he will in fact be Krapp's age of 69 and will play the role of Krapp at the age of 69. The first of his reveries is of course a triumphant success in London at the Royal Court Theatre "on the stage where it premiered eighty years ago"; his second self-prophesied reverie is quite the opposite, however, played to an audience of only five "at 'The Sarasota Multi-Media Festival for the Aged'" (364-A). So *Que Sera, Sera*: it is left for viewers or readers to decide their own preferred outcomes—and, ideally, to argue about them on the way out of the theatre.

Because Michael is an actor, the fragmented narrative of his life also includes a variety of venues where he has worked in less than stellar plays and/or films—far from the starring roles that every aspiring actor / star-wannabe envisions (at least initially). The insecurities of the acting profession are embodied in Michael's self-absorption, solipsism, narcissism, and/or neuroticism; cigarettes, alcohol, and self-doubts are unsurprisingly present, but opinions and amateur diagnoses are left for theatregoers to decide. His concerns are the inevitable anxieties about the next callback and the next successful acting gig to come along—wherever, whenever, and whatever it happens to be. Michael the character knows well what Michael the actor (as well as Michael the author) learned from years of hard-earned lessons about the acting profession.

The scrambled chronology of Michael's life gives *Krapp, 39* a distinctly cubist complexity as each segment provides a different disclosure about its complicated subject: himself. Accordingly, Laurence explains, "*Krapp, 39* ... is not a play in the conventional sense, but might be best characterized as an autobiographical theatre piece [: an] investigation of myself, of the famous character Krapp, and the psychological interplay of the two" (344-A).

With an obsessiveness worthy of Rousseau and his *Confessions* plus a compulsion to record virtually every working moment with the latest technology—in order to preserve on video even the most banal moments of his life—Michael's purpose is (in Rousseau's words) to display "myself as I was, as vile and despicable when I was so, when my behavior was such [and] as good, generous, and noble when I was so." As usual, especially post–Freud, the latter tends to be less frequent (and probably less interesting) than the former. Accordingly, given the nature of his profession, Michael—like every less-than-star actor—is never free of what might be termed Actors' Angst: the inevitability of uncertainty about when and/or if another role will be forthcoming, of how long the show might last, of less-than-choice or challenging roles, and of how to pay the bills *ad interim*. Yet in his segment dated October 28, 2004, Michael provides as eloquent a statement about his profession as can be found anywhere:

> I'm an *actor*, I'm an *artist*. I have this thing I do, that I scrape and claw, still, to get the chance to do, and that's all that matters. I have a religious devotion to these little black rooms, these tables, these pages of fantasy, these planks of wood, these cans of paint, and you know, I made a choice! And look at me now, I have no money, no fame, no family, except these temporary families on the road ...
>
> I look around this theatre. I look around this set. There's a *house* for a set. Look at that ... that house.... It looks for all the world like a *house*. It's structurally sound, people go in and out ... windows, doors....
>
> But then look, it's propped up by sandbags! Two-by-fours! I could *topple* it with a hard kick. And, you know, *that's* the house I live in. So! I made a choice ... you want to be in the theatre ... then *this* is where you live [355-B—356-A].

Yet after a few more such lines and a moment during which Michael "claws at the air, searching for words," he contends that "It's all bullshit. It's not about that. Deep down inside, I want to be alone" (356-A). In best modernist fashion, the matter is left for the audience / reader to decide—though one argument certainly seems more eloquent and impassioned than the other.

Whereas Michael's paean to the theatre has a certain universality, his contemplation of time in the "real world" is as distinctly twenty-first century as the technology that fills his room. He expounds on the nature of contemporary time itself:

> I think about how my every single human encounter of this day has lasted exactly *three minutes*. And how I had paid for each three-minute exchange—a quarter, three dollars, five dollars, a candle [for, respectively, a quarter for a pay-phone, a three-dollar three-minute shoe shine, a five-dollar three-minute peepshow, followed by a one-dollar votive candle purchased after a confession whose priest turned out to be absent, having gone to lunch]. And I think about time and children and love and work and that play [which he has recently finished] and how you have thirty-nine years to try to do something, forty-nine years to fail, fifty-nine years to love someone if you're lucky, and sixty-nine years to die [350-B].

Part Hemingway and part Meursault from Camus's *The Stranger*, this characterization may well epitomize Michael's personality when he is *not* in the theatre.

A quite unexpected plot twist occurs in the final moments of the play, when Michael opens a letter from Jane Miller, Esq., representing The Literary

Agency on behalf of the Samuel Beckett Estate in response to Michael's request for permission to use portions of *Krapp's Last Tape* in *Krapp, 39*. The reply includes the following:

> We've now had a chance to peruse all of the material you sent us, and I'm afraid we cannot authorize any use of Mr Beckett's copyrighted text in your project.
>
> I'm so sorry I couldn't be of help with this, but I must follow instructions from the Estate. Best of luck with "Krapp, 39" [365-A&B].

Those first two sentences have an unambiguous lawyer-like finality: any and all quoted words, phrases, stage directions, or other material of the text may not be quoted in Laurence's text. Period. Yet as we read, hear, or see it in the theatre, that third sentence seems blatantly incongruent, even contradictory. Given the denial of permission to use any of Beckett's copyrighted text, how and why exactly is Jane Miller (Esq.) expressing "best of luck with *Krapp, 39*"? Furthermore, how would the play ever have been produced under such unambiguous strictures?

(Spoiler Alert!) "Jane Miller (Esq,)" and "The Literary Agency" do not in fact exist. Michael Laurence did of course have to contact the representatives of the Beckett Estate, but he characterizes their discussion as amiable—and affirms that no quotations from Beckett's writing are used in *Krapp, 39*. For further details, see the interview that can be found at the end of this essay.

A particular synchrony between the two Krapps is explained when Michael notes further intricate textual and structural parallels:

> Specifically on that tape [the original] Krapp is recording on his thirty-ninth birthday [...] but when it comes to *love*, he's talking very specifically about two things: first, the death of his mother ... the loss of that *original* love ... that original love is gone ... extinguished in his thirty-ninth year [...] And second, the loss of or the *forfeiture* of, *romantic* love. He talks about several women [...] but then finally a *breakup scene* ... a breakup with a lover ... final moments with a woman who[m] he loves and she loves him ... in the boat on the lake. [...] I think, when you talk about what is extinguished, I think it's *love* ... [361-B]. [Note: in the above paragraph, ellipses in brackets denote that a passage of the text has been omitted; those that are single-spaced and without brackets are the playwright's own pauses in his text.]

Even beyond that passage, Laurence's intricately designed interactions between past and present necessarily must have an exceptional ending, as *Krapp, 39* definitely does. In fact, there are two endings, both set in the year October 28, 2038, in London as Michael fantasizes about "the scene of [his] rousing triumph! ... A brilliant opening night for my *Krapp's Last Tape* [at] The New Royal Court Theatre ... on the very stage where the play premiered eighty years ago today" (363-A&B). As his fantasy continues, his accolades include not only thunderous applause but also five curtain calls and "even [an] honorary knighthood bestowed on [him] by King William. He flies back to New York in time for the Tony Awards." Yet Michael's accolades do not stay for long, as he projects a starkly different scenario moments later. In this narrative, on Michael's sixty-ninth birthday, he is alone in a motel following his production of *Krapp's Last Tape* at the 'Sarasota Multimedia Festival for the Aged' whose "audience seemed to like the show, all five of them, although one guy said I didn't sound like me on the *Krapp, 39* tape. I told him I recorded it thirty years ago. He said *Yeah, that was a mistake*" (364-A). The point is not which of the fantasies is the more plausible, if either. Rather, it is a scenario with which surely every actor is quite familiar—another experience that comes with the profession, "another opening, another show."

Given the unique tripartite structure of Laurence's self-portraiture and the fragmented, non-chronological self-representations on which the play depends, *Krapp, 39* is arguably among the most complex, multi-faceted, and provocative portraits of the actor as a young(ish) man or woman. Michael obviously cannot be presented as a physically *fractured* obsessive while standing in front of the audience—with whom he quite deliberately does not make eye contact until very near the end of his performance (another of author Laurence's directorial specifications). Nevertheless, Michael the actor remains a complex, obsessive, and compelling character; each segment of Michael the playwright's non-linear, technology-obsessed narrative provides a new facet of the carefully constructed personality that becomes a worthy redaction of Beckett's own Krapp as a not-quite-young man.

## Notes on the Development of the Piece (Or Notes on Failure) by Michael Laurence

*Krapp, 39* started out as a birthday party. I was about to turn 39, and looking back over my life so far, I was haunted by my failures, both personal and artistic.

Maybe it's no wonder Samuel Beckett's *Krapp's Last Tape* was on my mind. I had studied the play as an acting student in college, seen several productions over the years, and now, as a professional actor coming into the middle age of my career, hoped for the opportunity to one day play the role. (Coincidentally, 2008 marked the fiftieth anniversary of the first production of the play, with anniversary productions happening around the world.)

All around me I saw theater and film tapping the vein of American triumphalism, but from my vantage point, perched on the edge of 40, alienated and adrift, I felt a perverse affinity with Beckett's strange and shambling anti-hero. I found myself becoming deeply introspective around the themes of the play—specifically fear of aging, loss of love, the death of a parent (which resonated particularly since the recent death of my mother), and, of course, *failure*.

That much of Beckett's play involves the 69-year-old Krapp ruefully listening to an older, autobiographical tape—one that he made on *his own* 39th birthday—only deepened my identification. Now, in most (if not all) productions of the play, the fact of this older recording requires the creation of a "dummy" tape, recorded by the actor playing Krapp, putting on the voice of his younger self. I thought about this as an interesting problem for every production of the play and for any 69-year-old actor. And then a possible solution occurred to me: what if the tape was an authentic one, recorded by the selfsame actor thirty years before?

Wishful thinking, maybe, but I wanted to create the artifact that could be used in my hoped-for production of *Krapp's Last Tape* in 2038. On February 12, 2008, my actual 39th birthday, I performed an early sketch of *Krapp, 39*. It had a few of the elements of the current version, and culminated in the recording of that tape. The invited (captive) audience was made up of friends and colleagues who were expecting a birthday party, but instead of balloons and cake they got a blast of Beckett. It seemed like a fun idea, and after all, your birthday is the one day of the year when your friends are happy to indulge your foibles. And I think I had some notion that I could alleviate my sense of failure by going public with it, as channeled through Krapp. Performance art as emotional exorcism.

Nursing my obsession, I decided to pursue the project throughout my 39th year. I cobbled together a script (basically transcribed from the video document of the birthday performance) and submitted it to The New York International Fringe Festival. I was surprised and grateful when it was accepted, but there was a stumbling block: I suspected I would not be able to use any of Beckett's copyrighted text. Without that text, the piece would lose its reason for being.

I fretted for weeks trying on increasingly absurd ways of getting around the problem. Could I project a video of me reading the text, for example? Or could I induce someone in the audience to read it and I remain an "innocent" bystander? Could the reading of it happen offstage like an inciting event in Greek drama? Could I read it inaudibly? I threw out each new ridiculous idea. Time was running out and I was failing. But then the Eureka: *Failure!* It's the place I started from, after all, the governing principle! My quixotic desire to record the text, and my inability to do so, would be the starting point for a newly structured version of the piece. *Krapp, 39* would be a "documentary" play in which I would explore the themes of *Krapp's Last Tape*, but in very personal terms. It would be a marker for my own "end of youth," and at the same time would shadow and pay homage to Beckett's masterpiece. And it would finish in *failure*. Or *might*. (I don't want to give away the ending here.)

Even my attempts to obtain the rights, my "Search for Beckett," so to speak, would become part of the story, and email exchanges with the Beckett estate could be woven in as narrative threads. If nothing else, my appeals would keep the narrative of failure alive. Actually, the more I was rejected, the better it would be. (Here I should mention that the agents for the Beckett estate were, in fact, very gracious to me.)

Since I wanted the structure to mirror *Krapp's Last Tape*, I kept the excuse of a 39th birthday party as the frame. This meant pretending that every night I performed the piece would be my actual birthday, but that seemed to be a fair and amiable fiction.

In terms of design, I also took my cue from Beckett: a tape recorder and desk would be center. But in a sort of transposition of technology, instead of using a reel-to-reel device, I would use modern digital playback/recording devices. And to add yet another layer of recording, I would capture the action of the piece as it was happening with digital video cameras.

Contemplating haunted Krapp and his tapes, I began to think about personal archivism of all sorts—journals, diaries, letters, audio and videotapes—and raided my own keepsakes, letters, and notebooks for material that could be relevant to the piece. I had tapes of my own: All the way back to the conception of the project, I had been having phone conversations with two friends and colleagues around the themes of the play; first with Jon Dichter, a brilliant writer currently living on the West Coast, and then with George Demas, my director. I had recorded all of these conversations onto cassette tapes using a flimsy little device I bought at Radio Shack. I edited the tapes on my computer, pulling sequences that could be incorporated as elements into the production.

As for the journal entries, they are all connected to my own actual journals, but sometimes I invented scenarios, or created alternate versions of my past. Names were changed, of course. The process of shaping the entries and juxtaposing them with the recorded phone call sequences involved a lot of trial and error: process dancing with content, the past dancing with the present. Though they are the most prominent element of the play, the journal entries were the final thing to fall into place. In fact, I was still shaping them up until the day of the first performance at the Fringe Festival, and continued adding and rewriting as the run went on. Sometimes my tinkering would unbalance the play, and I had to circle back, but I tried to keep in mind that there could never be a final version of the play, only a *next* version.

That mindset was the key to the project. For a play about process, I had to stay *in process*. And for a play about failure, I never wanted to be *afraid to fail*.

# An Interview with Michael Laurence
# by William Hutchings

**William Hutchings (WH):** Is *Krapp, 39* the first and/or only such redactive "prequel" that was created by an author other than the original creator of the character?

**Michael Laurence (ML):** As far as I know, yes. (Interestingly, when I was working on *Hamlet in Bed*, I was studying all kinds of derivative *Hamlet* fictions, "prequels" and otherwise. There were scores in that case.) The brilliant Austrian writer Peter Handke has written an "echo" of *Krapp's Last Tape* in the voice of Krapp's unnamed lover ("She") called *Till Day You Do Part*. It exists in conversation with *Krapp's Last Tape*, but I'm not sure Handke ever intended it to be performed, and as far as I know, it has not been.

**WH:** The Beckett Estate has historically been quite protective of its rights to insist on specific aspects of production details of the plays—such as its longtime refusal to allow female casting in *Waiting for Godot*, for example. When you first conceived of doing a play about Krapp as a younger man, how confident were you that such a play could and would be given permission to be produced?

**ML:** Well, if I may answer your question sideways—in the beginning I was not at all concerned with fleshing out a younger version of Beckett's Krapp, per se, but with exploring my own fascination with the character. My *cathexis* with the character, if you will. It was never a play about Krapp, really, but a play about actors in general, and how they, we, I prepare to take on a role, how we can get lost in a role. At least, that's how it started. It ended up becoming a very personal reflection / meditation on the themes of *Krapp's Last Tape*: aging, death of a parent, the artist in the world, etc.

I approached the project more as an actor than as a writer, if that makes sense, and saw it more as a performance piece than as a play in the *well-made play* sense. (I realize these distinctions are a little hazy.) As such, it was more assembled than written. Magpie style. Documentary style. The letters and recorded conversations were laid out first; the journal entries were fleshed out later. I *did* hope for permission to record the "Krapp at Age 39" voiceover/tape sections from Beckett's play, but held out little hope that I would be granted the rights. Indeed, when the rights to use "any copyrighted text" from the original play were denied, I structured the piece around that denial. In other words, the play is built upon a promise unfulfilled—a Beckettian structure, I think, if there ever was one! So the denial of rights ended up being a gift—I think the play would have been much less affecting if it had ended as I had originally hoped, with the recitation of Beckett's words.

**WH:** At the end of *Krapp, 39*, via a letter from the owners of the rights to

*Krapp's Last Tape*, we hear: "having had a chance to peruse all of the materials you sent us.... I'm afraid we cannot authorize any use of Mr. Beckett's copyrighted text in your project. I'm so sorry I couldn't be of help with this but I must follow instructions from the Estate." That seems quite absolute, unambiguous, and final. Yet the letter's very next sentence is "Best of luck with *Krapp, 39*." There seems to be a direct contradiction here—despite which the play was staged successfully in both Europe and the United States. How was this apparent contradiction resolved?

**ML:** In truth, the letter that I read at the end is not a real letter—there is no Jane Miller, Esq., and no "The Literary Agency." I made all that up. It is based on a real letter from a representative of the Beckett estate, but it is fiction in its particulars. An "amiable fiction," as I like to say. In fact, the representatives of the estate were friendly to the project from the first time I contacted them. I explained to them that I was not in any way going for a re-working of Beckett's play, and I think they recognized the respectful disposition of my piece and saw it as a loving homage—which in many ways it *is*. The apparent contradiction that you note was squared by the fact that the only restriction they put on me was that I lift no "copyrighted text." And, of course, I did not. Many moments in my play are redolent of the original or dancing near to Beckett's language. And of course, the whole point was to identify situations in my own life that rhymed with situations/memories in Beckett's play. But not a single actual line of *Krapp's Last Tape* is used in *Krapp, 39*. The closest it comes is the final line: "I feel a fire in me now, and anything could happen," which, of course, is close to Beckett's "I wouldn't want them back. Not with the fire in me now." But, in a way, my final moment is an inversion of Beckett's. His speaker is rueful—we don't get the sense that he believes himself or what he is saying. My closing line is something close to an opposite meaning in light of its own specific context.

**WH:** Even so, did the script have to be re-submitted to the Beckett Estate for approval?

**ML:** No, at that point there was nothing for them to approve. I did invite them to the show—one of the agents came when it was in London and was complimentary. I was very pleased that over the course of various runs in various cities (New York, London, Dublin, Edinburgh) many leading scholars and interpreters of Beckett came to the show and loved it—including, in London, the great David Gothard, who had been one of Beckett's best friends and most important champions in the later part of Beckett's life.

**WH:** There is a remarkable "time-warp" in the two plays' chronology of *Krapp's Last Tape* and *Krapp, 39*, in that the original "old" Krapp relies only on a reel-to-reel tape recorder to evoke the voice of his own past self amid the darkness—whereas "younger" Krapp lives in a room that is cluttered with sophisticated twenty-first-century state-of-the-art technology. Was that done in part to differentiate clearly your Krapp from Beckett's?

**ML:** Not exactly to differentiate, no. I like that in terms of technology and design my play rhymes with Beckett's, but inexactly. Since *Krapp, 39* is about an actor (me) trying to crack a role in the here and now, I thought it might be disingenuous not to use the tools available to me in the here and now. Beckett's play is pure poetry and the surrounding inky darkness is the *sine qua non* of the piece. Mine is a mix of poetic and prosaic, and as such, is more cluttered. It's a play about the making of play.

**WH:** You have mentioned that you hope to act the role of Krapp when you arrive at age 69 yourself. Would that be a later version of your own technologically enhanced Krapp in the now-unimaginable future? Or yourself starring in Beckett's play when you are "age-appropriate" for the part? Or both?

**ML:** No, here I am a purist. It is my hope to do exactly what I say in the opening phone call of the piece: I want to do Beckett's play exactly as he conceived it—reel-to-reel and all. And I will be using the tape I made of myself reading younger Krapp's lines. So, in a sense, I will be acting with myself across a thirty-year chasm.

**WH:** There are actually three other "speaking" characters in the play, though none of them ever appears on stage—and they are in fact recorded voices. Each speaks only via recorded telephone messages—not only a defining trait of the twenty-first century, but also an updated techno-counterpart of "old" Krapp's reel-to-reels. Is it also a deliberate manifestation of twenty-first century alienation and anomie?

**ML:** Hmm. Yes. I like your wording: "twenty-first century anomie." Recorded phone messages are literal "ghosts in the machine." I love telephones and answering machines, especially older, twentieth-century versions of each; they are charged, haunted objects. And *Krapp's Last Tape* is nothing if not a ghost story. All the best stories are.

**WH:** In one of your stage directions, you specify that your character avoids eye contact with the audience until nearly the end of the play. Why is that detail so specific and so important?

**ML:** Well, it was somewhat intuitive—but it felt important to really stick to the idea that Michael is in his own, private space—that all this business of reading journal entries and listening to tape-recorded phone calls is part of his own private preparation for doing the role, all leading up to the recording. And that he's videotaping himself as he goes through this preparation, as part of the preparation, and to create a record and an archive of this preparation. I wanted it to feel private and personal, not *performed*.

But then, of course, at the end, he reads the letter from the agent and the whole endeavor is rendered moot, although not meaningless! So, in *that* moment, he needs to burst the bubble on his whole project—to bring it down to the truth of the room in the new here and now. *Himself on this very night, with this very audience, etc.*

**WH:** So far, you are the only actor to have played your role and namesake—and you change the date of your character's 39th birthday to the actual date of the performance. If the occasion arose would you permit some other actor to be cast in your role, or do you consider the play to be exclusively your own?

**ML:** I would be thrilled for another actor to perform the piece—with updated names and dates!

### Note

*Acknowledgments:* I am grateful to Michael Laurence for his cooperation and support throughout my research—and specifically for his generosity in permitting me to quote from the script of *Krapp, 39*. His willingness to share his "Notes on the Development of the Piece (Or Notes on Failure)" has enhanced the understanding of our readership in thoughtful and candid ways—as does his extraordinarily insightful and candid interview.

### Works Cited

Laurence, Michael. *Krapp, 39. Plays and Playwrights 2009,* edited by Martin Denton. New York Theatre Experience, 2009, pp. 335–366.

# Waiting for Rothko

## Doug Phillips

### Abstract

*Every work of drama, by virtue of its temporality, keeps us waiting, but not every drama calls us back to its beginning, there to think about the play, once more, in its unfolding. It's the sort of repetition-with-a-difference that Didi and Gogo revile, but that theatregoers revere, for the simple reason that the very best drama is drama that not only keeps us returning, but keeps us thinking, and waiting. One such drama is John Logan's* Red *(2009), a play about the painter Mark Rothko and his acceptance, then rejection, of a lucrative commission in the late 1950s to paint murals for the posh Four Seasons Restaurant in New York City. But the play also dramatizes Rothko's artistic process, a process as dependent on waiting and thinking as it is on paint and brush. From this process came Rothko's color-field paintings, the work for which he is best known, the work he frequently characterized as "dramas." And the demand these dramas make of us (the demand, in fact, of all great theatre) is precisely the demand of* Red: *that we attune ourselves—for the sake of our future possibilities—to thinking and waiting.*

> Yes, we were now in that enchanted calm which they
> say lurks at the heart of every commotion.
> —Herman Melville, *Moby Dick*

> If I ever forget my lines in Shakespeare,
> I always say, "Crouch we here awhile and lurk!"
> —Carnforth Greville, *A Midwinter's Tale*

## Time's Winged Chariot

In milder, less murderous ways, the drama of your life is playing out in a manner best described as *Hamletian*. No, I'm not suggesting that you wish to kill your uncle, or that you have a *thing* for Gertrude, though—*who knows*? But whatever it is, something this moment in your life needs to be acted upon: something needs to get done, or, at the very least, something needs to get said. And you want desperately to say or do this thing, but you also know from experience, in particular your experience of *Hamlet*, that things said or done, the choosing, say, of this path over the other—however equally or unequally worn those paths appear to be—is to upturn (potentially anyway) the delicate balance of things as they are: to gather a storm, to set off a catastrophe, to sever a tie beyond repair. "Simply to choose," writes the poet Philip Larkin, stops "all ways up but one" (274). Worse yet, your choice, whatever it is, will come back to haunt: you will tell of it one day with a *sigh*, but whether that sigh will be of relief or regret is anyone's guess.[1] Haunting every decision, then, is not only something akin to the ghost of Hamlet's father, but to what Jacques Derrida calls the "ghost of the undecidable" ("Force of Law" 24), the notion that every decision, if indeed a *real* decision, could have been otherwise; and no decision, if a *real* decision, can be wholly justified.[2] Plus, insists Derrida, "the decision, if there is to be one, must advance towards a *future* which is not known, which cannot be anticipated" (italics mine; "Force of Law" 37). Of course, instead of acting you might do as Hamlet does and, for a time, delay; or as Didi and Gogo do, and wait. This is another way of saying (and saying what's obvious, I know) that drama, whether of stage or life, is often most fruitful when it compels us *not* toward acting but toward tarrying, toward hesitation—toward inhabiting (however briefly), alongside Ishmael, "an enchanted calm inside a commotion" (Melville 558). What's less obvious, in this age of rapidly melting ice caps and vapidly rapid un-presidential tweets, is whether we've any time left to wait, to think, to *crouch awhile and lurk*. To tarry, it seems almost certain to me, is to invite time's winged chariot to hurry-on near.

## Lean Forward, Lean into It

>...to stitch a caesura in the pulsebeat of the world.
>—Cormac McCarthy, *Blood Meridian*

John Logan's 2009 play *Red*[3] begins the way it ends, with the painter Mark Rothko standing before us, pausing, *staring*. Not at *us*, no, though it feels that way, this man clad in ill-fitting clothes, clothes "spattered with specks of glue and paint" (9), staring behind thick glasses at what we come to understand is a painting, one we might assume has been made in a similar mood and color (of bruising grays and blood maroons) as the other canvasses we actually do see on stage, all of them commissioned for the newly opened Four Seasons restaurant in New York, in 1959. Rothko's stare is keen and deep and accentuated by the sound of contemplative classical music, as well as by a long drag on his cigarette, when Ken, an aspiring young artist, arrives on the scene to take up his position as Rothko's newly hired assistant. Rothko's opening salvo toward both his new charge, and to those of us seated in the theatre who feel his gaze, is "What do you see?" (9). But before Ken can respond, Rothko tells him to "wait" (9). Then to "stand closer" (9). Then this:

> Let it work on you…. Let it spread out. Let it wrap its arms around you; let it *embrace* you, filling even your peripheral vision so nothing else exists or has ever existed or will ever exist. Let the picture do its work—But work with it. Meet it halfway for God's sake! Lean forward, lean into it. Engage with it! … Now, what do you see?—Wait, wait, wait! [9].

We, the audience, along with Ken the assistant, are commanded to *wait* upon the painting, to tarry in front of it for a time—to be, in Rothko's words, *embraced* by the painting, but also to *engage* with it, while again being told to *wait* upon it.[4] Rothko's approach—his process, his aesthetic considerations, indeed his *philosophy*—recalls Derrida's own "philosophy of hesitation."[5] Rothko was known in fact to sit and dwell before his canvasses for intensely long stretches of time before acting upon them, preferring to wait upon them instead. "Most of painting is thinking," he will tell Ken. "Ten percent is putting paint on the canvas. The rest is waiting" (16). But what exactly are we and he and Ken waiting for? How, in other words, might we think about the act of waiting, and about waiting to act?

On this subject, on advising others what to *think* about *waiting*, I am, I confess, the very worst person for the job. However, given my lifelong ineptitude for the practice of waiting, I'm someone who, lacking all expertise in the field, is most in need of the theory, which, I suppose, is why I'm taking it on here. Let me put it this way: Had I been a participant in that marshmallow experiment done years ago among wee ones to predict a correlation between their capacity to wait and their *future* successes in life, I would have failed *spectacularly*. There's no doubt in my mind, in fact, that as soon as the experimenter had closed the door behind her, I would have exhibited the same disciplined restraint toward the marshmallow that a lion does the meaty gazelle. If then I am here to ruminate on waiting as a way of life, which I am, it's not because I'm any good at it (no better than those tramps who, at every turn, want to hang themselves rather than wait any longer for Godot). Rather, I'm here because I've been wondering of late if I wouldn't be a little bit better at life if only I were a little bit better at waiting. For this reason, the drama that continues to interest me the most these days is drama that keeps me waiting—and thinking.

## Baby, What Did You Do That For?

> But wait. And only wait, Uncle Vanya, we shall rest.
> —Anton Chekhov, *Uncle Vanya*

As a way into this meditation on waiting, and its dramatic unfolding in Logan's play about Rothko, I want to begin first with a name. Actually, two names, both of them highly improbable, but absolutely *real*, I assure you. The first is Eddie Waitkus, baseball legend and inspiration behind the 1952 novel *The Natural*, written by Rothko's good friend Bernard Malamud. In 1949, Waitkus was lured to a Chicago hotel room by an obsessed and deranged fan named Ruth-Ann Steinhagen; upon entering her hotel room, he was shot in the chest with a .22 caliber rifle, barely missing his heart. Waitkus eventually recovered but he lost his game; he would never again be the baseball phenomenon he once was. After taking the shot in the chest and collapsing onto the floor, Waitkus, testified Steinhagen, looked up at her in disbelief and asked: "Baby, what did you do that for?" When, in 1972, he died of cancer at the age of 53, Waitkus had *waited* and wondered for 23 years why Steinhagen had done this to him, but he would never get an answer. On that subject, she was silent the rest of her life, channeling for the next 63 years, it seems, Wittgenstein's closing dictum to the *Tractatus*: "Whereof one cannot speak, thereof one must be silent" (189).

Which brings me to the second of the two improbable names.

A decade before Waitkus was shot in 1949, Samuel Beckett was walking in Paris when a pimp by the name of Robert-Jules Prudent stabbed him in the chest, nearly missing his heart. Beckett, like Waitkus, would eventually recover; but rather than lose his game, Beckett would go on to produce one of the world's great bodies of literature. Weeks after the stabbing, in court, Beckett had occasion to confront his attacker, asking Prudent, in effect: "Baby, what did you do that for?" (That's not quite the way he phrased the question, by the way; if my sources can be trusted, Beckett actually said: "What the fuck?"). To which Prudent-the-pimp replied: "I don't know why. I'm sorry" (Knowlson 283). Beckett, too, would wait and wonder his entire life for a meaningful explanation for why he was randomly stabbed by a random stranger, but Godot, we know, would never show.[6]

Waitkus's question, it would appear, is less a point of departure (as most questions are) than a terminus of confusion—and silence. It's the sort of thing said at the end of something, after the possibility of intervention is forever foreclosed, as when, that time, your friend tried to light fireworks from the top of his head: *Baby, what did you do that for?*[7] More than a baffled reaction to an irrational action, to life's absurdity, Waitkus's question also expresses, I think, a certain *tragic* vision of life, one which Rothko himself sought to evoke in his paintings, and which he dwells upon everywhere in *Red*. To begin, when Ken asks Rothko how he knows when a painting is completed, Rothko replies: "There's tragedy in every brush stroke" (12). Later, Rothko relays to Ken what he believes is the core of the human condition, which can only be understood as tragic: "Everything worthwhile ends. We are in the perpetual process now: creation, maturation, cessation .... The eternal cycles grind on, generations pass away, hope turns arid" (18). Rothko then mourns his own encroaching sense of Lear-like irrelevancy and loneliness: "Tragic, really, to grow superfluous in your own lifetime" (18). After insisting that Ken read Nietzsche's *The Birth of Tragedy*, Rothko berates him for failing to "think more" (30) in his assessment of Nietzsche's ideas about the Dionysian and Apollonian, especially as those ideas might be applied to an understanding of Rothko's work: "You miss the tragedy. The point is always the tragedy" (30). And "our tragedy," Rothko tells Ken, is that "we exist—all of us, for all time—in state of perpetual dissonance" (31–32), which recalls Derrida's notion of "the ghost of the undecidable" and its perpetual haunting.

Confronted with a real and meaningful and life-altering decision—"to be or not to be," for example—we may want to have it both ways (just as Hamlet wants it), but in the end we can only go in one direction. We must choose a path. And in choosing we're caught in what Derrida calls "the paradoxical condition of every decision: it cannot be deduced from a form of knowledge of which it would simply be the effect, conclusion, or explication. It structurally breaches knowledge and is thus destined to nonmanifestation; a decision is, in the end, always secret" (*Gift of Death* 77).

In other words, if a decision is in anyway programmatic—the result of a foolproof calculation that admits of no remainder, no ambiguity, no alternatives, no secret (in the sense that we're never entirely privy to *why* we do what we do)—then it wouldn't be a *real* decision after all, but rather a computed output determined by a computed input. In contrast, a *real* decision, writes Derrida, requires something like a *leap of faith*, because whatever reasoning there is behind a given decision, that reasoning can never be entirely accounted for; rather, every decision is the result of a multiplicity of reasons (even those we are unconscious of), in conflict with and forever haunted by a multiplicity of reasons for why we might have chosen otherwise. That is, any decision, like any dream, is *overdetermined*, which means for Derrida "the instant of decision is madness" (*Gift of Death* 65). One need only revisit *Hamlet* to know exactly what he's talking about.

To return, then, to Waitkus's question ("Baby, what did you do that for?"), it's a *tragic* rejoinder to the *tragic* proposition: *What should I do?* None of us can know with certainty the consequences of our decisions, of what will come of our actions, and it's this uncertainty that defines, in part, our tragic condition. Hannah Arendt explains this predicament of uncertainty in *The Human Condition*, first published in 1958, the year in which *Red* is partially set: "The reason why we are never able to foretell with certainty the outcome and end of any action is simply that action has no end. The process of a single deed can quite literally endure throughout time until mankind itself has come to an end" (233).

In light of this uncertainty we hear in Waitkus's question an indictment of the decision to act in the first place: an indictment of the decision to step *toward* the edge rather than to stay put, to wait, and to *think more*, as Rothko urges.

Orestes, in Aeschylus's great tragic trilogy,[8] has his own brief moment of stepping away from the edge, of forestalling the certainty of violence, before having his revenge. And while he waits, Orestes, like Hamlet after him, and like Beckett's tramps, weighs the question: "What should I do?" He knows, as the Chorus reminds him, that "the one who acts must suffer" (192). But *why* should this be the case? Again I defer to Arendt, who, in an extraordinary passage, writes of "the burden of irreversibility and unpredictability, from which the action process draws its very strength" (233). She adds that

> he who acts never quite knows what he is doing, that he always becomes "guilty" of consequences he never intended or even foresaw, that no matter how disastrous and unexpected the consequences of his deed he can never undo it, that the process he starts is never consummated unequivocally in one single deed or event, and that its very meaning never discloses itself to the actor but only to the backward glance of the historian who himself does not act [233].

For his part, Rothko feels intense *guilt*, horror even, for the potentially disastrous and unexpected consequences of his own deed, namely the betrayal of his paintings to the highest bidder, in this case the Four Seasons, where obscenely wealthy patrons will consume obscenely priced meals while feeling *cultured* (if utterly unmoved) in the presence of his work. When Ken calls him out—asking, in effect, *Baby, what did you do that for?*—Rothko attempts to rationalize, without much luck, his decision. "I didn't enter into this capriciously, you know. I *thought* about it" (57), he tells Ken. "And of course it appealed to my vanity. I'm a human being too. But still I *hesitated*. The very same thoughts: is it corrupt? is it immoral? just feeding the whims of the bourgeoisie? should I do it?" (57; italics mine). Despite his hesitation, his moment of delay, Rothko decides to accept the commission, though he fears he will meet the fate of the biblical Daniel: that he, Rothko, will be "weighed in the balance and found wanting" (47).

It's not until the final scene of the play, after Rothko returns from a visit to the Four Seasons, that he bewails his decision. He begins his lament with a description of the "voices" of the diners:

> It's the chatter of monkeys and the barking of jackals. It's not human ... and no one looks at anything and no one thinks about anything and all they do is chatter and bark and eat and the knives and forks click and clack and the words cut and the teeth snap and snarl [62–63].

He then confesses to Ken his great overriding fear: "In that place—*there*—will live my paintings for all time" (63). "I wonder," Rothko asks Ken, "Do you think they'll ever forgive me?" (63).

## Zugzwang

> Nothing to be done.
> —Samuel Beckett, *Waiting for Godot*

What, really, should any of us do? In the game of chess, "Zugzwang" is to be in a situation in which the most viable move is to do nothing—and yet we must eventually make our move in chess, just as we must in life. Though Pascal warned that "All of humanity's problems stem from man's inability to sit quietly in a room alone" (37), he also knew that such self-imposed confinement could never be a long-term solution to our tragic condition. In any case, to stay quietly alone in one's room, in solitary confinement, is itself an action, never mind a particular form of punishment—cruel and unusual—for the incarcerated. At the very least there's the suffering that comes with being left alone with one's own morbid thoughts ("caught without people or drink" [116], as Larkin writes in "Aubade") that may lead inexorably to one's own self-destruction via belt or shiv or an open window. Toward the end of his own life, Rothko gravitated increasingly toward solitude, accompanied always by a bottle, a pack of smokes, and an ever-deepening appreciation for the tragic, until at last, alone one morning in his studio, he did himself in by opening his veins. *Baby, what did you do that for?*

## There's No Future to That Question

> All other ways are closed to you
> Except the way already chosen.
> —T.S. Eliot, *Murder in the Cathedral*

Perhaps every work of drama, like every life, every love affair, every moment of being, and every suicide, bounces between these two questions for those caught in, and affected by, the action at hand:

1. *What should I do?*
2. *Baby, what did you do that for?*

The tension between them in *Red* arises not only in relation to Rothko's eventual suicide in 1970, a decade after the principal action (1958–1959) of this one-act play (and hinted at throughout its five scenes), but also in relation to three other central events of the play: (1) Rothko's acceptance of the Four Seasons commission (which occurs *before* the start of the play); (2) his later rejection of the Four Seasons commission; (3) his firing of Ken at the play's conclusion. Each course of action is in *reaction* to the question—consciously or unconsciously posed—*What should I do?* And in each case Rothko's action—because *act* he must—prompts Ken to ask (directly or indirectly): *What did you do that for?* Throughout *Red*, then, Rothko and Ken push one another, in Rothko's words, to "Think more" (30). Ken pushes Rothko to *think more* about the Four Seasons commission, and about his Oedipal-like rivalry with the up-and-coming Pop artists; and Rothko pushes Ken to *think more* about painting by way of a deep immersion in the works of Nietzsche, Freud, Jung, Aeschylus, Sophocles, Schopenhauer, Shakespeare, Byron, Turgenev—all of whom Rothko himself revered and thought foundational for anyone to become an artist in his own right. This, in effect, is the arc of the dialogue in the play, a play Logan might have aptly titled *Discourse on Thinking*, after Martin Heidegger's own book, first published in 1959—the year in which *Red* is partially set. In *Discourse on Thinking*, half of which is a dramatic dialogue, Heidegger makes a case for thinking—for *thinking more*—in relation to *waiting*. He also makes a case for waiting in relation to what he calls an "openness to the mystery" (55), which is another way of saying an *openness to the future*.

In her essay "Writing as Reading," Susan Sontag relays an anecdote about the jazz musician Duke Ellington, who, after being confronted with an unanswerable query, simply replied: "there's no future to that question" (qtd. 267). It's a retort I could easily imagine both Steinhagen and Prudent giving their respective victims as to why they did what they did. I hear it too in Rothko, in response to the *why* of his suicide: "There's no future to that question," he tells us. It seems also to be the retort to those other considerations of the play: to the *Why*, for example, of Rothko's acceptance of the Four Seasons commission in the first place. Was it for the money ($35,000), which, in today's dollars, would amount to nearly two million? Was it for the prestige—the fact that his work was chosen above anyone else's? Was it the prospect of having a place to house a series of his work, a place he initially envisioned as complementary to them—"a *place* created just for them. A place of reflection and safety.... A place of contemplation" (56)? Was it to avenge himself upon an obscenely expensive establishment—to create an environment, a predominant mood, in which a wealthy patron of the Four Seasons would feel "trapped in a room where all the doors and windows are bricked up, so all he can do is butt his head against the wall forever" (58)? Was it to put the patrons of the Four Seasons off their meals, a way of making them feel doomed? And did Rothko back out of the commission for the simple reason, as he tells Ken, "I do get depressed when I think how people are going to see my pictures" (55)? That is, did Rothko really worry "If they're going to be unkind" (55)? After all, he tells Ken, "Selling a picture is like sending a blind child into a room full of razor blades. It's going to get hurt and it's never been hurt before, it doesn't know what hurt is" (55). Or did Rothko back away from the commission on the strength of Ken's indictment: "Just admit your hypocrisy: the High Priest of Modern Art is painting a wall in the Temple of Consumption" (56)?

Could it be—as I have suggested already—that there is no one answer to any of these questions for the not-so-simple reason that every act, like every dream, is *overdetermined*—that is, every act, however it might be simply reasoned, is ultimately the result of a concatenation of events unfathomably complex and entangled? To say of a suicide, for example, that he killed himself because of x may offer closure for those who are grieving, but it conveniently obscures the long history and twists of fate that led to the suicide's last gasp. All of which is to say if there is a future to the question—*Baby, what did you do that for?*—what difference would it make in our knowing the answer? After all, warns Sophocles in *Oedipus Rex*, "How dreadful knowledge of the truth can be when there's no help in truth" (17). Perhaps here Elias Canetti's position should stand for us all: "I'm fed up with seeing through people; it's so easy, and it gets you nowhere" (49). There is, however, more than one way to conceive of the future. And how we conceive of the future has much to do, I think, with how we might experience Rothko's art, in particular the color-field paintings of his most mature work, which Rothko himself frequently associated with—and theorized as—a form of drama, tragedy especially.

Whatever its form, drama (drama = *dran* = *do, act*) is tethered at once to the past—to what has happened—and to the future: to what will happen, even if what happens next is nothing at all, as when Gogo and Didi (from Beckett's *Godot*) *do not move*. Drama is tethered, in other words, to Orestes's ever-pressing question, which always points to the future, and which haunts us all: *What should I do?* This, I have argued, is the question at stake in Logan's play, which, action-wise, centers around Rothko's uneasy acceptance of a commission to paint murals for the Four Seasons restaurant, "a place," Rothko lamented, "where the richest bastards in New York will come to feed and show off" (58). He also confessed: "I accepted this assignment as a challenge, with strictly malicious intentions. I hope to paint something that will ruin the appetite of every son of a bitch who ever eats in that room" (58). Rothko, however, could make no headway toward answering the question (*What will I do?*) until he took time off from his work-in-progress, in the spring of 1959, to *wait*. And *think*. In her study of Rothko, Annie Cohen-Solal writes of his hiatus as one "which unfolds as a play in three acts" (159). That is, he traveled to Naples where he tarried for a time among the ruins (especially among the Greek temples in nearby Paestum) and ruminated over the integrity of his artistic commitments, as well his own his tragic vision, neither of which fit the frame of a loud and obscenely priced restaurant in the service of millionaires. He concluded that his acceptance of the Four Seasons commission was nothing short of an abomination, an embarrassment. And so when he returned home to New York he promptly cancelled the commission—returning in full the $35,000 he had been paid in advance and telling his benefactors: "anyone who eats that kind of food for that kind of money in that kind of joint will never look at a painting of mine" (63). As for the nature of Rothko's long-held tragic vision, nurtured even further by his time tarrying abroad, it's one deeply informed by his reading of the ancient Greeks, Aeschylus especially, as well as his deep absorption of Nietzsche's *The Birth of Tragedy*, about which he spends much of the play schooling his assistant, Ken. "The point," Rothko tells him, "is always the tragedy" (30). And, he warns, tragedy *awaits*: "One day the black will swallow the red" (28). The irony of course is that Ken, whose parents, we learn, were brutally murdered when he was a young boy, hardly needs lessons in tragedy.

## The Absolute Future

> I think of my pictures as dramas; the shapes in the pictures are performers.... Neither the action nor the actors can be anticipated, or described in advance. They begin as an unknown adventure in an unknown space.—Mark Rothko, *Possibilities*

It's precisely this notion of tragedy in relation to *waiting*, and the notion of waiting in relation to the future, that most left me *thinking* after I had occasion to see a revival of *Red* last summer in London—the very city in which the play premiered a decade ago in 2009. And all of Rothko's ruminations on Nietzsche in the play led me to revisit the philosopher's work, wherein he writes: "There is only one hope and one guarantee for the future of humanity: it consists in his *retention of the sense for the tragic*" (213). But what exactly is this tragic disposition? What constitutes a tragic vision? In her essay "The Death of Tragedy," Susan Sontag offers the following: "the tragic vision ... is about the emptiness and arbitrariness of the world, the ultimate meaninglessness of all moral values, and the terrifying rule of death" (136). Defined this way, tragedy can no more be evaded than it can be understood. It escapes all reason, justification, explanation—which maybe explains why trying to *explain* a Rothko painting, infused as it is with a tragic sense of life, remains always a futile gesture to anyone who's ever tried. Two years before he took on the Four Seasons commission, Rothko himself had this to say about his own tragic vision: "I'm interested only in expressing basic human emotions—tragedy, ecstasy, doom, and so on—

and the fact that lots of people break down and cry when confronted with my pictures shows that I *communicate* those basic human emotions.... The people who weep before my pictures are having the same religious experience I had when I painted them" (119).

If what accounts for all this weeping is a confrontation with the tragic, with ecstasy, with doom—with, that is, a Messianic arrival of some sort—then the tragic so-defined is something that exists outside the realm of what Derrida calls the "future present"—the future, says Derrida, whose arrival we can predict or calculate or anticipate with some measure of certainty.

There is, however, another future in which to experience Rothko's work—and this future Derrida calls the "absolute." For Derrida, the "absolute future" is one we *cannot* predict or calculate, but that we must *wait* upon to arrive, to unfold itself; it's the coming catastrophe or capital-E Event that will so upturn our lives that life itself cannot go on as usual.[9] To exist in such a state of tarrying—to wait, say, upon a Rothko painting (just as he commands us to do)—necessitates, then, something akin to Keats's Negative Capability: the ability to exist in a state of uncertainty while remaining open to an uncertain future; it is to tarry without losing our minds—or, as the kids say, without losing our *shit*. It means embracing what George Steiner, in his book *The Death of Tragedy*, calls "the wanton, mysterious choice of destiny" (5); it means, therefore, being open to the *mysterious*, as Heidegger insists; it means, in Nietzsche's words, learning to love our fate. It's also what was meant, I think, by the poet Paul Celan (who, incidentally, killed himself the same year Rothko did), when he said of a poem that it "can be a message in a bottle, sent out in the—not always greatly hopeful—belief that somewhere and sometime it could wash up on land" (396). Once more, in Rothko's words: "Most painting is thinking.... Ten percent is putting paint onto the canvas. The rest is waiting" (16).

The drama of Rothko's paintings teaches us to wait in the way that the suicide teaches us to wait, for the very reason that, with respect to both, there is no *future present*—there is no *future present* to the question: *Baby, what did you do that for?* In *On Tarrying*, Joseph Vogl puts the problem this way: "Tarrying, we could say, is a program that searches for the unsolved question and problems behind given solutions and answers. In tarrying, the tragic hero is not only lost in the labyrinth of his actions and their consequences; he is also exposed to the urging of a violent questioning, to a problematic being that persists, disguised and deferred, in all instances of its dramatic solution" (36).

In other words, there's only the *absolute future*, the one we can only wait upon, but which, like Godot, may never arrive. And should it arrive we will, perhaps, like the young woman in Hopkins's poem, weep and know why.[10]

## Rothknow

> After Anne Sexton turned on her car's engine in a closed
> garage to commit suicide, she sat drinking vodka while waiting.
> —David Markson, *Reader's Block*

In his biography of Rothko, James Breslin reflects on the *drama* of suicide—Rothko's own, yes, but also the dramatic act of suicide in general, calling "it a *real* act, performed *theatrically*" (521). As for the drama of Rothko's own suicide, the details have been, for the last fifty years, well-established[11]: that he was discovered in his 69th Street (Manhattan) studio by his assistant on the morning of February 25, 1970. That the day of his death was the very day the murals originally painted for the Four Seasons arrived in London, at the Tate Gallery. That he had cut open both his arms, just below the elbows. That he used a double-edge razor, one side of which he held carefully with tissue. That there was a *hesitation* cut on his left arm. That otherwise he meant business, as evidenced by the veins he cut, and just how deeply. That there was lots of blood. That he had taken time to remove and fold his trousers across a nearby chair. That he was wearing only an undershirt, long johns, and long black socks. That he was ill of health. That he was alcoholic. That his second marriage was on the skids. That the first authority on the scene was a thirty-six-year-old Irish cop who had never heard of Rothko, but who appointed 24/7 security after being informed that the works in Rothko's studio were worth thousands upon thousands of dollars. That the medical examiner who determined Rothko's death to be suicide mistakenly misspelled Rothko's name, re-christening him in the case file with the improbable name of "Rothknow."

It's difficult to imagine what Rothko himself might have thought about the mistake—whether he would have read it ("Rothknow") as a claim for having known some dark impenetrable truth, of the sort to be experienced in his paintings; or whether he would have understood it as an omen, a warning, like that of Silenus's, whose hard capital-T truth about life is that it would be best never to have been born; and that the next best thing is to get out as quickly as you can. In any case, *there's no future to that question*. Rothko, painting as he did, remarked in an address to Yale University that he was "desperately searching for those pockets of silence where we can root and grow" (157). Those of us who find ourselves ever compelled toward his paintings, who, in the Rothko room at the Tate Modern, undergo all that we've ever known of a so-called religious experience, *wait* upon them: we wait and search for those pockets of silence where maybe, just maybe, we can root and grow.

# One Side Will Have to Go

> *ROTHKO is unsure.*
> *He looks at the painting.*
> *The moment is passing.*
> *He is getting desperate.*
> —John Logan, *Red* (stage directions)

The American critic Alfred Kazin noted that "What gets us closer to a work of art is not instruction but another work of art" (7). Philip Larkin's poem "Aubade" is one such work of art that can, I think, help us get closer to Rothko's own. It's as if the speaker of the poem, in his meditation on "unresting death," is bearing witness not only to the morning, but to the murals Rothko created for the Four Seasons. He embodies what Rothko had hoped for the person who was willing to meet his work halfway, to be embraced by it, to engage with it, but most of all to *wait* upon it, as one might death itself:

> And so it stays just on the edge of vision,
> A small unfocused blur, a standing chill
> That slows each impulse down to indecision.
> ...
> It stands plain as a wardrobe, what we know,
> Have always known, know that we can't escape,
> Yet can't accept. One side will have to go [116].

## Notes

1. In Robert Frost's most famous poem, "The Road Not Taken," the speaker anticipates a future—"Somewhere ages and ages hence" (105)—in which he is recounting his moment of *crisis* (in the root sense of "decision"), his hesitation before acting, his ultimate choice, and the "sigh" (105) with which he imagines himself one day explaining his choice to others. There is nothing in the poem, however, to suggest whether the "sigh" is one of joy or grief.

2. For more on Derrida's consideration (and deconstruction) of what it means to make a decision, see his books *The Gift of Death* and *Adieu to Emmanuel Levinas*, as well as his essay "Force of Law: The 'Mystical Foundation of Authority.'"

3. Much, if not practically all, of Rothko's dialogue in *Red* is comprised of things Rothko actually said or wrote, re-presented in the play verbatim. In 2018, *Red* was revived in London, with a reprisal of Alfred Molina's role as Rothko, which premiered a decade ago, in 2009, at London's Donmar Warehouse.

4. In his introduction to Martin Heidegger's *Discourse on Thinking* (1959), John Anderson offers the following commentary on "waiting" as it is analyzed in "Conversation on a Country Path," the dialogue that makes up the second half of the book:

> Waiting is a human activity, of course; but Heidegger wants to show that it has a deeper significance and involves a reference beyond the merely human, the subjective. Normally, when we wait we wait *for* something which interests us or which can provide us with what we want. When we wait in this human way, waiting involves our desires, goals, and needs. But waiting need not be so definitely colored by our nature. There is a sense in which we can wait without knowing for what we wait. We may wait, in this sense, without waiting for anything; for anything, that is, which could be grasped and expressed in subjective human terms. In this sense we simply wait;

and in this sense waiting may come to have a reference beyond man. The difference between these two kinds of waiting may be expressed by saying that when we wait in a merely human way we wait *for,* whereas in the deeper sense of waiting we wait *upon* [22–23].

    5. Simon Critchley, in *The Ethics of Deconstruction*, broadly describes Derrida's practice of deconstruction as a "'philosophy' of hesitation" (42). He also details Derrida's longstanding preoccupation with "undecidability," beginning with Derrida's earliest published essay, which, incidentally, was "originally given as a paper in 1959" (63), the year—it so happens—when *Red* is partially set.

    6. Coincidentally, Beckett was composing *Waiting for Godot* the year Waitkus was shot, in 1949. And *Godot* was first published in 1953, just six months after the publication of *The Natural*, Malamud's novel about Waitkus.

    7. In 2015, in Maine, a 22-year old man (boy?) celebrating the Fourth of July made the fateful decision to launch fireworks from the top of his head. It didn't go well. He's dead.

    8. *The Oresteia* is one of several ancient tragic works that Rothko deeply admired, was influenced by, and studied for what it could it teach him about the tragic sense of life. On the subject of Aeschylus and waiting, Rothko wrote: "The dramas of Aeschylus and Sophocles represent a *moment* of reconciliation when Apollo and Dionysus establish on this stage a *moment* of domestic bliss in which they *wait* for each other to speak… in spite of their irreconcilable strife at all other *moments* involving alternate triumphs and defeats for one at the expense of the other" (qtd. in Breslin 199; italics mine).

    9. For a detailed and pellucid explanation of Derrida's concepts of the "future present" and the "absolute future," see John D. Caputo's book *Truth: Philosophy in Transit* (107–108)

    10. Cf. Gerard Manley Hopkins's poem "Spring and Fall": "And yet you will weep and know why" (50).

    11. For details, see James Breslin's biography of Rothko.

## WORKS CITED

Aeschylus. *The Oresteia*. Translated by Robert Fagles. Penguin, 1979.
Arendt, Hannah. *The Human Condition*. University of Chicago Press, 1958.
Beckett, Samuel. *Waiting for Godot*. 1954. Grove, 1982.
Breslin, James E. B. *Mark Rothko: A Biography*. University of Chicago Press, 1993.
Canetti, Elias. *The Human Province*. Translated by Joachim Neugroschel. New York: Seabury, 1978.
Caputo, John D. *Truth: Philosophy in Transit*. Penguin, 2013.
Celan, Paul. *Selected Poems and Prose of Paul Celan*. Translated by John Felstiner. Norton, 2001.
Chekhov, Anton. *Uncle Vanya*. Translated by Vlada Chernomordik (adapted by David Mamet). Grove, 1988.
Cohen-Solal, Annie. *Mark Rothko: Toward the Light in the Chapel*. Yale University Press, 2013.
Critchley, Simon. *The Ethics of Deconstruction: Derrida and Levinas*, 3d ed. Edinburgh University Press, 2014.
Derrida, Jacques. "Force of Law: The 'Mystical Foundation of Authority.'" *Deconstruction and the Possibility of Justice*. Edited by Drucilla Cornell, Michel Rosenfeld, and David Grey Carlson. Routledge, 1992.
———. *The Gift of Death*. Translated by David Wills. University of Chicago Press, 1995.
Eliot, T.S. *Murder in the Cathedral*. 1935. Harcourt, 1963.
Frost, Robert. *The Poetry of Robert Frost: The Collected Poems*. Edited by Edward Connery Lathem. Henry Holt, 1969.
Heidegger, Martin. *Discourse on Thinking*. 1959. Translated by John M. Anderson. Harper & Row, 1966.
Hopkins, Gerard Manley. *Poems and Prose*. Penguin, 1985.
Kazin, Alfred. *Writing Was Everything*. Harvard University Press, 1995.
Knowlson, James. *The Life of Samuel Beckett*. Bloomsbury, 1996.
Larkin, Philip. *The Complete Poems Philip Larkin*. Edited by Archie Burnett. Farrar, Straus and Giroux, 2013.
Logan, John. *Red*. Oberon, 2009.

Markson, David. *Reader's Block*. Dalkey Archive, 1996.
*A Midwinter's Tale*. Directed by Kenneth Branagh. Castle Rock Entertainment, 1996.
Nietzsche, Friedrich. "Richard Wagner at Bayreuth." 1876. *Untimely Meditations*. Translated by R. J. Hollingdale. Cambridge University Press, 1997.
McCarthy, Cormac. *Blood Meridian or The Evening Redness in The West*. Vintage, 1985.
Melville, Herman. *Moby Dick or, The Whale*. 1851. Modern Library, 2000.
Pascal, Blaise. *Pensées*. 1670. Translated by A. J. Krailsheimer. Penguin, 1995.
Rothko, Mark. *Writings on Art*. Edited by Miguel Lopez-Remiro. Yale University Press, 2006.
Sontag, Susan. "The Death of Tragedy." *Against Interpretation and Other Essays*. Farrar, Straus and Giroux, 1966.
_____. "Writing as Reading." *Where the Stress Falls*. Farrar, Straus and Giroux, 2001.
Sophocles. *Oedipus Rex. The Oedipus Cycle: An English Version*. Translated by Dudley Fitts and Robert Fitzgerald. Harcourt, 1977.
Steiner, George. *The Death of Tragedy*. 1961. Yale University Press, 1996.
Vogl, Joseph. *On Tarrying*. Translated by Helmut Muller-Sievers. Seagull, 2011.
Wittgenstein, Ludwig. *Tractatus Logico-Philosophicus*. 1921. Translated by C. K. Ogden. Routledge, 1995.

# Review of Literature: Selected Books

Simon Critchley. *Tragedy, the Greeks, and Us.* Pantheon Books, 2019. Pp. 322. Hardcover. $26.95.

Behold your child, your only child, a son, let's say, and it's his wedding day. He's sharply suited, tall, a man almost, handsome. He's about to marry. He seems sure of himself, though not entirely, and nervous—in need of some advice, perhaps. Like Orestes, who hesitates before plunging, your son wishes to know: *What shall I do?* For the occasion you summon (with some hesitation) Søren Kierkegaard, whose ruminations on the pangs of indecision, of Hamlet-like paralysis—of taking or *not* taking the plunge—remain unsurpassed, summative, and most tragic: "Marry, and you will regret it. Do not marry, and you will also regret it. Marry or do not marry, you will regret it either way."

The drama above, my own, hasn't exactly the same weight of impending disaster, I realize, as Euripides's *Medea* (431 BCE) or Lorca's *Blood Wedding* (1933), but it does evoke a central concern of tragedy, both ancient and modern, which, in the words of the grieving mother in Lorca's play, is irreducibly double: "Two sides! There are two sides here!" This means something more, obviously, than Shaw's conception of marriage as "an alliance entered into by a man who can't sleep with the window shut, and a woman who can't sleep with the window open." In Sophocles' *Antigone*, for example, the matter of two justifiable claims in conflict with one another leads inexorably to a wedding ("a vaulted bride-bed in eternal rock") between Antigone and—her words—"sleepy death." When two rights make a wrong, thought Hegel, there is tragedy.

The disastrous collision between two equally justified claims features crucially in what Simon Critchley, in *Tragedy, the Greeks, and Us* (2019), calls "tragedy's philosophy." To help introduce this philosophy, Critchley turns to the poet and classicist Anne Carson, whose formulation for why we have tragedy in the first place is an object lesson in the fine art of distillation. Tragedy exists, she tells us, because we are full of *rage*. And we are full of rage because we are full of *grief*. Critchley, for his part, advances the formula a step further.

We, no less than the ancient Greeks, are full of grief because we are full of *war*. And war, whether with each other, or within ourselves, is the common source of our endless suffering.

In light of this perpetual state of division ("Two sides! There are two sides here!"), the "overwhelming experience of tragedy," writes Critchley, "is a *disorientation* expressed in one bewildered and frequently repeated question: *What shall I do?*" (4). That is, "What will happen to me? How can I choose the right path of action?" (4). The "mood of ancient tragedy" therefore "is *skeptical*," says Critchley; "it is about the dissolution of all markers of certitude" (35). But what was true for the ancient tragedians is true for us, too. Everywhere today, especially among the young, is an overwhelming mood of anxiety, of uncertainty about what to do in the face of an increasingly uncertain and even terrifying future. "In this sense—and this is my wager in this book—we are arguably the extreme contemporaries of those other skeptics, those other realists, the Attic tragedians, and perhaps we might learn something by spending more time in their company" (70), he writes. "The world is a confusing, noisy place," he adds, "defined by endless war, rage, grief, ever-growing inequality. We undergo a gnawing moral and political uncertainty in a world of ambiguity. To think in this spirit is to breathe a little of the air of Attic tragedy" (70–71).

In matters of great and grave importance, then, moral ambiguity is the rule rather than the exception, making every decision, every action, impossibly difficult if not impossible *period*. Not only can we *not* know the future consequences of any given decision, but whatever our choice, the one passed over is certain to haunt; late or soon, it will revisit unbidden, in quiet corners of the day, or at night, a balled-up question to unwind and terrorize: *What if I had chosen otherwise?* As Critchley puts it (borrowing from the film *Magnolia*), "We might think we are through with the past, but the past is not through with us" (3).

No matter our choice, we act always in partial if not complete ignorance of the ways we will be acted upon by our past, by our "transgenerational curse" (272), by what the ancient Greeks called "fate" (as far as Freud is concerned, the past *is* our fate). Echoing A.C. Bradley's argument in "Hegel's Theory of Tragedy" (1909), Critchley makes a case for the effects of fate in our lives, but only insofar as we conspire with it can fate do its thing. "What the thirty-one extant Greek tragedies enact over and over again," he argues, "is not a misfortune that is outside our control. Rather, they show the way in which we collude, seemingly unknowingly, with the calamity that befalls us" (12). To put it as the poet Philip Larkin does, the future is unlimited, but "only so long as I elected nothing; simply to choose stopped all ways up but one." Still, we *must* choose. We *must* act. We must throw our boomerangs. Which is why any so-called *life decision*—be it marriage, murderous revenge, or suicide—must give us pause. As one Dane might have counseled another, "Hang yourself or do not hang yourself, you will regret it either way" (Kierkegaard, *Either/Or*).

Simone Weil once offered a way out of the deadlock of indecision, advising that whenever we find ourselves confronted with an impossible choice, we should always side in favor of what's most difficult. This, she thought, is the best barometer of what's most ethical. Admirable as Weil's advice is, I think I prefer instead the stock response from the millennial who lives next door to me, whose own words of wisdom, however off-putting, express a tragic consciousness worthy of the ancients. To wit, whenever I ask her what she plans to do with her life, she replies: "Fuck if I know, dude." In her uncertainty she possesses—I'm sure of it—the terrible knowledge of tragedy: the "boomerang structure," Critchley calls it, "where the action that we throw out into the world returns to us with potentially fatal velocity" (15).

This "complicity on our part in the disaster that destroys us" (12) is reason enough to spend time with the ancients whose tragedies depict time and again what becomes of those who have forgotten that the world they inhabit can never be made intelligible to them, not entirely, anyway. Tragedy, writes Critchley, "permits us to come face-to-face with what we do *not* know about ourselves but what makes those selves the things they are" (1). Adopting for ourselves a tragic consciousness toward a world that is "only ever partially intelligible to human agency" (92) may be the first step, in fact, toward getting on in the world. True, spending time with Oedipus is no guarantee we will become any less blind, but, along with him, we may find ourselves better in touch. For Critchley, this tragic orientation to the world is the basis, once more, of what he calls "tragedy's philosophy," a minority pursuit in opposition to the long and predominant tradition of philosophy initiated by Plato.

"Tragedy's philosophy," like philosophy itself, has its wisdom to impart, but this wisdom comes accompanied always with Tiresias's caveat to Oedipus: "How dreadful knowledge of the truth can be when there's no help in truth!" Making his case for the value of tragedy's dark, dreadful knowledge, and why it matters still, Critchley opens window after window onto the longstanding battle between tragedy and those who, like Plato, have wished to banish it from the *polis*. This effort on philosophy's behalf to exclude tragedy from the life of the city state, as well as from the life of the individual, is what Critchley calls "philosophy's tragedy"—tragic because, by excluding tragedy from its purview, philosophy refuses to give "voice to what is contradictory about us, what is constricted about us, what is precarious about us, and what is limited about us. Philosophy, once again, beginning with Plato, appears to be committed to the idea and ideal of a non-contradictory psychic life" (9). But, adds Critchley, "Tragedy does not share this commitment. And neither do I" (9).

The long tradition of philosophy (exemplified by Plato, Aristotle, Aquinas, Spinoza, Kant, Hegel, etc.)—borne of Socratic optimism—is "premised on the idea that human beings can gain true insight into that which is" (91). For Plato, emotional indulgences (i.e., grief and lamentation) endemic to tragedy, along with its untruthfulness (tragedy = an imitation of an imitation), are inimical to the functioning of a well-ordered and rational *polis*, one he wanted to see governed by reason rather than undermined by upset. This exclusion of tragedy from life, however, is precisely "philosophy's tragedy" because philosophy neglects, or pretends to ignore, what is most fundamental about us, that "We are divided against ourselves in much of our living activity" (73). And tragedy "shows us human beings at odds with themselves, often in a state of profound contradiction" (73). But that's not all. This state of contradiction extends outward to the world at large:

> Tragedy presents a conflictually constituted world defined by ambiguity, duplicity, uncertainty, and unknowability, a world that cannot be rendered rationally fully intelligible through some metaphysical first principle or set of principles, axioms, tables of categories, or whatever. Tragedy is the experience of transcendental *opacity* [137].

In opposition to "philosophy's tragedy" is "tragedy's philosophy," a "style of philosophy," writes Critchley, "ultimately closer to the patterns of thinking, speaking, and reasoning that can be seen in Attic tragedy, especially the plays of Euripides" (91). "Tragedy's philosophy," a defense of which is the chief intent of Critchley's wide-ranging, intimate, and important book, "is premised upon a profound ontological skepticism: the world is only ever partially intelligible to human agency. Any philosophical dream of full intelligibility has to be given up" (92).

If, as Alfred North Whitehead famously remarked, philosophy "consists of a series of footnotes to Plato," then Critchley has joined the chorus with sixty-one notes of his own (dispersed among six parts), each of which ranges widely among and draws deeply from many of the ancient Greek tragedies. Doing so, Critchley wishes to "join Nietzsche" (the self-proclaimed "first tragic philosopher") in defending tragedy as a "form of philosophy that is destroyed by philosophy" (11). In the words of Nietzsche, which might serve as a stand-in for Critchley's overarching thesis, "There is only one hope and one guarantee for the future of that which is human; it lies in this, that the tragic disposition shall not perish." The proposition may sound initially counterintuitive, absurd even, especially—trust me—if pitched to a class of undergraduates who, many of them, raised on anti-depressants, will be mystified as to why anyone would want to nurture a tragic disposition rather than rid themselves of it. After all, wouldn't the best of all possible worlds, whether envisioned by Plato or Pangloss, be a world in which suffering is overcome through the powers of ratiocination, cheerful optimism, or prescription drugs? In short, shouldn't we structure our lives in such a way as to avoid the tragic, rather than to run toward it? For Critchley, for Nietzsche, for the ancient Greek tragedians (and that long line of pessimists borne in their wake), the answer is decidedly "No!" What is it, then, about tragedy that helps fortify, rather than nullify, a certain experience of what Critchley, in the last of section of his book, calls "aliveness"? For the psychotherapist Francis Weller, there "is a strange intimacy between grief and aliveness, some sacred exchange between what seems unbearable and what is most exquisitely alive." Which is why we should apprentice ourselves to sorrow and open ourselves to grief, just as the ancients did. This is another way of saying, with Nietzsche, that the "individual must be consecrated to something higher than himself—that is the meaning of tragedy."

"Ours is essentially a tragic age," begins D.H. Lawrence's *Lady Chatterley's Lover* (1928), "so we refuse to take it tragically." The age in question, in Lawrence's novel, is the aftermath of the Great War, a war that put the lie to narratives of human progress and the triumph of reason. But every age—our own, but also as far back as the time of *Ecclesiastes* and the *Iliad*—is essentially tragic, and always for the same reason. Tragedy, Susan Sontag observed, shows us "the emptiness and arbitrariness of the world, the ultimate meaninglessness of all moral values, and the terrifying rule of death and inhuman force." For most people, such knowledge, such a tragic vision, is simply too dreadful to bear. Therefore, Lawrence tells us, in a tragic age, we refuse to take it tragically. Better instead to keep up with the Kardashians or busy our time and minds with Netflix and online shopping. However, "when the age loses the tragic," warns Kierkegaard, "it gains despair." If instead we open ourselves to the experience of tragedy—to tragic theatre, in particular—then, writes Critchley, we can "look into the *core*, the core of life, of aliveness, in all its burning intensity, moral ambiguity, emotional devastation, erotic doubling, and political complexity" (279). Plus, says the mother in *Blood Wedding*, "We're all curious about what might hurt us." Then again, if tragedy teaches us anything, it's this: Embrace the tragic or do not embrace the tragic, *either way you will regret it.*

Doug Phillips<br>
*University of St. Thomas*

---

Trever Boffone, Teresa Marrero and Chantal Rodriguez, eds. *Encuentro: Latinx Performance for the New American Theater*. Northwestern University Press, 2019. Pp. 432. Paperback $34.95.

*Encuentro: Latinx Performance for the New American Theater* is not simply an anthology of selected plays produced during the *2014 Encuentro: A National*

*Latina/o Theatre Festival*, organized by the Los Angeles Theatre Center (LATC) in association with the Latinx Theatre Commons (LTC), but rather a depiction of past and current sociocultural, economic, and political adversities faced by Latina/o/x communities. *Encuentro* furthers the dialogue that revolves around the first question the editors make in their introduction: "What is the state of U.S. Latinx theater?" The editors follow with a concise history of the Chicana/o and Latina/o theater movements of the 1960s; the introduction also provides the origins and emergence of the Latinx Theatre Commons and the first Encuentro festival, proposed during the first LTC National Convening in Boston in 2013. More significantly, *Encuentro* provides not only a wide variety of aesthetics, but a common space to recognize the work of underrepresented and politically inflected theater groups in the United States. This anthology selects six plays out of the nineteen productions featured at Encuentro 2014. Each selected play is prefaced by a critical introduction by a scholar, focusing mainly on the performance during the festival.

The first play is *La Esquinita, U.S.A.* (2010), by Rubén C. González, which is described as "a *pueblito* stuck between the here and now, the always and forever," "a once-booming town but now forgotten like so many others" (10–11). This play adapts the space commonly identified as the *barrio*, a desolate place with broken and empty promises of prosperity made by big corporations that went into bankruptcy. A dominant narrative of pain reflects the reality of the characters who, due primarily to unemployment, push the boundaries of survival. These depictions of a reality surrounded by drug dealing and addiction aim to show the ruptured economic system that devastates marginalized communities. With a substantial degree of bitterness and dark humor, Lencho, "a shape-shifting, time-traveling narrator" (9), connects the stories of all nine characters at 40A Red Line, a bus stop that symbolizes an intersection of temporalities. More importantly, the bus stop, "la esquinita" (the little corner), represents not just a common space of human relations, but also of human degradation where hope seems to be absent. More than an American tale, *La Esquinita* unmasks the hidden stories of inequity and, above all, reclaims recognition of a community that has been living in those lands before the construction of physical and symbolic borders.

*Aliens, Immigrants & Other Evildoers* (2009), by José Torres-Tama, has been defined as a sci-fi Latino noir multimedia solo performance, which incorporates an overwhelming variety of short film projections, visual images, and ritualistic movements. "Ningún ser humano es ilegal! No human being is illegal!" is the *leitmotiv* of the play, which takes place in the present, "with a heightened era of post–9/11 anti-immigrant hysteria in FreedomLandia" (57). Torres-Tama tells the traumatic immigrant experience of injustice, hate, and racial discrimination based on real testimonies, such as the incident of Marcelo Lucero, who was stabbed and killed by a group of teenagers in Long Island on a "beaner hopping" right after the election of Barack Obama in 2008. Other cases include the death of an undocumented immigrant worker, the tragic accident of a Honduran working in New Orleans after Katrina, and the story of a Nicaraguan girl who was brought to the United States at age eight and after years of being "illegal," embraced the term and used it to empower herself. With the performative action of the Chicano and Pachuco tradition and a heavy use of satire and bilingualism, Torres-Tama deconstructs the use of controversial terms, such as Alien, Immigrant, and Illegal in a place he constantly refers as "The United States of Amnesia." *Aliens, Immigrants & Other Evildoers* is, to a greater extent, the most provoking act of political protest from all the plays included in this anthology.

*Dreamscape* (2010), by Rickerby Hinds, has been continuously produced since its first development in 2005. It was also adapted as a film production under the name *My Name Is Myeisha* (2018). *Dreamscape* is based on the factual case of Tyisha Miller, a victim of police brutality in 1998 in Riverside, California. The play consists of a prologue and twelve scenes, which are the twelve gunshots that killed the protagonist Myeisha, a nineteen-year-old Afro-Latina. What stands out in this poetical recital is the cross-cultural component of the hip-hop tradition, which also informs a significant aspect of the Afro-Latinx reality. Each scene starts with a detailed and disruptive description of every gunshot entrance. Under a surreal ambiance, wandering in limbo, Myeisha narrates how each one of the fatal and non-fatal gunshots killed her memories, dreams, and the possibility of a future. Although *Dreamscape* focuses on an irrecoverable existence, the play clearly advocates against the law enforcement's establishment of fear among minority communities such as Myeisha's.

*Patience, Fortitude, and Other Antidepressants* (2012), by Mariana Carreño King, is a contemporary tragedy, inspired by Federico García Lorca's classic tragedy *Yerma* (1934). Carreño King situates a New York's urban *barrio* as the space for self-identity encounter and patriarchy emancipation. The plot revolves around the character of Isabella and her three paintings called "Patience," "Fortitude," and "Bella," the last being the only unfinished painting and the symbol of Isabella's odyssey to find her true self. More than a discourse of escapism, these paintings are a surrealistic mirror and thus, an entrance to Isabella's subconsciousness. The past and present are juxtaposed by the presence of Isabella's adolescent friends and the sisters of her husband, Juan, who is a police officer and the authoritarian and passive-aggressive figure. In this context, Isabella tries to break the cultural ideology of marriage, including procreation and housewife duties. This fight against repressive systems of patriarchies ends tragically in the traditional carnival, which is another element used in the play to inform the game between illusion and reality. *Patience, Fortitude, and Other Antidepressants* transgresses and problematizes a significant cultural aspect among the *Latinidad*, but mainly it proclaims and returns the agency to women to own their bodies, minds, and identities.

Javier Antonio González's *Zoetrope: Part I* (2013) takes the reader and audience back to a crucial decade of political battle and cultural reaffirmation in Puerto Rico's history. The 1950s witnessed events such as the proclamation of Puerto Rico as a U.S. Commonwealth and the beginning of one of the biggest migrations known as "La Gran Migración" (The Great Migration). In this context, the love story of Inés and Severino allegorizes the division between those who leave to pursue the American dream and those who stay to support the pro-independence movements. The American dream, however, proves to be an illusion for Severino, who first served in the U.S. army and then lived miserably in New York. Following the annotations, "a zoetrope is a device that produces the illusion of action from a rapid succession of static pictures. This play is written as a series of scenes that skip back and forth though the years and settings" (261). Thus, *Zoetrope* intends to be a collective journey to a challenging and static past that is still relevant for the Puerto Rican diaspora.

*Premeditation* (2014), by renowned Chicana playwright Evelina Fernández, started as a one-act play in 1992. The full version of the play premiered on April 2014 by The Latino Theater Company, directed by José Luis Valenzuela. *Premeditation* differs from the rest of the plays in this anthology by distancing from socioeconomic factors, cultural conflicts, and political discourses. In fact, there is only one cultural reference throughout the play; the character Fernando claims about his cultural heritage, "I love the opera and classical music, fine art, and I appreciate and cherish the wonderful things about being Chicano and I love our culture" (373). Otherwise, the play detaches from stereotypes and introduces a distinctive middle- to upper-class Latino perspective that has adopted the American way of life. In the form of a melodrama, the plot is developed around universal topics, such as domestic disputes and marital miscommunication. However, it stands out for the presence of strong female characters who are not afraid to kill in order to restore happiness.

*Encuentro* means "encounter," broadly defined as a meeting or finding, but above all, it is an engagement with conflict in need to be recognized. These plays encourage the reader to take risks and both expect and accept discomfort as an opportunity to expand awareness on challenging topics that include politicized and vulnerable characters succumbed to a "bare life," as construed in Giorgio Agamben's *Homo Sacer* (1995). As a pedagogical tool, these plays empower education around anti-racist and anti-oppressive systems. Furthermore, they foster the diversity of human experience and open the discussion to understand each other's narratives, build a joint narrative, and learn effective strategies to communicate across communities of cultural and social difference through theater making.

"What is the state of U.S. Latinx theater?" *Encuentro* intends to answer this question by situating a long-standing Latinx theater history that is in the process of reaffirming its presence and revitalizing its aesthetics. From solo-piece performances to full-length plays, *Encuentro* also informs a fast-growing theater movement that reflects other collaborative initiatives, such as the subsequent *2017 LTC Encuentro de las Américas International Theatre Festival*, the *2018 LTC María Irene Fornés Institute Symposium*, the *2018 LTC Carnaval of New Latinx Work*, the *2019 LTC Theatre for Young Audiences Sin Fronteras Festival*, and the most recent *2019 LTC Miami Regional Convening*, to mention only a few.

OSVALDO SANDOVAL-LEON
*Colgate University*

---

Lopamudra Basu. *Ayad Akhtar, the American Nation, and Its Others After 9/11: Homeland Insecurity*. Lexington Books, 2019. Pp. 193 + xiv. Hardcover $83.85.

Contemporary playwright Ayad Akhtar is phenomenally successful at melding the commercial and the literary in theater: he has acted in, directed, and written award-winning movies, plays, and a novel, and, by his own admission in an interview, "falls a little more profoundly on the commercial side of things," seeing his own work as a form of entertainment with the goal being to connect with "the simply human aspect of every single person in the audience" (See Srila Nayak, "Pulitzer Playwright Ayad Akhtar on Aristotle and Islam," *HowlRound* 11 May 2014). Ironically, the xenophobic political climate and anti–Muslim racism of the past years has seen a profusion of productions of *Disgraced*, his play centered on a Muslim protagonist, in regional and global theaters; it became the most produced play in the 2015–16 season. His intriguing writing—with its provocative themes, tormented characters, mounting dramatic conflicts, and the unsettling beats of dialogue in his scripts—has been effusively received, and he has been feted in glowing reviews and countless interviews.

With *Ayad Akhtar, the American Nation, and Its Others After 9/11: Homeland Insecurity*, Lopamudra Basu, professor of English at University of Wisconsin–Stout, readily fills a vacuum of literary discourse on individual Muslim-American artists like Akhtar, to whom scant scholarly attention has been paid.

In analyzing Ayad Akhtar's controversial early plays and the connections between global capitalism and radicalism, Basu looks at the form of tragedy used by Akhtar in his cultural production. In Basu's analysis, Akhtar's plays enact national mourning and he "uses performance as a mode of disrupting the hegemonic discourse of American exceptionality which undergirds the structure of the Homeland Security State" (5). Basu states that the 9/11 literary archive has lacunae in the literary representation and literary criticism of South Asian, Muslim, and Arab-American experiences of 9/11; the narratives of these racial and religious minorities "still tend to remain peripheral to the developing 9/11 canon" and, within the field, drama "continues to be a marginalized genre" (9).

Basu's monograph on Ayad Akhtar is graced by a portrait of Akhtar by the Pakistani-American artist Shahzia Sikander, which visually ties together the motifs of art, faith, and nation analyzed in Basu's book. For those unfamiliar with the full body of Akhtar's oeuvre, the book is divided into four chapters focusing on themes of racial and religious identity in all of Akhtar's works, followed by an interview Basu conducted with him in 2016. Basu begins with applying theories about the sublime, spectacle, terrorism, and sexuality to an incisive analysis of Akhtar's earliest cinematic works, where she claims he challenges the American Dream by exhibiting the embattled nature of masculine Muslim identity.

The second chapter connects Akhtar's portrayal of the over-determined South Asian Muslim-American male identity in *Disgraced* to the performance of race in *Othello*, showing Akhtar's canonical counter-discourse to Shakespeare's play functioning as "a metafictional commentary on the politics of representation" (60). Basu asserts that Akhtar's wrenching ending of the play dramatizes the social contradictions of "the underlying disorder of American society" and advocates for change by "promoting a critical consciousness in its audience" (77), even if the writer himself resists any moralizing.

Basu's study of rage at emasculation in Akhtar's work shifts in the next chapter to his interrogation of progressive female agency among Muslim-Americans in the novel *American Dervish* and the play *The Who and the What*. Basu deepens her analysis of Akhtar's play by showing his revision of the comedic marriage plot in *The Taming of the Shrew*. Although Basu acknowledges that Akhtar ascribes "a fair portion of the blame for misogyny and oppression faced by women to Islam" (94) which can create potentially anti–Islamic readings, she frames her own analysis of Akhtar's work within a restricted conception of Muslim feminists examining Islam-focused female agency, social change, and resistance. Her disclaimer of Akhtar's disdain for female autonomy in Islamic spaces leads to a peculiar statement on the play as "a metacommentary on the role of the Muslim writer" who explores complex truths without "seeking to vindicate the minority group's reputation within the fabric of the multicultural nation" (119).

In the last chapter, Basu comprehensively inspects the global financial networks of jihadi terrorist ideology and capitalism in the play *The Invisible Hand*, and the 2008 debt crisis created by the market crash and the tragedy of declining American manufacturing in the 2016 play *Junk*. If terror and capital are globally intertwined in *The Invisible Hand* (133), Basu deftly shows how in *Junk*, Akhtar turns a trenchant eye on domestic myths of American innocence and moral superiority undercut by the shrinking of American democracy. Basu suggests that with this last play set in the 1980s, Akhtar's posing of questions of national belonging and exclusion "foreshadow the post–9/11 predicament of Muslims in America" and current Trumpian "nativist, anti-trade, anti-immigration" hostility (151).

Another highlight of the book is Basu's interview of Akhtar as "a dramatic storyteller" (153): here, Basu engages with the audience's relationship with Akhtar's Aristotelian character reversals and recognitions, presenting a thoughtful depiction of Akhtar's intricate relationship with his faith. In his creative conversation with Jewish American writers and performers, Akhtar finds ethnic equivalencies of faith-oriented othering of the position of Muslims in the U.S. (153); even the seemingly sensational evisceration of Islam in his plays occurs from a place of inspiration from the Muslim experience. The interview also reveals Akhtar as a writer of the hybridity of commerce and dramatic storytelling, one partaking in the global North and South, who understands that "union with the audience represents a fulfillment" of his task as an artist (163). If in his quest to repurpose classical tragedy for modern audiences Akhtar may seem nihilistic in his rejection of forms of protest such as discursive or grassroots activism, he realizes that the totalizing reach of global consumerism can easily co-opt opposition as merely reactive since "there is no ground for agency in that oppositional relationship" (159), which still precludes any alternate imagination of resistance on his part.

Basu provides a dramatic overview of Akhtar's plays in the Conclusion that addresses his work within both classical Aristotelian tragedy and the communal role of theater. Basu proposes that Akhtar writes to communicate with an immediate audience in a reaction against global capitalism. His plays work as Aristotelian tragedies, in which Basu sees the suffering of characters from the rage and violence of the post–9/11 Homeland Security state as allowing the audience to "tarry in grief, mourn for the loss of life, property, or a vision of the nation" (173). Even though no alternatives are provided by Akhtar, Basu argues that he "faithfully records the scars and documents the sufferings to initiate his audience to reflect and think about these conditions of suffering and envision paths toward liberation" (173).

Although Akhtar situates himself in dialogue with classical Western theater, his work could also be examined within Islamic classical theatrical traditions of tragedy, such as the passion play tragedies of *ta'ziehs*. In the Introduction, Basu briefly places Akhtar with his contemporaneous male Muslim-American playwrights, Aasif Mandvi and Yusuf El Guindi. Another comparison of Akhtar could be formed with veteran writer, director, and actress Bina Sharif and her politically relevant and socially conscious performance plays at the Theater for the New City, which Basu perhaps avoids because of the commercial tenor of Akhtar's plays. Basu also reports the varying criticisms of pandering in Akhtar's work but, like the playwright himself, dismisses such criticisms in the service of art and appears to conflate the multiple modalities of modern Islam (especially in America) with its cultural interpretations across the globe. Evaluating Akhtar's texts without ample critical deconstruction risks disregarding his tendency to play to the most anti–Islamic and paternalistic paradigms in his quest to appeal to a universal audience, with hardly any inclusive concern for Muslim-American audiences or an attempt to balance with complementary nuanced Muslim characters.

Basu's study of Akhtar's work touches on the burgeoning complexity of his faith and reveals that the more profound dramaturgical analysis of the evolution of Akhtar's thought is in his comprehension of the global matrices of power and neo-imperial capital in his later work. The recognition accorded to Akhtar's plays pushes the narrative of fraught race relations in America onto the stage for minorities considered outcasts by their religious, racial, class, or immigration status, and his success opens up the performative space for other Muslim-American voices to be heard. His theater seduces the audience and then makes it viscerally confront its own expectations and biases. In this process, as Basu reminds us, Ayad Akhtar shatters representational tropes and forces a mainstream audience to acknowledge the dynamic minority discourses that are defining America.

MAHWASH SHOAIB
*Central Piedmont Community College*

---

Max Shulman and J. Chris Westgate, eds. *Performing the Progressive Era: Immigration, Urban Life, and Nationalism on Stage*. University of Iowa Press, 2019. Pp. 298. Paperback $90.00.

Max Shulman and J. Chris Westgate have edited a "chimera of literary and cultural history" (215) which, in eleven chapters by established and emerging scholars, illuminates the centrality of performance during the Progressive Era from 1890 to 1920. Part of the revisionist turn in theatre history, the book works to recover and revitalize the Progressive Era as well as to "undercut the reassuring myth of progress" and "remind all of us that we may not have come all that far from the Progressive Era as we believe" (219). Indeed, the central cultural debates of the Progressive Era—immigration and citizenship, changing familial roles and obligations, and the ethical dilemmas posed by emergent medical technologies—remain unresolved to this day.

The essays collectively argue that "the Progressive Era was brought into being through the ubiquity of performance" (3). The book takes a capacious view of performance and tours theatre and dance halls, parade routes, world's fairs, Little Theatres, wealthy neighborhoods, and amusement parks in major U.S. areas. Most chapters employ interdisciplinary methodologies grounded in history and performance studies as well as "textual analysis, manuscript studies, performance analysis, reception theory, cultural history, spatial analysis, and archival research" (5). The central argument that performance "brought into being" the Progressive Era is most convincingly proven in chapters which reveal how particular performances anticipated cultural anxieties, problematized political issues, and reframed ethical dilemmas for Progressive Era audiences—how, in other words, performance forecast the future.

Amy Arbogast's opening chapter, "Rural Life with Urban Strife: The Evolution of Rural Drama in the Late Nineteenth Century," sets the tone for this main argument by revealing how rural plays evolved as U.S. cities experienced increasing industrialization. She defines rural plays as those set in the country that "provided urban audiences with nostalgic portrayals of simpler times and patriotic images of the country's rustic citizenry" (17) and argues that beginning in 1890, rural plays moved away from a romanticized view of rural America and instead emphasized an increasing national interconnectedness.

As examples, Arbogast discusses August Thomas' *Alabama* (1891), James A. Herne's *Shore Acres* (1892), and David Belasco's *The Girl I Left Behind Me* (1893). These plays share three important traits: they are hopeful about the possibilities of industrialization in rural areas, they feature a promising younger generation poised to write a brighter and more unified chapter in American history, and most interestingly, they de-emphasize the past to urge a conciliatory view of the Civil War. Arbogast draws on recent Civil War scholarship by Nina Silber and David Blight which focus on "conciliation culture" (21) in her discussion of this third point. Considering their wide popularity, Arbogast presents a compelling case for these three plays as optimistic on-stage inaugurators of the Progressive Era.

However, this rosy and unified national outlook did not last long. In Chapter Three, "'Wasn't America Crowded Enough Wid Out You Forriners?' Staging Immigration, Assimilation, and Social Mobility in the Rooseveltian Nation," J. Chris Westgate investigates James Halleck Reid's *From Broadway to the Bowery*, a comic melodrama which exposes "the vicissitudes of immigration, assimilation, and social mobility of the Progressive Era" (54). The play premiered in 1907, the same year the Dillingham Commission was formed to study the economic and cultural consequences of immigration—lending compelling evidence to the thesis that performance "brought into being" the debates of the Progressive Era.

Westgate considers the play in light of what historians call the Rooseveltian Nation, defined as the attempt by the President's administration to align two competing traditions through which the U.S. viewed immigration during the Progressive Era. The first tradition, defined by Gary Gestle as "civic nationalism," saw immigrants as the backbone of American identity and argued that all immigrants, regardless of their background, deserved political freedom and economic opportunity. The second tradition, "racial nationalism," took a more conservative position and viewed citizenship as the exclusive right of descendants of Anglo-Saxon ancestry. While Roosevelt publicly recognized civic nationalism, his administration adhered to a conservative racial nationalism and implemented severe immigration restrictions.

Westgate argues that Reid's play both "accelerated the shift toward the conservative tradition of racial nationalism" and, more importantly, "delineate[d] the superiority/inferiority of Anglo-Americans and non–Anglo-Americans through reference to heritage and inheritance in accordance with the Social Darwinism of the time" (55). To Westgate, the play is asking which immigrant groups deserve the advantages of American citizenship and which are incapable of assimilation. Irish, Chinese, and African character groups are simultaneously connected and set against each other in this dilemma, while the Anglo protagonists remain secure in the American-ness regardless of the other misfortunes they undergo. This imbalance underscores connections between Social Darwinism, racism, and immigration policy during the Progressive Era. As Shulman and Westgate note in the co-authored conclusion, such attitudes and policies "continue to cause pain, poverty, and sectarian dogmatism today" (219).

In addition to stage plays, the collection considers less traditional forms of performance as well. Chapter Seven, "New Women and Girls of Today in Motion: The 'Strenuous Clasping' of Tango Teas" by Ariel Nelson, focuses on "tango teas": events hosted by department stores, restaurants, cabarets, and hotels which combined tea drinking with tango dancing to hybridize ladylike and more scandalous activity for young urban women of the Progressive Era.

Tango teas were a source of concern for moral reformers for three main reasons: their overtly sexual choreography, tango's imagined nonwhite origins (although the dance form as practiced in American cities was largely a mash-up of the Argentinian tradition with what ex-pats living abroad brought back), and the upending of male-female roles in tango teas during which professional male dancers were brought in to teach the dance to women in "an inversion from the usual exchange" (126). Nelson focuses on this final point and suggests that what was most dangerous about tango teas was the accompanying sense of economic empowerment for women who attended tango teas.

Some reformers nevertheless chose to defend tango teas, perhaps because of their widespread popularity. But Nelson points out that the negotiation to oppose or support tango teas hinged on shifting definitions of femininity centered in the image of "The Girl of Today": a young woman single by choice and free from tradition. Nelson's final and most intriguing argument, that tango teas "could be opportunities for exercising independence in leisure activities during the political moment when women advocated for their legal right to suffrage" (140) elegantly proves the collection's overall thesis that performance "brought into being" Progressive Era reforms.

Shulman and Westgate appropriately conclude with the most uncomfortable chapter, "Monstrosity or Medical Miracle: Incubator Baby Sideshows and the Contradictions of the Progressive Era" by Susan Kattwinkel, an unnerving survey of the incubator baby shows of the early 1920s. Kattwinkel describes these exhibitions as a "microcosm" of the debates surrounding child-rearing, entertainment at the expense of the Other, and the perceived American ideal of physical strength as a symbol of superiority during the Progressive Era.

Incubator baby shows were associated with freak shows in the popular imagination. Both types of spectacle were popular with mass audiences during the Progressive Era but were coming under increasing scrutiny from reformers. Incubator baby shows in particular straddled two competing perceptions: one which viewed the incubator as an amazing technology that could improve human life, and another which feared incubators as "a dehumanizing machine" (181). Kattwinkel characterizes this tension as an oscillation between "excitement and anxiety" (192) which typifies the entire Progressive Era. As spectators peered down upon incubator babies, Kattwinkel suggests, they beheld the awe-inspiring human capacity for sustaining and improving human life. In the same moment, however, they were forced to recognize the disquieting power of technology and contemplate the ramifications of such powerful, life-giving tools. More than any other in the collection, this moment reveals how performance "brought into being" the debates, reforms, and moral ambivalence of the Progressive Era.

Any review of this collection would be incomplete without mention of Laurence Senelick's masterful introduction. Senelick defines the Progressive Era in personal terms, enlarges the contradictions deeply embedded within that troublesome term "modernity," and articulates the value of historical research and writing for scholars of performance. Senelick cautions against "getting lost in the pastness of the past" and argues that "without having to belabor issues of 'relevance' or 'timeliness,' the best histories reveal points of relation and identity that alert readers can apply to their own culture" (xii). This eclectic edition should rightly be considered, then, among the best histories. It will prove indispensable to scholars interested in the Progressive Era's performances, of course, but also for those aiming to understand the role of performance in the formation of twentieth (and twenty-first)-century American culture.

PATRICK MIDGLEY
*Texas Tech University*

---

Selby Wynn Schwartz. *The Bodies of Others: Drag Dances and Their Afterlives*. University of Michigan Press, 2019. Pp. 300. Paperback $34.95.

In our moment when there is political fervor over policing bodies—trans, black, immigrant, female, gay, etc.—a book such as *The Bodies of Others: Drag Dances and Their Afterlives* by Selby Wynn Schwartz is timely. When the public debates which bathrooms trans people are "allowed" to use, yet still ostracize gender-neutral restrooms, or when a homophobic attack ends in what was then the largest mass shooting in the United States and still the deadliest large-scale attack on gay bodies, or when a nationally syndicated talk show host makes fun of a young royal for taking a ballet class, it is a stark reminder about the damning attitudes that persist in niches of dominant society about non-heteronormative, non-cisgender, or non-gender conforming persons, in reality or in perception. Published with this ongoing backdrop, *The Bodies of Others* examines the intersection of gender and dance, and the politics that are inherent when these topics are merged.

Spanning four decades of drag dances, *The Bodies of Others* delves into five bodies of work in drag dance: Mark Morris's solo-performed duet *Dido and Aeneas*, Richard Move's drag séance animation of Martha Graham in *Martha @*, Kazuo Ohno's channeling of La Argentina in *Admiring La Argentina*, Anthony Bassae's cofounding of drag ballet troupe Les Ballets Trockadero de Monte Carlo, and Fauxnique/Monique Jenkinson's feminist dance theatre *Faux Real* (not to mention a bonus sixth case in the introduction: Jane Comfort's *S/He* danced with Andre Shoals). The case studies presented are from concert dance, rather than ballroom, club, or drag shows. *Jeté*-ing through club mothers, butoh divas, drag ballet, and dance theatre, *The Bodies of Others* explores questions about gender, dance, theatre, and performance, which ultimately culminates in the body expression of artists being discussed.

Schwartz's book is not a comprehensive history of dance and drag, but rather an in-depth examination of five distinct case studies that span time, continent, and style for the purpose of analyzing the politics of gender in motion. The book is written in the language of an ethnographic insider to the communities which Schwartz discusses. Drawing from queer theory, dance history, and dance practice, *The Bodies of Others* is a text befitting a gender or performance studies graduate survey course but is accessible enough to find its home in other academic settings.

As revealed in the title, a central theme of the book is the "afterlives" of drag dances. Schwartz chronicles how drag dance is an embodiment not only of past drag performers through drag mothers (and their drag houses), but also through the dancers who came before them. Through this embodied historiography, Schwartz constructs the narrative of how it is impossible to extrapolate the performing body from history (or herstory); drag dancers have the ghosts of those that came before them channeling through them figuratively via dance séance (Richard Move) or channeling animation (Kazuo Ohno), or consciously through a continuance of mission of subversion of gender, and race via Les Ballets Trockadero de Monte Carlo or Fauxnique/Monique Jenkinson. "Afterlives" are more than the recalled phantasm or specter of drag kings and queens and the LGBTQIA+ community who fought for representation, rights, and respect; "afterlives" are embodied historiography in addition to new ephemeral creations. In this way, Schwartz questions the notion of dance being an ephemeral art form especially when it is being used to embody qualities that are ever present: hope, memory, and mourning.

Schwartz spends a great deal of time dissecting gender and, with a thorough understanding of a variety of Judith Butler's texts on the topic, succinctly presents a discussion on constructs of gender, gender norms, and gestures. Turning to dance to consider the language of the body—is it a language, Schwartz poses—she presents the learned language of movement and positions it against how people can "read" physical movement to denote gendered movement. Adding layer upon layer, Schwartz gets the reader to question what it means when a gendered gesture that has been constructed for a particular body is performed by another body.

The book begins with a discussion about Mark Morris's solo-performed duet *Dido and Aeneas*. The chapter asks and answers questions such as how bodies communicate; how can male-bodied performers be perceived as female through gesture; and without a gendered costume, what did Dido do to communicate multiple female characters? Ultimately, it was not enough to be feminine, because there is a spectrum of femininity rife with various codes and Schwartz goes on to explain the implications of the answers.

Next, in Chapter Two, Schwartz focuses on Richard Move's drag séance animation of Martha Graham in *Martha @*. This chapter presents the concept of creating space in one's body for the body of another person, which in Move's case, is legendary choreographer and dancer Martha Graham and even members of her company. Move does not simply replicate Graham's movement; he goes beyond to channel her vocal qualities. Schwartz examines theatrical femininity and asks, "when 'straight' dance genealogies fail, how can queer claims on inheritance give us models for preserving dances in a way that acknowledges bodily difference, loss, aging, and mortality?" (26).

Chapter Three continues the theme of reincarnated dance genealogies. Various styles of dance collide when Japanese butoh dancer Kazuo Ohno channels the Spanish flamenco and bolero dancer La Argentina (1888–1936) in *Admiring La Argentina* (1977). Ohno embodies La Argentina more than forty years after her death, or in his words, has a séance. Schwartz uses Ohno's unique interpretation of drag dance to highlight two branches prevalent in twenty-first century drag dance: synchronicity of drag dance performance and reincarnation beyond re-performance (i.e., fictional archiving, as Ohno's successor calls it).

Turning to a company, rather than particular choreographer/dancers, Chapter Four focuses on Les Ballets Trockadero de Monte Carlo (1974–present), giving particular attention to Anthony Bassae, who cofounded the drag ballet troupe. This chapter examines how the troupe conceives itself as a way to change the lineage of ballet through creating a new ballet genealogy via dance, gender, gender roles, race, size, non-heteronormativity, and overall, a more inclusive place and space.

Chapter 5 is different from the previous chapters in that it focuses on a cisgender female faux queen drag dancer. Schwartz explores Fauxnique/ Monique Jenkinson's feminist dance theatre *Faux Real* (2009) and the etymology of the terms "faux queen" and "realness." Diving into ballroom history, focus on realness, a term that belongs to queer black and brown trans communities, this chapter untimely makes a full circle and returns to the questions posed in the first chapter and builds upon them, for example, by asking and answering how gender can be performed as if it were not self-identical (168).

Schwartz's work goes a step further: when gender is removed from its ontological basis, it is possible to examine the many layers that go into a gendered performance of the body: movement, gesture, costume, attitude, race, age, ability, and so on. All of these are explored over the course of the book, especially in the chapter on Les Ballets Trockadero de Monte Carlo. It is clear that Schwartz holds the Les Ballets Trockadero dear to her heart as her writing in this chapter pulses with a love for what this revolutionary company was built on and how it continues its work. While the entire book is clearly written from a place of passion, this chapter in particular reveals just how engrained into the research (and even preparation) for this book Schwartz was; it is a refreshing writing style that should be used more often as it allows for an accessibility to readers who may be encountering the subject matter for the first time.

A book about movement and life is presented through static words; however, Schwartz is able to paint picturesque scenes through words for readers to visualize the specific people and dances discussed. She translates movement in such a way that a reader who has not seen drag dances or taken a dance class will be able to visualize the case studies with ease. Furthermore, readers of this book will have vocabulary about drag, dance, gender, and trans issues, and an expanded literacy of these topics as they intersect. For example, readers will learn about the term "bioqueen" in Chapter Five and why its association with gender is problematic and transphobic.

Readers will also learn about how performers who are cisgender women can be drag queens (faux queens)—after all, as Schwartz beautifully argues, drag is a specific type of gender-affect performance that people choose to do. By moving beyond perceived notions of "woman," "real woman," or "man," etc., drag dances are able to hold up gender in a liminal light that is beyond the reach of gender norms.

ALICIA M. GOODMAN
*Texas Tech University*

---

David Palmer, ed. *Visions of Tragedy in Modern American Drama*. Bloomsbury Methuen Drama, 2018. Pp. 272. Paperback $26.95.

It is not often that a work which so significantly contributes to the ongoing dialogue on dramatic criticism is also one that can be easily adopted for use in the undergraduate classroom, but that is exactly what *Visions of Tragedy in Modern American Drama* has been designed to do. Edited by David Palmer, this volume features eighteen essays by some of the leading critics and scholars of American drama, each covering select works from a different playwright, and all are short and approachable enough for use by undergraduate students. Despite their accessibility, the essays do not lack in scholarly rigor; taken separately, each essay casts a critical eye on the way that each playwright engages with the genre of tragedy, and, more significantly, together they constitute an insightful conversation about what might define a uniquely American version of tragedy. While all the essays rely heavily on the seminal ideals of the tragic as laid out by Aristotle, each moves beyond the classical confines of the genre, using a wide array of modern criticism—ranging from the expected (Arthur Miller and Raymond Williams), to the more contemporary (Rita Felski and Harvey Young)—in order to address the question of whether or not "there is something about America that causes its dramatists to write their tragedies from a certain perspective or a set of attitudes that make American tragedy distinct or peculiar in some way" (7).

The project's approachability lies in the fact that contributors were tasked to focus on the plays themselves to explore each playwright's "vision of the nature and sources of human suffering" (7), so while theory is surgically employed, the primary thrust of the essays lies in close readings of the plays. Authors mine the words of the playwrights, not only in their dramas but in essays, letters, emails, speeches and interviews, as they attempt to situate their own work, and the work of other playwrights that have influenced them, within the tragic genre, allowing readers to readily make connections between iconic American writers. This not only allows readers to trace the historical development of the genre, it also prompts authors to explore the temporal characteristics of the genre itself, exploring the place that the past, present, and future each occupy within the tragic formula. At the heart of many of these essays is an exploration of both the foundational ideals of America as a nation and the continued, and corrosive, effect of the American Dream on its people. Many essays point to America's "glorification of the individual's potential and experience" (8), as creating an inherent demand for its people to not only survive but to flourish that is at odds with existing material, social realities, thereby setting Americans on an inevitable path towards a tragic fall. The book's focus on more contemporary dramas is strengthened by its continued acknowledgment of the fluidity of genres within the field of modern theatre, exploring how the historical development of genres, particularly Absurdism, has philosophically altered our perceptions about mankind's place in the cosmic order, and thus, the social function of tragedy. And while the essays vary on the defining tragic principles that they address, as a whole, they assert that the continued appearance of the classical tragic formula and tropes in contemporary American drama demonstrates "the universality of the human experience of tragedy" (7).

One of the book's strengths is the wide range of playwrights that it examines; the usual, tragic subjects are here (such as Eugene O'Neill, Tennessee Williams, Arthur Miller, and August Wilson), but so are writers like Susan Glaspell, Adrienne Kennedy, Amiri Baraka, and Suzan-Lori Parks to name a few, allowing the book to provide more inclusive dramatic perspectives that take into account what effect the uniquely American iniquities of race, class, and gender have had on the tragic form. However, while the breadth of playwrights examined allows for more diverse viewpoints, not every essay is as persuasive in its attempt to position the work of its playwright within the genre. Another strength of the collection is the connections made in each essay between the other playwrights covered in the book. Students who are assigned several essays from the volume will find that many are in a kind of conversation with one another over the various elements of the tragic form, allowing even the most neophyte of readers to see the historical and cultural transformation of the genre over the history of American drama.

Perhaps the most commonly addressed theme explored in the essays is that of an individual's response to social forces, with authors locating the tragic in "the struggle between what man feels he is or ought to be and what society says he is or ought to be" (76). Exploring the nature of the individual within the specific cultural/social context of America, some authors assert that it is most often "the conflict of intersecting identities" within an individual character that is the both the social context for, and the tragic result of, the American identity (127), while others see the isolation of a character from society as having the greatest portent of tragedy. Several essays point to the fact that, historically, the decline of religion in the latter half of the twentieth century and its effects on our beliefs about the cosmic positioning of mankind, necessitated a change in the ideals and the social function of classical tragedy. Still others interrogate the potential use-value of tragedy within society, including redemption, transformation, forgiveness, and hope, insisting that American drama's "lack of [a] convincing resolution to disorder points to a meta-context of social injustice" that, in part, defines the contemporary tragic structure (117).

Of the many excellent essays in the collection, one standout is Claire Gleitman's essay on the "genre-fuck" of Tony Kushner's *Angels in America*, whose aesthetic of "fabulousness" "features conventions of the tragic form while subverting tragic expectations" (190). Gleitman argues that no tragic catastrophe is necessary for the anagnorisis in this tragedy, but rather it requires audiences and characters alike to recognize the absurd and inseparable nature of living and suffering. Further, she suggests that *Angels* substitutes forgiveness for redemption in the tragic formula and resists a tidy resolution because, as Kushner's character Prior tells the Angel, "'We can't stop. We're not rocks. Progress, migration, motion is ... modernity'" (194). Another exemplary essay is Soyica Diggs Colbert's examination of Suzan-Lori Parks's attempts to reconfigure "historical narratives to not only redeem the present but to place purchase on the past" (199). Colbert points to Parks's purposeful conflation of dramatic heroes with historical figures, her use of the Chorus, and her signature, jazz-inspired "Rep and Rev" style to provide audiences with the possibility of both "individual and collective freedom in futures still tethered to unrecognizable pasts" (201).

The collection concludes with a survey of "American Theatre since 1990," in which Toby Zinman points to the future of tragedy in American Drama. Her choice of representative dramas is impressively contemporary in scope, and are primarily those concerned with American history, allowing her critical focus to be more sociological than emotional in nature. "Tragedy," she reminds us, "demands more of us than tears" (213). The relevancy of this project is readily apparent in the topics that permeate the plays and musicals with which Zinman engages—war, politics, and immigrants—and in her exploration of the way these tragedies "portray the hope America promises," as well as "its betrayal, and renewal" (12).

MELISSA RYNN PORTERFIELD
*Valdosta State University*

# Index

abolition 49–51, 54–57, 59
adaptation 115, 116, 121, 122, 133, 134, 135, 136, 146, 147
Adorno, Theodor 81
Aeschylus 179, 187
Ajax 60
American Civil War 49, 50, 53, 58, 59, 61
Arendt, Hannah 53, 178, 179
Artaud, Antonin 136
Atkinson, Brooks 32, 33
*August: Osage County* (Tracy Letts) 8
authenticity 134, 135, 144
authorship 131, 134
autopoeisis 133

Bakhtin, Mikhail 72
Barilla, Anthony 80
Barthes, Roland 132
Beckett, Samuel 7–8, 161–173, 177, 187; estate of 170–171; *Krapp's Last Tape* 161–173; *Waiting for Godot* 7–8, 170
Bell, Daniel 80
Benét, Stephen Vincent 50, 57–61
Bernancoce, Marie 144
biopower 84
*Black Mirror* 80
Bortolotti, Gary 135, 146, 147
Boucicault, Dion 12–16
Boulez, Pierre 147
Bradby, David 131
Braunschweig, Stéphane 136
Brown, John 49–61
Brown, Lenora Inez 31
buffoonery 141

*Camille* (Dumas) 66–9, 75
Canetti, Elias 182
Caravaggio 68
Carlson, Marvin 61
Carnivalesque 72–3
Carr, Marina 113–118, 121–122, 124, 126–127
*Cat on a Hot Tin Roof* (Williams) 64
Chaplin, Ralph 57

Chemers, Michael Mark 33
*Chicago Sun-Times* 78, 88
*Chicago Theater Beat* 78
*Chicago Tribune* 79, 88, 92
Childress, Alice 18–19; *Trouble in Mind* 42
Clum, John 151, 153
*Clybourne Park* (Bruce Norris) 9, 32, 39
Cohen-Solal, Annie 182
communitas 93
Critchley, Simon 187; 189–193
*The Crucible* (Miller) 134
Curry, John Steuart 50

Dahlhaus, Carl 81
D'Amour, Lisa 78–81, 84, 86–89, 93; *Airline Highway* 80–81, 87–93; *Detroit* 78–87, 91, 93
De Francesco, Joseph 59
Demas, George 169
Derrida, Jacques 175, 176, 178, 184, 186
Dichter, Jon 169
*A Doll's House* (Ibsen) 66, 69–71, 75
dramaturgy 31–33, 36, 38, 40
Dumas, Alexandre *fils* 66–67
Duplessis, Marie 67

*The Eccentricities of a Nightingale* (Williams) 148, 152–160
*ecriture scénique* 131
Eliot, T.S. 59
Enders, Jody 60
Erlich, Leandro 73
*Etiquette of Vigilance* (Robert O'Hara) 32, 45, 47
Euripides 114–117, 122–123, 126

*La Farce de Maître Pathelin* 137, 142, 143, 144, 145, 146
Foucault, Michel 51, 84
Friedman, Michael 134
Fuchs, Elinor 65–66, 68
Futurama Exhibit 81

Gillette, J. Michael 64
Goffman, Erving 90, 94

Goldman, Lucien 94
Gothard, David 171
Greco, Loretta 80
Greenburg, Phoebe 141
Grieve-Carlson, Gary 59
Guattari, Félix 132, 133

Hall, Florence Howe 55
*Hamlet* 175, 178
Handke, Peter 170
Hansberry, Lorraine 18, 27–48; *A Raisin in the Sun* 27–48; *The Sign in Sidney Brustein's Window* 37, 38
Harpers Ferry 50, 58
Heidegger, Martin 78, 86–87, 89, 93, 94, 181, 184, 186; *Being and Time* 78; *Discourse on Thinking* 181; Mitsein 93
Herrington, Eldrid 50, 61
Hippolytus 114–117, 119–121, 123–124, 126
historiographic metafiction 114, 121–122, 124
historiographic metatheatre 124–125
Howe, Julia 56
Hutcheon, Linda 114, 121–124, 135, 146, 147
hybridity 138, 139, 145, 146

Ibsen, Henrik 66, 69–70
Industrial Workers of the World (IWW) 49, 57
Infernal Bridegroom Productions 80
Ingham, Rosemary 64–65, 68
Isherwood, Charles 79, 88
Isin, Engin F. 78, 84

Jacobs-Jenkins, Branden 5–26; *Neighbors* 38, 39–40
Jameson, Fredric 78, 80–81, 86, 93, 94
*John Brown's Body* 57–61
Jones, Chris 79, 88, 92

Kennedy, Adrienne 18, 45
Klaic, Dragan: *The Plot of the Future* 79
*Krapp, 39* (Michael Laurence) 161–173
*Krapp's Last Tape* (Beckett) 161–173
Kusama, Yayoi 68

Larkin, Philip 175, 180, 186
late capitalism 80–81, 86
Laurence, Michael *Krapp, 39* 161–173
LeCoq, Jacques 137, 141
*lecture mise en espace* 142–146
Leinberger, Christopher 81
lisibilité 143, 144, 146
Logan, John 174, 175, 177; *Red* 174–186
*Long Day's Journey into Night* (O'Neill) 8, 40
Lukács, Georg 94

MacCannell, Dean 90
Malloy, Kaoime E. 64
Marcuse, Herbert 94
Marx, Karl 83–84
Mayakovsky, Vladimir 79
Merleau-Ponty, Maurice 94; *Phenomenology of Perception* 94
Merlo, Frank 156–157
Metcalf, Laurie 78
Miller, Arthur 8, 44, 134
Miller, James 94
Minotaur 115, 117–120, 125–126
*mise en performance* 136, 146, 147
*mise en scène* 132–133, 135–136, 142, 147
*Miss Julie* (Strindberg) 66, 72–75
Molière 137, 138, 146
*musee mecanique* 152, 158
myth 113–118, 120–127
mythographic metatheatre 113–114, 121, 124, 127

neoliberalism 80, 84
neuroliberalism 84
neurotic citizen 78, 84, 86
New York Women's Project 80
New York World's Fair 81
Nietzsche, Friedrich 178, 183, 184
Norris, Bruce 9; *Clybourne Park* 9, 32, 39

*Oedipus Rex* 182
O'Hara, Robert: *Etiquette of Vigilance* 32, 45, 47
O'Neill, Eugene: *Long Day's Journey into Night* 8, 40

Parks, Suzan-Lori 42, 44–45
Pascal, Blaise 180
Pavis, Patrice 136, 144, 146
Pawling, Christopher 94
Phaedra 113–127
*Phaedra Backwards* (Carr) 113–127
Phelan, Peggy 54
Planchon, Roger 131, 137, 139
*Les Précieuses ridicules* (Molière) 137–142, 146
Preston, John T.L. 52–53
*Princess Butterflies* (Scott Taylor) 138–141
proto-intersectional dramaturgy 36, 38, 40
Puchner, Martin 131–134

Racine, Jean 114–117, 123–124, 126
*A Raisin in the Sun* (Hansberry) 27–48
*Red* (John Logan) 174–186
risk societies 84–85
Rokem, Freddie 60
Rothko, Mark 174–188
Rousseau, Jean-Jacques 164

San Quentin Prison  49, 50, 59–61
Sanborn, Franklin B.  55
Schubert, Franz  163
semiosis  133
Seneca  114–117, 123–124, 126
Shakespeare, William  134
Shaw, George Bernard  79
Shepherd, Heyward  50
Slumburbia  82
Sontag, Susan  181, 183
Sophocles  182
Soskis, Benjamin  55–56
*Station Eleven* (Emily St. John Mandel)  96, 98–99, 106–112
Stauffer, John  55–56
Steiner, George  184
Steppenwolf Theatre Company  78, 80, 88
*Stick Fly* (Lydia Diamond)  8
Stoppard, Tom  162
Strindberg, August  66, 72–73
Sullivan, Catey  78–79
*Summer and Smoke* (Williams)  148–160

théâtralisibilité  143, 144, 146
Theseus  113–121, 124–126

Thoreau, Henry David  50
touristic consciousness  90
tragedy  113–114, 116–117, 119–120, 123, 125, 127, 189–193
Turner, Victor  93

uncanniness  86–87, 89, 92–93

Warren, Robert Penn  51, 56
Washburn, Anne  21; *Mr. Burns*  96–99, 101, 103–112
Weiss, Hedy  78–79, 88
Whitman, Walt  52, 58
Williams, Edwina  157
Williams, Tennessee  64–65, 148–160; *Cat on a Hot Tin Roof* 64; *The Eccentricities of a Nightingale* 148, 152–160; short stories 153; *A Streetcar Named Desire* 8–9; *Summer and Smoke* 148–160; "The Yellow Bird" 151
Wilson, August  18, 44–45; *The Piano Lesson* 9
Winemiller, Alma  148–160
Wittgenstein, Ludwig  177
Wolfe, George C.  40, 44–45
Wooster Group  133, 134, 147